The ABC's of Retail and Restaurant Site Selection

How to Pick WINNERS and Avoid LOSERS

Your Guide To Making

Smart Location Decisions   **FRANK RAEON**

I

Print information available on the last page.

Publication Date: May, 2025

To order additional copies of this book, contact:
Luna Global Media ,LLC
Lunaglobalmedia.com
Paperback: 979-8-9923634-5-6

Table of Contents

IV

DEDICATION

This self-help guidebook is dedicated to the seemingly endless legions of men and women who (a) possess a strong desire to go into business for themselves, (b) currently operate a small retail or restaurant business, (c) wish to see their multi-unit companies grow larger as well as more prosperous, and (d) are either thinking about becoming franchisees, or are intent on expanding the number of franchise locations they operate. They are the real entrepreneurs - the people who have not only a DREAM, but a strong DESIRE and DRIVE to succeed in spite of the many obstacles and risks they will encounter.

These are the people who, after reading my book, will gain a new set of insights as well as skills which will better enable them to find, and potentially secure, "Home Run" locations.

PREFACE

The idea for "The ABC's of Retail and Restaurant Site Selection" originated many years ago. Beginning with the Alibi, the busy, very successful "mom and pop" restaurant which my parents operated, I have always been intrigued with why businesses either succeeded or failed at their respective locations.

Before becoming involved in commercial real estate I had the good fortune to work at the municipal level as a City Planning Director for two communities - one in southwest Ohio and the other along the central coast of California. Together, they provided me with the opportunity to ask anyone and everyone who came into my office a very important question: what were your reasons for selecting a particular retail or restaurant location?

Having worked over many years with numerous multi-unit national retail and restaurant companies, I quickly learned that making "smart" location decisions always originated with a detailed set of site selection criteria - s o m e t h i n g which is not well - known among people starting a new business, and not always embraced by businesspeople who operate one or perhaps only a handful of retail stores or restaurants. In addition to choosing locations which are not typically considered "prime," I have learned that cheap rent, vacant space, a sense of urgency, and proximity to home repeatedly explain how the great majority of small businesspeople end up making their location decisions.

After establishing a working relationship with McDonald's real estate representatives, I was taught to never bring them a site which I would not personally invest my own money in. Ever since then this has been the "gold" standard I have used when making retail and restaurant site selection recommendations.

In the future, retail and restaurant businesses will continue to open and close. This is one prediction that is extremely easy to make. It is also a statement that no one ever disagrees with me about because it is factual as opposed to being based upon opinion. With the hope of helping both existing and would be business decision makers succeed, I've written what I consider to be an *instructive guidebook* - one which I believe has the capacity to save readers not only significant time, but potentially lots of money.

We live in an impatient world, one where getting things instantly has become the new mindset. Quick and fast are well established buzzwords. However, when it comes to making "smart" location decisions, nothing could be further from the truth! The sooner you understand that there are **no shortcuts** in retail and restaurant site selection the more successful you will be.

Site selection is not a simple process. Rather, it is a time-consuming process which requires doing lots and lots of *homework*. As a result, you need to commit to not only making countless site visits, but undertaking a significant amount of analysis. In doing so, I hope you'll remember something I can attest to: making "smart" location decisions is much more similar to running a *marathon* than running a *sprint*.

I have learned over many years that disappointment, disillusionment, and failure are all preventable. However, to ensure that none of these negative consequences occur, you'll always need to do your *homework*. Indeed, this is the only way to build a strong foundation.

If you ignore my advice, especially what I refer to as **The Six Keys,** you may well end up having either a short and unproductive business career, or, never achieve the store or restaurant expansion you once envisioned.

The inspiration for this guidebook comes from three sources: the **authors** of various site selection books which I have read over many years, including John Thompson, Luigi Salvaneschi, John Melaniphy, and Richard Fenker; the many **companies** whom I have helped find "home run" retail and restaurant locations during my thirty plus years working in commercial real estate; and the large number of **entrepreneurs** I have not only talked with, but periodically assisted.

The first group indirectly acted as my early mentors and provided me with a strong and continuing interest in learning more about retail and restaurant site selection - something which will, no doubt, continue to be a passion of mine for the rest of my life.

The authors whose books I read and the companies I worked with taught me that a *systematic* approach was essential for making "smart" location decisions. These were people who left "no stone unturned." They are the people who understood, beyond any doubt, which locations had the potential to become either *winners or losers.*

As for the entrepreneurial group, I quickly observed that the great majority of them had very little understanding of how site selection works. Furthermore, these were people who were much more likely to make independent decisions rather than rely on the advice and expertise of one or more professionals. Perhaps it's this type of decision-making which helps explain why so many small businesses fail within a relatively short period of time.

Preventing business failures while helping business succeed led me to realize that there was a definite need for the types of professional services which I pride myself on providing.

To each and all of the aforementioned groups, I am deeply indebted and very thankful. Collectively, they have enriched not only my knowledge, but my passion for finding "home run" locations.

It's primarily because of the many hours I've spent over the years working with emerging multi-unit companies who are intent on successfully growing their retail and/or restaurant footprint that I determined there was, indeed, a market for my real estate advisory services. Accordingly, I decided to establish my consulting company *Location Decision Advisors.*

When looking to find a "home run" location, my advice to decision-makers is to not overlook the option of working with two very important resource groups: commercial realtors and consultants with an expertise and track record in retail and restaurant site selection. In addition to helping you find "home run" locations, each of these important resource groups is capable of helping you negotiate (a) favorable lease terms, (b) favorable rents and purchase prices, and (c) favorable build out and tenant improvement allowances.

I want to wish you **good luck** in your quest to either launch your retail or restaurant business, or expand its footprint - whether locally, regionally, or nationally.

Before you proceed with reading my book and applying what you've learned, I want to make one thing perfectly clear: **good operations** are, without a doubt, a cornerstone for future retail and restaurant success. A good location which suffers from poor operations is only destined to disappoint. On the other hand, a good operator has the potential to elevate an average location to a better location if it passes the **PASTA V** test which is identified in *Chapter Two*.

INTRODUCTION

This guidebook is directed at each and every person who is involved in making retail and restaurant site selection decisions. Anyone who owns a small business, is interested in starting their own business, or advises people on buying or leasing commercial real estate is invited to become familiar with not only its terms, but with the methodology which it identifies for selecting profitable locations - the kind which have long runways.

Over a long period of time, I have learned that for many small businesspeople site selection is more about emotion, convenience, and cheap rent than it is about working with a commercial realtor or a real estate consultant - two groups who are capable of employing a helpful systematic and disciplined decision-making approach.

Please note that site selection is neither an art nor a science. Rather, it is a combination of both. It is a process which involves doing a significant amount of *homework* - something which a few people are willing to invest a lot of time doing while, regrettably, many others are only interested in spending a little time on. In the long run, doing your *homework* is the only way to justify making what will surely turn out to be a significant investment of not only time, but money.

This guidebook is intended to be comprehensive in scope while being basic in its description of terms. It is meant to give you, the small businessperson as well as the person who is contemplating opening a new business, the *tools* which are required to make "smart" location as well as "smart" site selection decisions. Indeed, if you understand and employ the very helpful information which I have identified you will greatly increase the likelihood of achieving success.

As you look through this guidebook you will see that I have divided it into Fourteen chapters. In *Chapter One*, I describe the highly popular but little understood phrase **Location, Location, Location**. After reading through the information in *Chapter One* you will have a much better understanding of the three pillars of real estate that determine which retail and restaurant locations will become Home Runs, and which ones are destined to fail.

Whether you are a member of the real estate profession, a small businessperson, or an entrepreneur with the desire to start your own business, it is absolutely essential that you understand that while the same word is being repeated three times, each word means something different. If that sounds confusing don't be alarmed. You're not alone!

In *Chapter Two* I identify some of the most important information in my book – **The Six Keys (PASTA V)** to retail and restaurant site selection. Ignore them and you may as well forget about not only staying in business for any length of time, but ever having the opportunity to add future locations. In short, they are paramount to selecting "home run" locations.

Incidentally, many years ago I chose to personalize my license plates by featuring the phrase **PASTA V**. I can't tell you how many times over the years that people have asked me the significance of these important letters. After I explain their meaning, a light bulb seems to come on and a smile breaks out on many of their faces.

In *Chapter Three* I define what **trade areas** are. For your information, all retail and restaurant businesses include a primary as well as a secondary trade area. Briefly, these are the geographic areas from which the great majority of customers are coming from throughout the day and evening.

While many commercial realtors choose to use 1-3-5 mile rings to define trade areas, it's important that you understand that *minutes* are another gauge of where customers are coming from. In many instances, if you ask a customer how many miles they've driven to a particular retail or restaurant destination you may get a confused look accompanied by a moment of silence. On the other hand, many people can tell you, without any hesitation, how many minutes it took them to arrive at a particular destination.

Chapter Four has a twofold focus. The first of these is **demographics.** This critically important set of data informs you not only about how many people live within a defined trade area, but identifies other essential information such as people's ages, their education levels, and their income levels.

The second focus, and arguably of equal importance, is **psychographics.** They reveal something fascinating - the different *lifestyles* of people living within a particular trade area. This is where you'll learn something which is very revealing - people's spending habits. Examples include where they shop, which restaurants they patronize, what publications they like to read, and what types of entertainment they enjoy.

The focus of ***Chapter Five*** is to understand as much as possible about who your customers are. One of the easiest and most helpful ways to accomplish this is to conduct **customer surveys.** Whether detailed or brief, customer surveys need to be an essential component of how you conduct business.

An often-overlooked reason for conducting **customer surveys** is their ability to help you determine exactly where your customers are coming from. In most cases, people will be coming to your place of business from their homes or apartments. In other instances, they will initiate their visits from places where they are employed. Other potential points of origin you need to know about include shopping centers, sports, cultural, and entertainment venues, as well as other stores and restaurants.

Once you know where your customers are coming from you can easily pinpoint their points of origin on a map - something which will result in your having a much clearer understanding of both your businesses' primary and secondary trade areas.

Chapter Six is all about creating and using a variety of **site selection tools**. These include criteria, guidelines, standards and checklists. Collectively, their purpose is to help existing retail and restaurant owners as well as aspiring businesspeople avoid costly mistakes while simultaneously establishing a platform for success.

Creating these important tools is something you can do either independently, or by employing the services of a real estate consultant who has deep site selection skills.

In *Chapter Seven* you'll learn why **walking and talking** is such an important task - i.e., a really "big deal." As a result of "knocking on doors" you're guaranteed to learn a lot from people who are very familiar with the area you are considering as a potential location for your business. They can do something very important: help "educate" you.

Chapter Eight talks about the many different factors that need to be taken into consideration when evaluating an Area, a Site, and a Space. Using **a Site Selection Scorecard** will enable you to make better, more informed decisions while, at the same time, eliminating emotion and "gut" from playing a role.

Chapter Nine provides you with details on **how to estimate sales**. Be forewarned, this is one of the most important exercises you'll ever conduct. Developing a reliable system for accurately estimating future sales is absolutely critical. It is a task which needs to be completed prior to either signing a lease or purchase agreement. Otherwise, how will you have a good idea of what you can realistically afford to pay for expenses such as rent, build out, and FF& E (furniture, fixtures and equipment).

Having been a member of the commercial **real estate and consulting** professions for more than thirty years, I'm happy to talk in *Chapter*

Ten about the important roles they play in helping retail and restaurant business owners make "smart" site selection decisions. If you are open to establishing a "partnering" relationship with them you'll be doing yourself a big favor! Don't dwell on the cost of their services. Instead, focus on the value of the return on investment they can provide.

As a former City Planning Director, I feel well qualified to talk, in *Chapter Eleven*, about the critical **role the public sector** plays in partnering with the private sector in order to facilitate new shopping and eating options for area residents, employees, and visitors. Meeting and getting to know planners and zoning staff, economic development staff, and engineering staff can make the approval process not only less intimidating, but smoother and a lot easier.

In **Chapter Twelve** I describe the many different types **of location options** which are waiting to welcome start-up as well as existing retail and restaurant businesses.

In **Chapter Thirteen** I'm proposing that major colleges and universities consider offering the opportunity for commercial realtors to earn a **Certificate in Retail and Restaurant Site Selection** as a way of incentivizing veteran commercial realtors to earn a designation which will help differentiate them from less qualified commercial realtors as well as help them "win" more assignments.

In *Chapter Fourteen* I've chosen to share a variety of wide ranging **career experiences** - the kind which have not only taught me a lot, but have provided me with many **wonderful memories**.

Towards the end of my book, I provide readers with (a) some closing thoughts and (b) information about myself before (c) describing the audience I hope will read and benefit from my book. This is followed by three important Appendix items: *Site Selection Influences, Words and Terms You Need to Know About, and Other Sales Influences and Related Factors.* I close by providing readers with three important exhibits which

I hope they'll consider using at a later time: a *Sample Letter of Intent*, a *Sample Real Estate Representation Agreement,* and *Meaningful Quotes and Educational Pictures.*

As you read through my book, I hope you'll understand why it is critically important to spend hours and hours, weekdays as well as on weekends, doing lots of "homework." In the process, I hope you'll "take to heart" the following advice:

Making site selection decisions without doing your "homework" is like starting a new job without any training!

In closing, I want to once again take this opportunity to wish you **Good Luck** as you embark on your site selection journey.

Chapter One
Location, Location, Location

The most ubiquitous phrase in all of real estate is **Location, Location, Location**. In spite of most people's familiarity with this popular phrase many don't have a good understanding of its true meaning.

If you conduct a Google search on **Location, Location, Location** you will find page after page of entries. Most of what you see or read is focused on residential real estate, especially single family homes. Very little mention is made of such commercial real estate stalwarts as retail and restaurants. After reading many pages of explanations, it became apparent to me that there is no common definition for this ages' old axiom. Not only is this surprising, it's disappointing.

Whether your area of expertise is residential, industrial, office, retail, restaurant, or investment real estate, it is absolutely imperative that you understand the real meaning of **Location, Location, Location.** The same holds true if you are a businessperson or prospective businessperson, an appraiser, a lender, a city planner, a geographer, an economic development official, an executive with your local chamber of commerce, a property manager, a builder, a developer, or, a professor at the college level.

I am prepared to explain the real meaning of what is widely regarded to be the #1 rule in real estate. When I think of the phrase **Location, Location, Location** I picture a hierarchy of locations. To me, each of the three locations mean something different. With that in mind, I want you to think of the geographic landscape being divided into three segments: large, mid-size, and small.

While my goal is to describe **Location, Location, Location** from a retail and restaurant perspective, it behooves me to start off by providing you with a residential example. Why? Because what I'm about to describe is something I believe everyone can relate to. Assuming that you either own or have owned a single family home, I'm going to describe the three location factors which I'm confident led to your decision to buy.

No doubt the first thing you thought about was where (in which **area** or **community**) do I want to live? If you have children or have thought about starting a family, you most likely began your house search by looking at the quality of local schools. In addition, you probably looked at a number of other influential factors such as community size and character, walkability, proximity to major roads, shopping, and/or parks, and maybe even the extent of the street tree canopy. Doing this kind of time-consuming homework helps explain what Location Step *#1* is all about.

Next, you probably drove through several **neighborhoods** as well as up and down countless **streets** - grid streets, curvilinear streets, no outlet streets, cul-de-sac streets, and boulevards - looking at a variety of houses while paying particular attention to those that were for sale. In doing so, you made a series of observations about curb appeal, the presence or absence of both sidewalks and street lights, street trees, landscaping, speed limits, etc. This combination of driving and scouting illustrates *Location Step #2.*

Lastly, more than likely, you visited each of the **houses** for sale which met your search criteria such as price, lot size, house size, kitchen size, number of bedrooms, number of bathrooms, garage size, and, the presence or absence of amenities such as a family room, basement, deck, patio, back yard, views, etc. Collectively, these attributes describe *Location Step #3.*

As a result of the aforementioned three step process, you used **Location, Location, Location** to guide your search efforts. Starting off by looking at a community (*macro*), then proceeding to looking at a particular neighborhood and/or one or more local streets, and ultimately to looking at one or more houses (*micro*), you demonstrated, knowingly or unknowingly, that there is no better way to achieve the American dream of home ownership than by relying on **Location, Location, Location** - the single best foundation for making "smart" location decisions.

Now, with respect to retail and restaurants, I want you to picture a geographic **"area"** where a person or a company is interested in opening a business. This will require you to think at the *macro* scale. For example, think about a regional **"area"** or perhaps a downtown **"area."** These are destinations which are capable of attracting lots of people for lots of different reasons. Now, ask yourself why this particular "area" is an attractive location? Could it be because of the presence of one or more anchor stores, a large critical mass, an affluent surrounding population, a high traffic count, a significant number of retail stores, lots of restaurants, a large daytime population, or simply, because it is located in the path of growth?

For most professionals and experienced businesspeople, identifying this part of the location process is an essential first step in retail and restaurant site selection. As a result of having done their *homework*, they are capable of pinpointing a desirable **"area"** - in this case, a particular business corridor or street - fairly quickly and with relative ease. By performing this important exercise, you have taken *the first step* in the **Location, Location, Location** process.

Identifying *the second step* in **Location, Location, Location** is where the hard work really begins. Now you need to focus your attention on a specific **"site"** - something which is much more difficult for the untrained person to do. Here is where you need to determine if a particular retail or restaurant **"site"** meets the critical **PASTA V** test which is identified in Chapter Two. As previously mentioned, **"P"** stands for Parking, **"A"** for Access, **"S"** for Signing, **"T"** for traffic, **"A"** for Activity, and **"V"**

3

for Visibility. Only if all of these attributes receive high marks will the **"site"** you are evaluating merit further consideration.

The third step in the **Location, Location, Location** process is not difficult to analyze but is often overlooked. It describes a specific **"space."** This is where you need to look both long and hard at the adequacy of critically important factors such as building setback, building frontage, building depth, window area, storefront signing, curb appeal, and, if you are in the restaurant business, an increasingly important amenity - outdoor seating. This is where you will need to determine whether or not a particular **"space"** receives a passing grade.

Because site selection is all about paying attention to details, I religiously rely on a **Site Selection Scorecard** like the one identified in Chapter Eight. This important tool keeps me not only organized but focused on the task at hand. It also allows me to make the best use of my time. Very importantly, it provides me with a **systematic** approach for making factual rather than emotional decisions.

Unlike buying a house, there's no room for emotion when it comes to making a "smart" retail or restaurant location decision - a lesson some people never learn. If their business fails, they are quick to blame failure not on the quality of food or merchandise or service, but on one factor - their location.

Retail and restaurant site selection pros know for a fact that **"area,"** **"site",** and **"space"** play a primary role in the location decision-making process. Very importantly, they understand that the strength of their real estate strategies and the *homework* they complete can result in success.

Unfortunately, very few start-up businesses as well as some expanding businesses, including more than a few retail and restaurant franchisors, don't have detailed or adequate site selection criteria, standards, and strategies to help guide their real estate decisions. Many of them stop doing their *homework* once they've identified a particular **"area."** They

4

believe, incorrectly, that if they have identified the right **"area"** that they can't go wrong and can justify making a major financial investment. Sadly, nothing could be further from the truth!

Other, wiser individuals proceed to the second location step and are satisfied that they'll succeed for the simple reason that they've found the right **"site."** However, they may be in for a big surprise if they haven't completed all of their *homework*. For instance, a "danger" signal will occur when one or more of the variables comprising **PASTA V** is either missing or ranks poorly.

Steven Tanger, CEO of Greensboro, North Carolina based Tanger Factory Outlet Centers, Inc., sums up the key importance of **"site"** when he says that "…the best tenant mix is ultimately contingent upon the quality of the site." He continues by saying that "the quality of any development… is primarily contingent upon the quality of the site."

This is a good time to re-emphasize that the quality of a **"site"** has a lot to do with the future success of a retail or restaurant business. I think it is arguably the single most important component of the **three location steps** which I've previously identified.

In the long run, it's the people who master not only **"area"** and **"site"** but the third and final location step who end up sleeping well at night. These are the people who do their *homework* (due diligence) in order to make sure they have the right **"space."** These are the individuals and companies who are the best equipped to see their respective businesses not only grow, but prosper.

The most effective, but least common, way for you to find the right **"space"** is to become involved in the early planning stages of a new retail and/or restaurant development. Being engaged early in the process will provide you with the rare opportunity to not only educate a developer, but educate the people he or she works with, such as his or her project architect, about your requirements. Being a participant from the start will enable you, in many instances, to customize to some degree the space you decide to lease.

There is one other very important location component which needs to be mentioned. It has to do with the type of **"space"** a business ends up selecting. The three types of retail and restaurant **"space,"** from the most to the least common as well as least to most expensive are: inline, end cap, and freestanding. In most instances, the type of **"space"** which is the best positioned to generate the highest sales volumes is freestanding. Next in order of sales productivity is end cap **"space."** Inline **"space"** is typically the least productive type of retail or restaurant **"space."**

Among the reasons why freestanding **"space,"** the type drugstores and many chain restaurants invest in prolifically, is the most desirable type of **"space"** is because such **"space"** is likely to (a) enjoy outstanding visibility, (b) benefit from having the ability to display more sign area, and (c) offers customers not only more parking but more convenient parking. Freestanding **"space"** which is located in the right **"area"** and on the right **"site"** can turn out to be a "home run" location, perhaps even a "grand slam" location. If you want a quick lesson in retail site selection, my advice is to pay particular attention to where chain drugstores have made location investments.

If you follow the evolution of drugstore site selection, you will find that these businesses have a history of moving "up the ladder" from one type of location category to another. In other words, over a period of many years, they have graduated from inline to end cap to freestanding **"space."** In the process, they have been able to grow their sales.

Drugstores help illustrate why not all seemingly similar locations are created equal. The fact of the matter is that two similar drugstore **"spaces"** located on two similar **"sites"** within the same general **"area"** can produce two different sales levels. Taking a page out of McDonald's site selection playbook, drugstores understand that the four corners of an intersection are, by no means, created equal. They know, depending

6

upon which **"site"** is selected, that there will be a variance in sales levels. What is the explanation for this? It starts with a comparison of **PASTA V** attributes followed by a determination of which store prototype (model) **"space"** is most capable of producing the highest sales and profits.

One other **Location, Location, Location** distinction you need to understand is that the meaning of this important phrase can change depending on whether it is daytime or nighttime. If, for instance, you are in the sub sandwich business, you need to be in an **"area"** with a strong daytime population in order to thrive. If the **"area"** you are considering doesn't have a large number of daytime employees you need to think long and hard about whether this is an **"area"** where you should make a major investment.

Conversely, if you are in the pizza business, you need to be in an **"area"** where a strong nighttime population exists - regardless of whether your business is dine-in, caters to pick up/carry out customers, or delivers to surrounding households. If you choose an **"area"** without a lot of nearby rooftops you are making a decision which will, no doubt, cost you dearly. Instead of remaining in business for a long time, you stand the risk of being what I commonly refer to as a "short timer."

The real learning curve in retail and restaurant site selection occurs when you have acquired a level of skills which enables you to consistently differentiate between location types. These location types consist of what I like to call "A+" **(Grand Slam)** locations, "A" **(Home Run)** locations, "B" **(Triple)** locations, "C" **(Double)** locations, and "D" **(Single)** locations.

From a frequency perspective, both "A+" and "A" locations are the most sought out, the least common, and the most expensive types of locations. Next in order of importance are "B" locations. On the other hand, both "C" and "D" locations - typically low rent locations which reflect a host of **"site"** and **"space"** related problems - are plentiful and, to use an old cliche, can be found "here, there, and everywhere."

My advice is to never let cheap rent or bargain deals prompt your decision to either lease or acquire real estate. If you don't heed my advice you will not only be guilty of poor judgment, but of "rolling the dice." In site selection, minimizing risk and maximizing return on investment is "the name of the game."

Learning how to differentiate between two or more locations is not an easy task. By doing your *homework*, starting with data collection and extensive fieldwork, and by learning to be picky, you can eventually become a member of a relatively small group of people who have distinguished themselves by consistently making "smart" location decisions. In the process, you can take great pride and satisfaction in making the leap from being an amateur - someone who "thinks" a particular location is a good one, to being a pro - someone who "knows" that a particular location is, in fact, a good one, a *winner!*

I think this is a good time for me to share a very important thought with you regarding **Location, Location, Location.** It's something I've been thinking about more and more as I reflect not only on suburban development but the growing amount of redevelopment which is taking place within the beltway areas of our large cities. I'm talking about the impact transportation improvements have on **Location, Location, Location.** Whether changes are being made to accommodate the automobile or mass transportation, the bottom line is they can positively help or negatively impact the quality of a location.

With regards to the automobile, a new highway interchange, a new road or street, the addition of a traffic signal, and/or the widening of a road or street will all have a *positive* impact on not only the **"area"** but the multiple **"sites"** along a corridor. Such improvements can provide greater convenience, and, over a period of time, (a) lead to new retail and restaurant development, (b) prompt other kinds of development and/or redevelopment such as an increase in both rooftops and daytime employment, and (c) increase the local tax base.

8

On the *negative* side, an overriding concern for safety can result in (a) limiting curb cuts, (b) requiring one-way streets, (c) adding medians, and (d) reducing site access to right turns in and out of a site. Whether individually or collectively, these types of changes can not only limit the overall desirability of a "site", but act as a deterrent to (a) future development, (b) negatively impact sales revenues, (c) lead to short-term as opposed to long-term use, and (d) adversely affect local property values.

The introduction of, as well as upgrades to, intracity light rail and subway systems can also lead to changes in the attractiveness and desirability of both an **"area"** and a **"site."** Being at or near a transit stop can lead to all kinds of opportunities, including mixed use development. Here, you can expect to see the clustering of some or all of the following types of land uses: retail, restaurants, apartments, offices, residential condominiums, hotels, bars, cinemas, fitness facilities, and even sports complexes. I like to call the grouping of four or more synergistic uses a "game changer." Especially in core urban areas, these types of uses are capable of (a) not only repopulating our cities but (b) helping transform the urban fabric.

People who make site selection decisions understand that "time can change everything." With respect to the strength and viability of an **"area,"** a **"site,"** and/or a **"space,"** the quality of a business location may fluctuate over time. In other words, over a short, intermediate, or long period of time, a particular location may transition from being outstanding, to being average or perhaps mediocre. What was once a "home run" location may, from time-to-time, be reduced to nothing more than a "double" or a "single" type of location.

In order to better understand this phenomenon, all you need to do is look at older commercial corridors. Whether they are a few blocks in length or extend mile after mile, with few exceptions, the dynamics of these once thriving business corridors will have changed over time. As a result, noticeable differences in the quality, vibrancy, and viability of a location may become more apparent.

People who make location decisions will remain amateurs if they pick the right **"area"** but the wrong **"site"** and/or the wrong **"space."** Likewise, they may not rise through the ranks if they select the right **"area"** and right **"site"** but end up selecting or developing the wrong "space." Picking the right **"area,"** the right **"site,"** and the right **"space"** is what - to cite another overused phrase - ends up "separating the men from the boys."

The next time you hear somebody talk **about Location, Location, Location,** ask him or her to explain its meaning. I can say, without any hesitation, that you won't always hear the same answer. In some instances, you're likely to find people who will be honest and tell you that they have either a limited understanding or no real knowledge of what it means. But, by asking them, there's a good chance you'll learn something helpful.

Now that you have a better appreciation for, as well as a much better understanding of the real meaning **of Location, Location, Location,** you are in the unique and enviable position of being able to separate yourself from the large number of people who think that picking a profitable retail or restaurant location is not that difficult. Believe it or not, some of these individuals include (a) commercial realtors with limited knowledge of retail and restaurant site selection, (b) "rookie" developers, (c) new franchisees, (d) small businesses who don't employ any in-house real estate staff, and (e) start-up businesses.

After a few years of making profitable retail and restaurant location decisions, your experience will eventually qualify you for membership in a small and select group, one where individuals take great pride in knowing that they are, in fact, members of an exclusive club. Given their expertise, some of these people are justified in thinking of themselves as "site selection snobs." Quite frankly, I think such a "credential" is something more real estate people and more business owners should aspire to. With that in mind, *I firmly believe the time has come for the real estate profession to create a new designation: the* **Certified Site Selection Specialist (CSSS).**

In the future, I hope you will share your new found wisdom about **Location, Location, Location** with your friends and business associates. In doing so, I hope you won't feel shy about reminding them that making the right location decision is like putting *money in* the bank. Conversely, choosing the wrong location is the equivalent of taking *money out* of their pockets - something they are likely to regret for a long, long time.

For those of you who are interested in learning the origins of the phrase **Location, Location, Location**, I'm going to briefly cite an article which was written by columnist William Safire. It appeared in the New York Times on June, 26, 2009.

The first written citation in which the popular **phrase Location, Location, Location** appeared was in 1956 in the Yale Book of Quotations. Its origins date to **1926** when a real estate classified ad appeared in the Chicago Tribune. It read: "Attention salesmen, sales managers: **location, location, location**, close to Rogers Park."

 If you are unfamiliar with metropolitan Chicago, Rogers Park is a dense urban neighborhood which is located nine miles north of downtown Chicago. It borders Lake Michigan on the east and the city of Evanston on the north. Rogers Park is home to Loyola University. If you ever visit this area, you'll find a dense mix of apartments, condominiums, and single-family homes, as well as retail, bars, and restaurants.

In closing, here are a series of final thoughts regarding the memorable phrase **Location, Location, Location.**

"Smart" location decisions are made with Location *Enhancement* and Location *Enrichment* in mind.

Careful site selection, coupled with comprehensive market research, helps distinguish retail and restaurant *winners* from *losers*.

Remember, all locations are **not** created equal. Some will be more productive than others, meaning they will generate higher sales per square foot.

McDonald's and other successful restaurant and retail companies understand that site selection is not just about finding a site. It's about knowing what kind of **sales** a site can produce.

Christine Day, the former CEO of Vancouver, Canada based Lululemon, says:

"… the strength of our real estate strategy drives the strength of our business."

When considering which location to choose, my advice is to never *focus on rent. Always focus on sales.*

I've got one final piece of advice: always count on paying more for the best real estate. You'll be doing yourself an immense favor by remembering that neither "grand slam" nor "home run" locations come at bargain prices. In the long run, you get what you pay for.

Chapter Two
The Six Keys to Making "Smart" Site Selection Decisions

Throughout my real estate career, I have tried to be a "quick study" as a result of continuously asking the people with whom I was working a series of questions starting with why? The answers which they provided gave me a good understanding for the processes which were used in order to make "smart" site selection decisions and reinforced what I already knew: **there are no shortcuts**.

The **Six Keys** which follow should be committed to memory as soon as possible. If you do so, I can guarantee you that you will be saving yourself a lot of time, a lot of anguish, and, potentially a lot of money.

ACCESS. Every business needs to be easily accessible to its customers. Today's consumers demand convenience. Sites which are hard to get into and/or out of will not only end up jeopardizing repeat business but will have a strong negative impact upon both customer traffic counts and sales volumes. As a result, the likelihood of your business succeeding will be greatly diminished!

When you visit a prospective business site make sure that you **get out of your car and walk around**. Then, start recording your observations either with a recorder or on paper. In addition, taking a series of photographs from different vantage points is recommended. Start by counting how many curb cuts there are and exactly where they are located in relationship to the space or the property which you are interested in leasing or buying. In addition, you should note whether they accommodate full or limited turning movements.

Be careful about choosing a site which is restricted exclusively to right turns in and right turns out. Unless you are planning on opening a destination type business - one where convenience is not an important factor in generating customer traffic - such access will definitely reduce the number of people who visit your business.

The presence of a median - a barrier which can severely restrict turning movements into and out of a site - is a potential "danger" signal. As such, a location which has thirty thousand vehicles a day driving by may realistically find itself directly accessible to only fifty percent of that number. This means that potential customer counts are likely to be diminished by a similar amount. Remember that **reduced traffic** results in **reduced sales**. And, **reduced sales** typically mean **reduced profits**.

Many busy streets and roads incorporate exclusive middle turn lanes. These are customer friendly and are an attractive, safe, and effective means of prompting increased levels of customer visits.

Another important observation you need to make is whether traffic stacks (meaning it backs up) in front of one or more of the curb cuts which serve the site you are evaluating. If a traffic stack does exist - especially during non-rush hour periods - then you should either cut your site visit short or proceed with extreme caution.

ACTIVITY. Diverse land uses such as shopping centers, office buildings, post offices, hotels/motels, schools, libraries, churches, grocery stores, drugstores, bookstores, cinemas, hospitals, amusement parks, banks, convenience stores, gas stations, and restaurants all have something in common - they create activity. And, activity is what generates potential customer traffic.

Determining whether or not activity exists in the immediate as well as in the nearby business area you are considering appears, on the surface, to be a fairly simple exercise. However, depending upon when- meaning what time of the day or evening you visit - you will experience different levels of activity. Therefore, in order to be as informed as possible, it is very important that you make a series of location and site visits rather than relying on a single visit. Furthermore, you are advised to make your location and site visits on weekdays as well as on weekends.

When conducting your visits it is important to understand that you aren't looking exclusively for motor vehicle activity. Rather, you are also trying to determine whether a high, medium, or low level of customer activity is present. Are businesses like retail stores, restaurants, lending institutions, convenience stores, bookstores, grocery stores, and drugstores busy? Are their parking lots full or half full or not very full?

Making your observations and impressions either in writing or via voice recording is highly recommended. Please do not try to remember everything that you see - especially if you are trying to record your thoughts a few days after you make one or more field visits. Remember there is no time like the present. Otherwise, remind yourself that the human mind tends to fairly quickly forget a lot of detail - something which you cannot afford to do when making an informed decision is your primary objective.

While two heads are sometimes better than one, your initial site visit should not include any company. This is a time for you to focus your efforts on making and recording observations rather than on talking to or with a family member, another businessperson, a friend, or a trusted advisor. Each of them can become a distraction - something you cannot afford to have happen. Instead, it is recommended that you invite people whose advice you respect to accompany you only after you have substantially completed your homework and have narrowed your choices to one or two potential sites.

PARKING. A lack of parking or inconveniently situated parking can turn out to be the "kiss of death" for most businesses, especially in suburban settings where people are extremely dependent upon the automobile in order to get around. Here, off-street surface parking is king - something which has become not only ubiquitous but has increasingly become a dominant element in the suburban landscape.

Customers typically like to find off-street and on-street parking spaces which are located either close to or reasonably close to the front door of a retail store or restaurant. In many instances this means providing as many parking spaces as possible within one hundred to one hundred fifty feet of the front door of a particular business. Parking which is located more than two hundred and fifty to three hundred feet away from a business is typically taboo unless such a business is located either in a pedestrian friendly destination environment such as a lifestyle center, or in a popular mixed-use neighborhood.

Businesses which are freestanding can, in most instances, accommodate not only the greatest number of parking spaces but the most convenient parking for customers. Here, customer parking can be situated in front, in back, and potentially on both sides of a building. Maximizing customer parking opportunities out front or on the side of the building which is located closest to the front door is advisable rather than locating any significant amount of parking in the back.

End cap shopping center locations are also prized by businesses because customer parking can typically be accommodated not only in the front but on one side of a building. On the other hand, inline shopping center locations are pretty much restricted to providing required parking in a single area - out front.

In urban areas where neighborhood business districts tend to predominate, the fact that limited on-site parking exists means that conveniently situated on street parallel or angled parking is absolutely essential. In order to encourage significant use by prospective customers these parking spaces should either be free or cost relatively little. Unfortunately, metered parking can sometimes result in the issuance of a traffic ticket - a scenario which does not bode well for building either repeat customer trips or customer loyalty.

Garage and deck parking is not only very expensive to build, but isn't always customer or employee friendly. Cost is certainly the most prohibitive factor. However, concern for safety can also raise some eyebrows. Yet, garage and deck parking are vital to many businesses which are located in suburban lifestyle centers, upscale malls, neighborhood business districts which are surrounded by high density populations, and downtown areas. Without a garage or a parking deck the ability of businesses to attract a steady flow of customers would not only be limited but would result in irreparable harm.

Generally speaking, all retail and restaurant businesses need to provide as much customer parking as possible, whether it is located on or off the street and within approximately one hundred feet of their front doors. Unless a street scene looks to be interesting, inviting, and safe, or, people are spending time going from one business to another, only a limited number of people will choose to walk very far from where they have parked. In commercial real estate, the rule of thumb is never more than three hundred feet - the length of a football field.

Different levels of parking exist for different types of businesses. Full-service restaurants and sports bars require a lot of parking in order to adequately accommodate both customer and employee parking. Sometimes they can require as many as 15-20 parking spaces per 1,000 square feet of floor area.

Beauty salons are another example of parking intensive uses. For the most part, 5 parking spaces per 1,000 square feet of floor area is adequate for retail and service retail businesses. However, this ratio doesn't work for beauty salons.

In all instances, employee parking should be separated from customer parking - perhaps even identified in a different manner. In particular, employee parking should be restricted to only those locations which have the least convenience appeal to customers. Generally, this means that employee parking needs to be located either in back of a shopping center or restaurant, on the street a required distance away, in a distant part of a parking lot, or in a nearby parking garage or parking deck.

The lack of parking in urban areas can definitely have a negative impact on retail and restaurant sales. Unfortunately, too many businesspeople overlook the lack of convenient customer parking because the property they are interested in renting or purchasing is cheap or has some other attribute such as architectural character, attractive colors, lots of windows, significant signing, etc. that they find appealing. Don't make this mistake! If a reasonable amount of parking isn't nearby then you should definitely proceed with caution.

To truly comprehend the importance of conveniently situated parking you need to think about how much each parking space represents in sales. For example, does an individual parking space generate $15,000, $20,000, $25,000 or more in annual sales? Conveniently situated parking is "money in the bank." Generally speaking, the more you have the greater your sales will typically be. Similarly, the more parking spaces you have the higher your return on investment is likely to be.

SIGNING. Almost every small businessperson I know of thinks that the number of signs and their sizes (the more-the-better philosophy) are the real secret to generating customer traffic. While this is a bit simplistic, their importance cannot be overlooked. Signs are definitely helpful. Indeed, they play an essential role in creating not only business identity but in helping build name recognition.

Every business, regardless of its location, should feature front facade signing which can be seen from at least one hundred to two hundred feet away during the day and evening. Zoning regulations in the community where you are opening your business will regulate the size, total sign area, and placement of your sign(s). In addition, some property owners may also place restrictions on signs. Hopefully neither will tie your hands with respect to colors and materials. However, if your business is located in an older or historic business district then you may well need to comply with certain restrictions.

Facade signing, whether mounted flush to or projecting from a building, and whether in an older urban area or in a newer suburban location, represents your best option for displaying identification signing. Due to space limitations a business will typically only have room for its name. In other instances, a business will be able to feature a symbol. In a best-case scenario, a sign may also be permitted to display a brief message.

If your business is located in either a freestanding building or an end cap location, chances are pretty good that additional facade signing opportunities will be available on one or both sides of a building.

Based upon local zoning codes, such signing will almost always be smaller than the front facade signing which is permitted.

Oftentimes, freestanding buildings will also have the advantage of being able to display freestanding or pylon signs either near or at the edge of the street right of way. The only caveats here are to make sure that such signing isn't the same height as neighboring signs and is set back a little further, perhaps three to five to seven feet, than the other freestanding or pylon signs which line the same street. In order to maximize visibility and avoid getting lost in the crowd, such signing should be easily recognized by motorists from a minimum distance of one hundred to two hundred feet away in one or more directions.

Where multi-tenant signing opportunities exist, businesses are typically able to reserve a sign panel to advertise their presence. Because little or no variation may exist in panel size, your best bet is to differentiate your business by making your sign stand out. Certain colors, such as red and yellow, attract more attention throughout the day and evening than others. For proof of this look no further than McDonald's and Wendy's. Their signs are not only easily recognized, but easy to remember.

As for positioning, try reserving a sign panel which is located either at the top or the bottom of a multi-tenant sign. People driving by a site tend to look at the top or the bottom of a sign which has multiple businesses identified. As such, you should make every effort to ensure that your sign won't be buried somewhere in the middle - a place where it is guaranteed to get very little notice.

Individual sign letters which are capable of being lighted, whether mounted on a raceway or on the building itself, are very effective. While neon signs are more expensive, they are also very appealing. Plus, they really stand out. This is exactly what you want! On the other hand, the least attractive, least expensive, and most unimaginative building signs available for fabrication are box signs. If you are looking to maximize your image and can spend a little more money you are advised to stay away from this type of signing.

When starting work on your sign package please don't overlook the opportunity to add one or more window signs. While such signs tend to be small, they are typically very affordable. Incorporating one or more symbols or messages in your windows is an especially effective means of building name recognition for your business as well as promoting the products you sell.

TRAFFIC. Every business needs to have traffic going by its front door. Put into perspective, more is better than some, and some is better than a little. Many city and county engineers as well as metropolitan planning organizations can provide you with current or relatively current traffic count information.

Traffic volumes will be higher on primary arteries than on either collector or local streets. Whereas ten thousand vehicles a day might be adequate to support some businesses, others might require that a minimum of twenty thousand vehicles a day drive by their front door. Typically, streets and roads with these kinds of traffic volumes are two lanes - one in either direction.

A site where thirty thousand or even forty thousand vehicles a day go by may sound like an ideal situation. However, you should remember that the key is not so much the quantity of traffic but the *quality* of traffic. You need to ask yourself if the people who are driving by the site you are looking at can get in and out easily as well as safely? Typically, four lane streets and roads featuring two lanes in either direction carry higher volumes of traffic.

Other important observations you want to make when evaluating your prospective site(s) include: the posted speed limit, proximity to nearby streets, the presence of medians, and whether or not a traffic signal is located close by. All of these have the potential for either negatively or positively impacting customer traffic counts.

VISIBILITY. No single site selection factor is more important than visibility. Nothing, I repeat, nothing could be more accurate than the oft stated phrase "out of sight, out of mind."

Visibility is something a site either has or doesn't have. Those with lots of direct visibility as well as visibility from two hundred to three hundred feet away have a much higher probability of succeeding than sites with some or only limited visibility. Sites with no visibility are the "kiss of death." They should be avoided at all costs.

In strip shopping center settings, the most desirable and most expensive sites are building pads (out lots) and end caps. One of the reasons for their popularity is their heightened visibility. The least desired and cheapest spaces on the other hand are typically inline spaces, in part because they can be largely indistinguishable from their immediate and nearby neighbor businesses, especially when located in large, multi-tenant shopping center buildings.

While facade and sign visibility are absolutely essential, parking visibility is also important. Collectively this trio of factors represents a "package" of impressions which can either "make or break" a site. The ideal is for all of these factors to enjoy high marks for visibility.

Sometimes street trees can block storefront and sign visibility. In other instances, trees which are planted in landscape islands in parking lots can have the same negative impact. In such instances, businesspeople need to be vigilant if good site visibility is to be retained and potentially maximized.

In certain cases, slope can negatively affect visibility. Sites that sit a little higher than the street do not generally present a visibility problem. On the other hand, sites that sit more than a few feet lower than the street generally represent an insurmountable obstacle to visibility even if their roofs are easily seen.

Distance and timing are two other important ways of determining the amount of visibility a business enjoys. Typically, the further away from the street a business is located the less visible it will be. Similarly, the longer the period of time that a person sees a business while driving by it, the better.

Another means of evaluating visibility has to do with storefront windows, glass wrap, and walls. Both of the former are great ways to welcome customers and increase visibility. On the other hand, large expanses of walls on the side and front of a building can turn off and even turn away customers - something no business can afford.

In older business districts, storefront differentiation is an important means of increasing visibility - something today's lifestyle centers have been quick to copy. Here, different building materials, recessed entryways, appealing colors, bay windows, nighttime lighting and customized awnings are great ways to not only create a unique and more memorable identity but to increase storefront visibility.

A fun way to remember all of the **Six Keys** which have been identified is to create a simple system. For instance, if you choose to remember them in alphabetical order you can classify them into the following pairs: AA, PS, and TV. Otherwise, you might classify them into three different groups of very short words such AS, AT, and VP or AS, PA, and TV. If you prefer, you can even separate them into two groups of three letters, like PSA and TVA or ATV and SAP. Perhaps the easiest way to remember the six keys, however, is to create an acronym or a word which is followed by one or more letters. For example, **PASTA V** or PAST VA.

Your immediate goal is to focus as much of your attention as possible on the combination of the **Six Keys** in order to establish a strong foundation for future business success. If the site which you are considering does not satisfy all of these important criteria, then you should redirect your efforts to other potential business addresses. Alternatively, if each of these important factors has been satisfied, you are ready to proceed to the next step: evaluating the influence which primary and secondary site selection variables will have on future sales.

Satisfying each of the **Six Keys** will provide you with the confirmation that you are on the right path - one which will substantially improve the odds of your achieving long-term business success.

Chapter Three
Defining Trade Areas

A retail store or restaurant serves a customer base which is typically divided into both a primary and a secondary trade area. Collectively, they account for where the great majority of customers come from.

The former typically accounts for the lion's share of customer traffic, meaning anywhere from sixty (60) to seventy (70) percent. On the other hand, the latter typically accounts for most, but not all, of the balance of a store or restaurant's customer traffic.

You also need to know there's a hierarchy when it comes to differentiating trade areas. Very simply, they range from small to large. Specifically, I'm talking about the following: convenience, neighborhood, community, and regional retail trade areas.

Convenience is, indeed, king. Increasingly, time or lack of it, is becoming a major influence in determining how we make our convenience, shopping, and eating decisions. Every minute is valuable, especially during busy periods like the morning rush hour, the lunch hour, and the always busy late afternoon/early evening rush hour.

Convenience locations focus on the immediate needs of customers. In addition to convenience stores and gas stations, or a combination of the two, today's convenience locations are increasingly likely to include freestanding banks, coffee shops, beauty salons, and fast food (quick service) restaurants.

Being able to easily get in and out of a convenience location is absolutely essential to not only attracting customers, but to boosting sales. If your fieldwork reveals that finding a parking space is a problem or that traffic stacking leads to congestion, then the smartest thing you can do is to begin looking elsewhere.

For the most part, convenience trade areas are defined by their small geographic size. They are most often visited by people who live in the nearby or immediate area, and by people who are passing through on their way to work, shopping, school, play, etc.

Convenience types of locations can range from a single user to several businesses. As such, a building footprint ranging from 2,500 - 15,000 square feet is the norm. Here, buildings are built close to the street in order to maximize visibility, feature easy ingress and egress, and offer lots of convenient front door type parking.

Moving up the hierarchy, there will always be strong demand for **neighborhood business locations** because of the convenience and choices they offer, primarily to residents living in the nearby area. At some point, it seems everyone either drives or walks by them on their way to get somewhere else.

Some of the characteristics of neighborhood serving locations are: limited critical mass, little direct competition, and affordable rents. These are the types of locations which foster more than their fair share of start-up as well as mom and pop businesses.

Small grocery stores and small drugstores can function as anchors in neighborhood locations. This type of location is also home to a variety of businesses which pride themselves on offering friendly service to a steady flow of repeat customers. They include local bakeries, dry cleaners, beauty and nail salons, coffee shops, ice cream shops, and small restaurants which serve a variety of food.

While neighborhood locations can be good or even excellent places to operate a business, they tend to be parking challenged - a real drawback which can inhibit small businesses from maximizing store or restaurant revenues. Here, on street parking is the norm.

Serving a much larger population than **neighborhood locations, community serving locations** are most often anchored by a mix of market leading grocery stores as well as a wide variety of retail stores and restaurants - many with either regional or national name recognition. Banks, home improvement stores, tire stores, liquor stores, coffee shops, gas stations, and a wide range of service types of businesses are some of the businesses which prioritize being located on a busy, easily accessed "main drag."

Regional serving locations are usually the first choice of national retail and restaurant chains - all of whom are interested in taking advantage of not only the surrounding area's large population and critical mass, but its anchor stores, synergistic neighbors, connectivity, mix of land uses, and high traffic counts. Another distinguishing factor is that regional locations are usually at or very near an interstate highway interchange - something which makes them very accessible to a large or very large trade area population.

Regional malls oftentimes anchor these types of destination locations. Expensive, but definitely worth considering, is how I would classify regional serving locations. Besides having the advantage of year-round temperature control, malls are bright, clean, interesting, and busy places to visit. Generally speaking, mall owners understand tenant mix and synergy better than most other shopping center owners. They also have a better understanding of marketing and programming. As a result, the best regional malls typically generate some of the highest square foot sales in the shopping center industry.

Except for kiosk and seasonal operators, opportunities for local merchants to rent space in regional malls is typically pretty restricted. While retail and restaurant operators can expect to pay high rents and pass-through expenses here, the beauty of a regional mall location is the unmatched guarantee of seven day a week, year-round traffic.

As is true of other business areas, remember that not all locations are created equal. Here you can find "home run" locations as well as average performing locations. While being close to anchor stores and food courts is typically high on every merchant's priority list, you're bound to pay a premium in rent if you want to be close to therm.

Regardless of the type of trade area location your business is in, it is imperative that you learn as much as possible about your customers. As such, you are advised to periodically conduct what I refer to as a short form in-person survey - something which might consist of 3-5 questions and provides you with the opportunity to make a series of observations. My recommendation is to conduct in store surveys over a multi-day day period. Note: I believe such surveys are superior to conducting telephone surveys.

Regardless of the type of trade area your business serves, it's always important to learn where your customers are coming from. While many customers will be coming from their homes, others will be coming from their places of employment, nearby shopping centers, educational institutions, hospitals, or perhaps, a sporting event, cultural, or entertainment function.

Once you've gathered customer information you are encouraged to map it - something which is commonly overlooked by members of the small business community. On the other hand, it is a visual tool which is relied upon religiously by multi-unit operators.

From my perspective, customer spotting maps provide business decision-makers with what I like to refer to as "market intelligence." Indeed, they form the foundation for visually identifying both customer origins and business trade areas.

When you create a customer spotting map, you'll see something that's easy to grasp. I'm talking about an odd shaped "boundary" map - something which might be amoeba shaped. You'll see that its borders extend primarily along the major street and/or road network which surrounds your business. That's because driving on primary streets and roads is not only faster, but accommodates higher volumes of traffic than secondary streets and roads.

TRADE AREA MAP

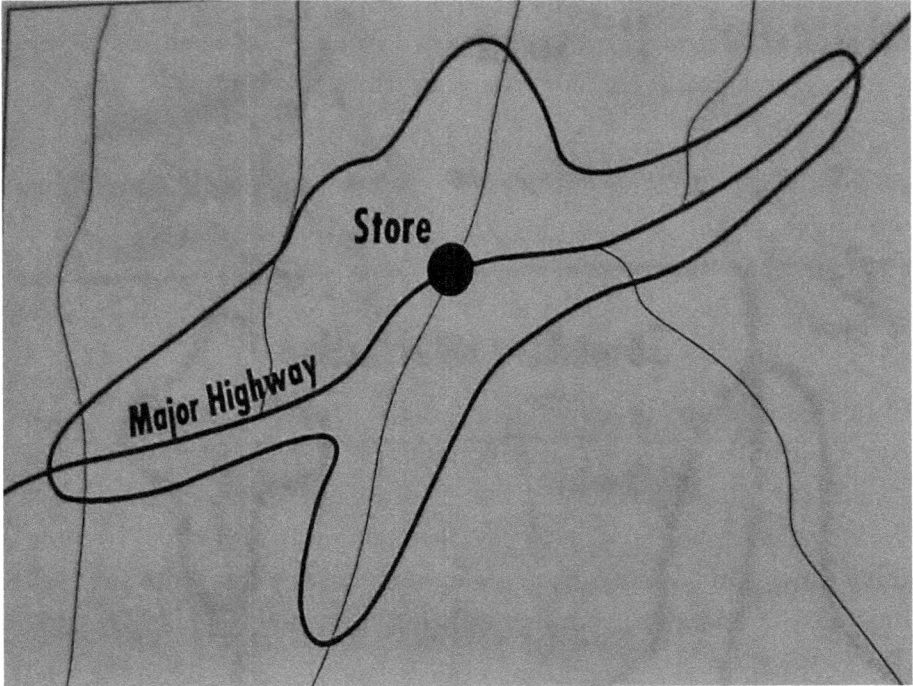

If you want to create some "fun" customer interaction when inquiring about where their visits originate from, you might ask them to place a pin on either a map or an aerial photograph.

One of the questions you should always ask your customers is how frequently they visit your store or restaurant. It should be no surprise to learn that repeat or frequent customer visits are much more important to business success than occasional or infrequent customer visits.

Depending on time and the number of questions you want to ask, you might also ask your customers to tell you where they are going to next.

Incidentally, I always chuckle when I hear a business owner or manager tell me that his/her customers come from all over. While that might be true, customers traveling from further away more than likely represent only a very small/tiny percentage/fraction of total customer visits. What really matters is learning where your most frequent/best customers, as opposed to infrequent customers, are coming from when establishing the trade area boundaries for your retail store or restaurant.

Many, many small businesspeople have never either (a) taken the time or (b) spent any money to document where, in fact, their customers are coming from. Nor do they know the frequency of their visits. As a result, when they get ready to look for expansion locations, they are unable to utilize customer-based data to make one of the most important decisions they'll ever make.

Data gleaned from drive time maps, rather than ring area maps that are based on miles, are a good compliment to customer trade area maps - especially if you are in the fast food or quick service business. In such instances, you'll want to pay close attention to the 5-7-10 minute drive times. On the other hand, when it comes to most retail stores, it's much easier and more common to justify prioritizing 10-15-20 minute drive time maps.

Regarding drive times, the information you learn from conducting customer surveys is essential to creating meaningful site selection criteria. For example, if 50% or more of your customers are coming from five (5) minutes away, this should become a standard you apply whenever you are looking at other locations.

Once you have mapped your primary and secondary trade areas, it's time for you to begin thinking about ordering both demographic and psychographic information - important data which is discussed at length in Chapter Four. In particular, you want to pay close attention to (a) the size of both the male and female population, (b) age groups, (c) income levels (d) education levels, (e) occupations, and (f) rates of both homeownership and renter occupancy.

If you decide to open more retail stores or restaurants, make sure you don't have any trade area overlap with an existing location. Cannibalizing existing sales is not recommended. This is one of the major reasons why mapping trade areas is a very, very important exercise.

You may be interested in learning a long-established fact prior to making any future site selection decisions: *sales decline with distance*. Since rooftops play such a pivotal role in generating customer traffic as well as sales, the more rooftops which either surround your business or surround the location you are considering, the better. The same is true for being in close proximity to employment centers such as professional and medical offices, manufacturing, industrial, and warehouse facilities, etc.

When looking to create a meaningful data base, one of the easiest ways to collect customer information is to establish a loyalty membership program. In doing so, you'll have access to not only names but addresses, visit frequencies, money spent, goods or products purchased etc. In the case of addresses, you can easily create a customer loyalty map. As for the other data, you are advised to make them a part of your site selection criteria.

Something you may not realize or be convinced about is that retail and restaurant businesses can expand their respective trade areas and revenues by locating in clusters. Automobile dealers are a good example of generating more customer visits as a result of grouping together in an auto park or on auto row. The same can be said for restaurants such as Wendy's and Burger King wanting to be near McDonald's. Banks, gas stations, and home improvement stores are other examples of businesses that like being close to their competition.

Top performing businesses are usually the ones that competitors like to follow because it provides them with a comfort level that they too will thrive.

Simply stated, you need to remember the following. "Where there's smoke, there's fire." Also applicable is, "Activity generates more activity." Yet another way to embrace **the power of clustering** is to think of it as a "magnet" which is capable of generating more demand.

Grocery stores are a prime example of the cluster principle. Since they generate constant traffic, they are a magnet for drugstores, fast food restaurants, coffee shops, gas stations, and banks, to name a few.

I pity the suburban business owner who decides to pick a secondary location in order to avoid competition. In such instances, the trade area for his/her "loner" location will be relatively small. Conversely, where several competing suburban businesses are clustered close to each other they will draw customers from a much larger geographic area.

It's important to note that in urban areas, the denser the area around your retail store or restaurant location, the smaller it's trade area will be. Conversely, low density urban areas will have larger trade areas.

An important take away from the above example is that as trade area boundaries grow in size, they end up generating higher levels of sales for competing businesses. So, the next time you get the urge to be a "pioneer," my advice to you is to resist going into an area which lacks a cluster of similar or synergistic types of businesses.

If you harbor any doubt about the power of clustering, I suggest you look no further than your local mall. Malls offer visitors not only food courts, but lots and lots of retail stores where customers can "shop until they drop." Indeed, malls are the preeminent example of how a grouping of similar business can not only boost sales, but expand the size of their individual trade areas.

DRIVE TIME MAP

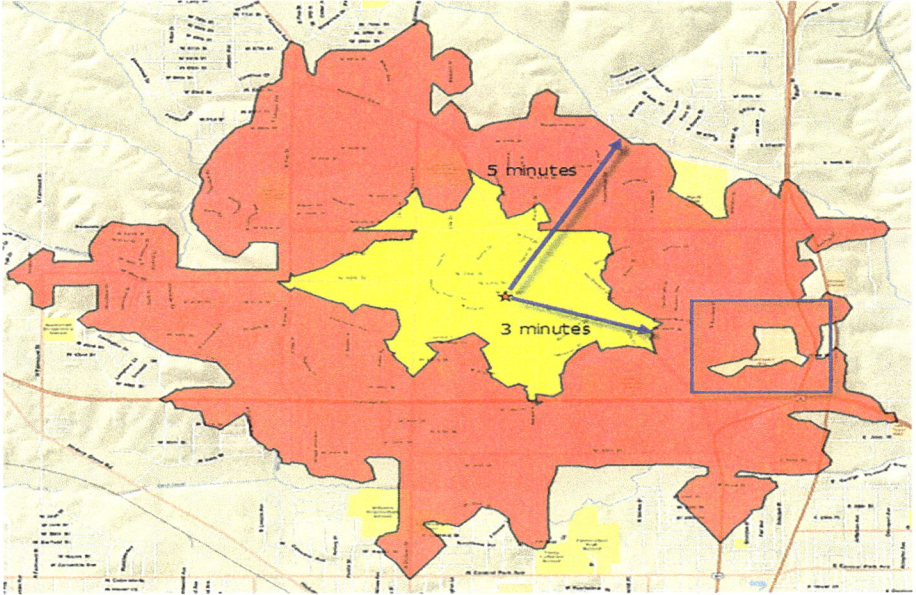

Chapter Four
The Importance of Demographics and Psychographics

Conducting demographics and psychographics research should be looked upon as an "insurance policy." My advice is to never make a retail or restaurant site selection decision without first learning more about the important data these two guideposts can provide.

While demographics and psychographics can help guide you to desirable market areas, they must always be accompanied by comprehensive area as well as detailed site evaluations. Collectively, these tools represent essential elements in building the type of foundation which is required to make "smart" location decisions.

Demographics - both **nighttime** and **daytime** - can be ordered from many different market research firms including well established companies such as Claritas, ESRI, Sites USA, and Buxton. Two additional resource groups you would be wise to contact in order to acquire demographic and psychographic data are (a) site selection consultants and (b) commercial realtors who possess a strong track record for picking "home run" retail and restaurant locations.

Demographics are based upon United States Census information and are updated periodically by companies such as Claritas in order to offer customers current information as well as much in demand demographic projections. They consist typically of multi-page reports which go into significant detail about the composition of the study area's population. In addition, most demographic packages typically include maps, charts, and graphs.

In order to compare "apples and apples," - one location to another - the most common analytical approach is to rely on *radius* based demographic reports. As an example, obtaining 1-3-5 mile radius based information can provide an individual or company with a wealth of valuable information. While *radius* based demographic reports are what most commercial realtors favor, I've found that most established businesses rely on *drive time* demographics.

Sometime, I hope you will ask your customers two questions: how many miles did you drive to get here, and, how many minutes did it take you to get here? While most people guess at the number of miles they drove, they can much more easily tell you how many minutes it took them to get to your business. To me, drive times are more reflective of a business' trade area.

While commercial realtors, market research analysts, and market leading companies all rely on demographic reports for important insights, many start-up and small business people oftentimes are overwhelmed by the many different kinds of data they contain. This is one of the reasons why you should seriously consider contacting and working with a professional - someone who is either a site selection consultant or an experienced commercial realtor - before you become actively involved in the retail or restaurant site selection process.

A word of caution; when you look at demographic reports you want to **pay particular attention to numbers as opposed to percentages.** While percentages can wow you, numbers are not only more insightful, but more meaningful. This is the reason why I've chosen to show you numbers instead of percentages in the statistical information which follows.

The beauty of demographic reports is that they identify lots of variables. Your job is to determine which variables are the most relevant to your site selection system or model, and then use them to *compare one or more existing business locations with one or more potential business locations.*

One very important thing I learned a long time ago was to **pay special attention to the number of people who live and work in close proximity to a location.** Typically, people who live and work nearby are much more likely than people who live and work farther away to become your customers. That's because, convenience plays an important role in people's purchase decisions.

The following information identifies a short list of key demographic variables for an existing "unnamed" *grocery anchored shopping center* located in an urban setting. For illustration purposes, **it includes both radius and drive time data.**

Variable	1 Mile Radius	3 Mile Radius	10 Minute Drive
Total Resident Population	17,706	103,574	55,853
Total Daytime Population	16,895	125,108	69,427
Population per Household	1.8	2.1	2.0
Median HH Value	$73,440	$55,859	$61,865
Median Home Value	$338,665	$213,804	$267,277
Bachelor's Degree	39.0%	28.2%	32.4%
Graduate Degree	31.6%	19.6%	24.4%
White Population	88.4%	67.9%	73.4%

The following is an example of key **drive time** demographics for an existing "unnamed" *mini lifestyle center* which is located in a suburban setting and is anchored by two table service restaurants and an ice cream store.

Variable	5 Minute Drive Time	10 Minute Drive Time
Resident Population	22,137	99,434
Total Households	9,385	41,547
High School Graduates	5,705	22,560
Associate Degree	1,340	5,833
Bachelor's Degree	2,547	11,909
Master's Degree	689	3,870
Home Value $150,000 $299,999	1,834	9,114
Home Value $300,000 $499,999	251	1,679
Home Value $500,00 $749,999	25	253
Home Value 750,000 $999,999	11	56
Home Values $1,000,000	20	78
HH Income $250,000 +	67	419
HH Income $150,000 $149,999	329	1,547
HH Income $100,000 $149,999	28	4,171
HH Income $75,000 $99,999	1,204	5,510
Average HH Income	$58,367	$59,411

Median HH Income	$45,587	$45,413

What follows is a comparative analysis for three different shopping center sites. The information which is provided is for a two-mile radius around each site, and identifies what the author considers to be the most relevant set of variables.

Demographic Variables	*Long Cove*	*Buttermilk*	*The Pointe*
10 year Projected Population	29,996	17,516	20,969
5 year Estimated Population	26,564	17,276	20,476
Existing Population	21,271	16,026	20,009
Estimated 0-17 Age Population	7,514	4,047	5,835
Estimated 18-24 Age Population	2,034	1,405	1,779
Estimated 25-34 Age Population	3,518	2,212	2,417
Estimated 35-44 Age Population	4,803	2,255	3,193
Estimated 45-54 Age Population	4,117	2,881	3,394
Estimated 55-64 Age Population	2,325	2,325	2,243
Estimated 65+ Age Population	2,155	2,181	1,616

Psychographics offer an invaluable insight into consumer spending habits. They provide insights into people's *lifestyles*. They provide both new and expanding businesses with the opportunity to not only understand who their customers are, but where they shop, where they eat, what they read, what they buy, etc., etc.

Psychographics are both a powerful and influential decision-making tool. Unfortunately, not every commercial realtor or small business operator relies on psychographics when making important location decisions. This is not because of high costs or lack of availability. Rather, it's due primarily to the fact that, unlike demographics, psychographics have not yet become a household word to many existing or prospective small business decision-makers.

Because psychographics can generate tremendous consumer insights, I have relied upon PRIZM information when completing consulting and site selection assignments. I am absolutely convinced that they should be a part of everyone's site selection evaluation process.

PRIZM is a proprietary system which has been developed by Claritas. Using Census information, PRIZM provides users with a variety of segmentation information which describes as well as groups customers according to *lifestyle* behavior. In total, nearly seventy *lifestyle* segments have been identified and ranked according to a series of socioeconomic factors which have been given not only interesting, but memorable names.

The very top PRIZM customer group is **Upper Crust**. It is the wealthiest *lifestyle* group in America. It is home to empty nester couples age 55 and older. No group has a higher concentration of residents earning over $200,000 annually or possessing a postgraduate college degree. Only about 1.5% of all U.S. households are classified as **Upper Crust**.

Blue Blood Estates, **Movers and Shakers**, **Young Digerati**, and **Country Squires** round out the Top 5 most affluent PRIZM groups. Collectively they account for only about 5.71% of all U.S. households.

Other desirable PRIZM groups which high end retailers and fancy restaurants would like to be able to claim as part of their customer base are **Winner's Circle**, **Money and Brains**, **Executive Suites**, **Big Fish/Small Pond**, and **Second City Elite**.

According to Claritas, the three largest lifestyle groups - **Traditional Times**, **Simple Pleasures**, and **Back Country Folks** - account for approximately 7.61% of U.S. households. The first two of these segmentation groups rank in the middle of the pack, meaning that their affluence level skews average. However, the last PRIZM group ranks at the lower end when it comes to incomes.

In order to give you a better insight into the different kinds of *lifestyles* which exist in the United States, I have chosen to identify a randomly selected listing of PRIZM groups. Each group features household index scores. An index score of 100 indicates the norm or average while increased index scores identify higher than average patronage.

New Empty Nests: Lifestyle Group #14 - listen to all news radio (230), belong to a country club (222), order from Lillian Vernon catalog (186), watch tennis on television (178), own vacation/weekend home (175).

Pools & Patios: Lifestyle Group #15 - buy from the Home Shopping Network (280), read **Kiplinger's Personal Finance** magazine (223), listen to Oldies radio (166), enjoy cruise ship vacations (159), watch soccer on television (153).

Bohemian Mix: Lifestyle Group #16 - shop at Banana Republic (233), buy from Dunkin Donuts (163), shop at Victoria's Secret (163), watch MTV (155), buy rap music (151).

Kids & Cul de Sacs: Lifestyle Group #18 - shop at Disney Store (272), watch Nickelodeon on television (264), go to the zoo (248), shop at Kohl's (189).

Home Sweet Home: Lifestyle Group #19 - read Inc. magazine (202), go downhill skiing (197), eat at the Cheesecake Factory (189), listen to alternative rock radio (186), member of frequent flyer group (164).

Gray Power: Lifestyle Group #21 - order from Reader's Digest Association (229), enjoy foreign travel by bus (177), play bingo (161), contribute to PBS (145), read *Golf Digest* magazine (136).

Young Influentials: Lifestyle Group #22 - read Maxim (216), watch

VH 1 (176), eat at TGI Friday's (151), order from Barnes & Noble (150), shop at TJ Maxx (132).

Suburban Sprawl: Lifestyle Group #30 - listen to classic hits radio (191), read *Road & Track* magazine (181), eat at Pizza Hut (142), watch pay per view sports (141), shop at Old Navy (138).

Like demographics, psychographics information can be ordered either by drive times or radii. And, similar to demographics, psychographics can be used to establish something which is very important - customer profile information. Collectively, demographics and psychographics provide small business owners and multi-unit operators with crucial *market intelligence*. I regard demographics and psychographics as extremely important tools for building a success story in today's constantly changing and increasingly competitive marketplace.

One other variable I want you to be aware of is nearby **visitor traffic**. Oftentimes, visitors can help boost customer sales at nearby restaurants and retail stores. Think of people who are in town to attend sporting events, concerts, and festivals. They are all prepared to spend money. From a sales perspective, think of visitors as "icing on the cake."

Here's a closing thought about demographics that I hope never leaves you. Site selection consultant John Melaniphy, in his book *Restaurant & Fast Food Site Selection,* wrote: "One of the primary **secrets** for successful site selection is targeting areas with demographics that match your most frequent visitors' characteristics." This statement underscores beyond a doubt why developing customer profiles is the "smart" thing to do.

Chapter Five
Customer Surveys and Customer Profiles

One of the most disappointing things about small retail and restaurant businesses is how little they actually know about their customers. If there is any group that needs to know as much as possible about exactly who their customers are it is the small business community. Big companies know their customers - that's one of the reasons why they are "big" companies.

Why has collecting customer information often been overlooked by so many small business owners? The primary answer is because it is something that very, very few of them have ever had direct experience with or been trained in. The other primary answer is cost. Quite frankly, most small business owners don't think about spending money on research. This rationale is one of the reasons why many small businesses are destined to never become bigger, multi-unit businesses.

If your restaurant sells pizza and offers delivery you have a lot of very valuable customer information at your fingertips. For instance, you know who your delivery customers are and where they live. You know how much they spend and how often they have pizza delivered. As a result, it should be very simple to collect and analyze such data. In addition, you can now create something which is absolutely essential - customer spotting maps. You don't need to stop here, however. Armed with such information you can create a series of illustrative charts and graphs. By doing these simple things you will be "head and shoulders" above your competition.

41

I like to regard such information as market intelligence. Collecting data is not rocket science. Rather it is something that every business owner can accomplish relatively easily and relatively inexpensively. The beauty of market intelligence is that it allows you to understand who your customers are and what their buying habits are. I can't tell you how many times over the past thirty or so years I've asked small business owners to tell me who their customers are and have either received a blank stare or have received only a very general response. They just don't know. Sadly, the "light bulb" has never gone off.

I love customer surveys because they allow me to build a preliminary customer profile. And, once I add in demographic and psychographic information, I can finalize my customer profile. Doing so gives me not only a vital insight into my current customer base, but the opportunity to begin looking at where I can replicate the same type of customer base for my next location. Ladies and gentlemen, knowing who your customers are is the foundation upon which "smart" location and "smart" site selection decisions are made!

Having a profile of who your customers are puts you in a unique competitive position. It allows you to look at specific geographic areas where, if you can locate the right site(s), you can confidently look forward to opening one or more potentially successful retail stores or restaurants. And, if you're either a good or a great operator, you should be able to turn the locations you have chosen, with the help of my Site Selection Scorecard, into even better performing locations.

Once you begin expanding, you need to continue conducting customer surveys. Don't expect that every location is going to generate exactly the same types of customers. However, what you are after is the opportunity to discern common similarities and overlaps in customer characteristics. Doing so will allow you to sharpen your customer profile focus and potentially to do an even better job of site selection in the future.

Possessing market intelligence information also enables you to eliminate guessing. It also means that you will no longer need to be dependent upon blanket marketing and advertising in order to reach existing and potential customers. Now, you can take a "rifle" as opposed to a "shotgun" approach to reaching people who live in, work in, and/or visit your trade area. In the meantime, you can take satisfaction in knowing that most of your competitors will likely continue missing the mark with respect to not only marketing and advertising, but site selection and profitability.

Short form customer surveys can be designed either in house or by a company which specializes in market research. The same choices exist with respect to administering long form customer surveys as well as analyzing their results. While budget is oftentimes the deciding factor on how you wish to proceed, the most reliable information comes from employing professionals.

I typically favor randomly sampled exit surveys - the kind where a customer is asked several important questions on their way out the door. Most people will feel complimented that you are asking them to help you out, and, will be willing to answer a short list of questions. Nonetheless, you cannot expect their cooperation unless you postpone their exit for no longer than approximately forty-five to sixty seconds.

While men are certainly capable of administering customer surveys, I prefer hiring females to complete this important assignment. People are more willing to talk to a woman, especially a young woman, than to a man. Also, they are more likely to say yes to a smiling person - someone who is polite, dressed in a professional manner, and typically young as opposed to being middle age or older.

Short form surveys start with two observations that precede any introductions or questions. The first observation notes a person's sex; are they male or female? The second observation has to do with race; is the person Caucasian, African American, Asian, Hispanic, or Native American?

Next, I like to find out what food item or retail item they purchased and how much they ended up spending? Afterwards, I like to find out where exactly they came from prior to visiting the subject restaurant or store? Was it from home, from work, from shopping, from a nearby restaurant, from visiting a friend, or, from being at some form of entertainment like the cinema, a play, a concert, or perhaps a sporting event?

I always want to know approximately how many minutes (five or fewer, six to ten, eleven to fifteen, or more than fifteen) it took a customer to get to the subject restaurant or retail store. This is one of the single most important questions that customers will be asked to respond to.

As I near the completion of the exit survey, I like to find out how frequently the person being interviewed has been a customer? Is it weekly, monthly, quarterly, twice a year, annually, or longer since their last visit? If you are asking yourself why the responses to this question are so important the answer is simple: you need to know who your repeat customers are. They, as opposed to the very occasional customer, are the people you want to target. They are the ones you want to reward. Indeed, they are the ones who will provide you with the best platform for growing as well as expanding your business. Very simply, these are the people who will end up putting money in your pockets. By now, I hope you realize something very important – not all customers are created equal.

Now, for the hard questions. You want to find out the age group of the person you are interviewing. Generally, age groups can be broken down in the following manner: under twenty-five, twenty-five to thirty-four, thirty-five to forty-four, forty-five to fifty-four, fifty-five to sixty-four, and sixty-five and older. Next, you want to ask them what street they either live or work on, and what is the nearest cross street? (If you wish, you can also ask them for their zip code.) The responses to this essential question will not only help determine the size and the extent of your customer trade area, but will enable the preparation of a highly informative customer spotting map.

The last question is one that you won't end up asking. Rather, it is one where you will show them an index card with various income groups identified and ask them to point to the one which best describes their current annual household income. The following illustrates the various income groups your customers could be asked to select from. Less than $25,000, $25,000-$49,999, $50,000-$74,999, $75,000-$99,999, $100,000-$149,999 and $150,000 or more.

Why is this information so important? The answer is really quite simple: you want to create a customer profile. This important information will enable you to not only know the answer to the question "who are your customers" but, provide you with an accurate tool for helping assess the potential of other locations and sites if you decide to expand your geographic footprint.

If you are wondering how many interviews constitute a valid sample, I would say that largely depends upon your customer count. Generally, I like to base my analysis on not less than 200-250 customer surveys. However, I enthusiastically embrace the phrase "the more the better" when it comes to determining the number of survey responses.

At this point, you are probably asking yourself two very important questions: is there a best day of the week to complete my short form customer surveys, and, is there a certain time during the day or evening when customers should be participating in such surveys?

The answer to both of these questions depends upon the type of business you are operating. Most lunch-oriented restaurants will want to take advantage of when the great majority of their customers are present. On the other hand, restaurants which do a substantial amount of dinner business will want to conduct their surveys during the evening. Retailers, on the other hand, have the luxury of conducting surveys over a longer period of time, such as from late morning to early evening.

For the most part, late week and weekends trump early weekday periods for conducting surveys, primarily because most restaurants and the majority of retail stores see their customer traffic peak late in the week and on weekends as opposed to during the early part of the week.

If you are interested in learning only one or two things about your customers, like how many minutes it took them to get to your business, or what their zip code is, you can ask them these questions at the cash register while they are checking out. If you are interested in learning a little more about your customers you might consider having them complete a short five to seven or seven to ten question survey after they have placed their food order and sat down. Afterwards, be sure to offer them a free beverage, small salad, or dessert item as a thank you for their participation. Believe me when I say they won't forget about having been rewarded.

If you are in the pizza delivery business you already have a wealth of point-of-sale information that you can "mine" in order to learn a whole lot about your customers. Neglecting to assemble, review, and analyze such information is inexcusable. On the other hand, I'm willing to bet that outside of defining their delivery area many mom & pop businesspeople have never invested either the time or the money to harvest such data.

Other avenues for collecting customer information are telephone interviews, drawings, contests, and customer loyalty cards. While different venues will end up producing different levels of information, they are all valid exercises for learning more about not only who your customers are, but who your "best" customers are.

Regardless of what type of survey instrument you decide to use, you need to assure each respondent that all of the information which has been gathered will be held in the strictest of confidence.

While long form surveys can occasionally be distributed to a random sample of customers at your retail store or restaurant, they are typically completed at home within a stated time frame such as three to five days.

In order to prompt widespread customer interest in completing each of the dozen or more questions that should be contained in the long form survey, it is common practice to motivate your customers by giving them some kind of gift certificate, purchase discount, or even cash. However, I recommend that your customers should only be eligible to earn a reward after they personally return the completed long form survey to your place of business within a specified period. Setting a deadline of two or three days should motivate them to revisit your place of business and turn in their survey responses.

Today, it is not uncommon for both restaurants and retailers to ask their customers to complete some type of internet survey. This is a very convenient way for customers to provide important feedback. Again, to motivate them to respond, business owners need to provide customers with some form of "reward" for their valuable time and input.

Each long form survey is intended to build upon the information which is contained in the short form survey. In the case of observation items which appear in the short form survey, they will need to be asked as questions in the long form survey.

Like the short form survey, the information which is contained in the long form survey is meant to remain confidential. Nonetheless, you want to capture each customer's name and residential or business address. This is especially important if you intend to build a customer spotting map in order to learn more about the geographic area which constitutes your trade area.

Please note that some customers will be reluctant to provide their address. In such instances, they should be asked to identify (a) the street they live on, and (b) the name of the closest intersecting street. Doing so will enable you to develop the always important customer spotting map.

The long form survey should start off by telling the person who is completing it exactly what its purpose is. For instance, "Your survey responses will be combined with those from other customers to help us better identify who our customers are, what they spend their money on, and the quality of their experience." It may even choose to state that "The responses which are provided will help influence where else we decide to look for and potentially open a new location."

If you are in the ice cream business you might ask survey respondents to name what their favorite flavor or treat is. In addition, you might ask them if there are any other products they would like to see you sell. Examples might include smoothies, ice cream cakes, coffee, flavored iced teas, baked goods, ice cream sandwiches, etc. You might also probe how often they would be inclined to use a drive thru if one were provided.

Another question you might consider asking is which type of nearby businesses would prompt your visiting us more frequently? Examples might include cinemas, bookstores, restaurants, etc. Similarly, you might ask them to identify one or two businesses they would like to see become your next door or nearby neighbor(s). Furthermore, don't be shy about asking them to identify who they believe your primary competitor(s) is/are.

If you want to learn even more about **customer demographics** ask survey respondents "What is the highest level of **education** you achieved? (Answer categories might include a high school degree, some college, a college graduate, or a postgraduate degree).

You might also ask the **occupation** of the head(s) of household? (Answers might include Professional, Manager, Sales, Business Owner, Educator, Retired, and Other).

If you are interested in gaining important insights into **customer psychographics,** consider asking the following. Are you a homeowner? Do you listen to talk radio? Do you watch reality TV? Do you attend professional sporting events? What kinds of music do you like? What type of car(s) do you drive? What is your favorite magazine? Do you own a laptop computer? Where do you like to go on vacations?

Incidentally, try using an iPad, as opposed to paper, when conducting customer surveys. The information they capture can easily be downloaded to an Excel spread sheet.

The information which is provided by short and long form customer surveys is full of insights - some of which can turn out to be unexpected. After conducting customer surveys, one restaurant company I worked with was able to document that most of their lunchtime customers came either by themselves or in pairs - something which encouraged them to rearrange their seating to include more two top tables rather than installing more booth or table seating capable of accommodating four or more people.

In another instance, customer surveys found that instead of attracting primarily male or primarily female customers to their restaurant, their customer base was split 50-50 between the two groups.

A pizza pick up/carryout restaurant I worked with had a busy location which was surrounded by apartments. Accordingly, they presumed that renters made up the majority of their customer base. After conducting customer surveys, we learned that the opposite was true. Subsequently, their plans to open another pizza restaurant became more focused on homeowners and less focused on renters.

One of my most memorable customer survey assignments involved an upscale ice cream company that wanted to learn more about their customers as an important step in developing site selection criteria. While we learned a lot of good demographic related information, we also learned that their customers preferred dining at a small hometown pizza chain more often than eating at other pizza restaurants. This important finding quickly led the owners of the two businesses to establish a working relationship which resulted in "paired" locations in amenity rich, upscale mini lifestyle centers where customers could enjoy being in a "Third Place" type of environment.

I hope I'm wrong when I say I'm betting that most small business owners will never invest in administering either a short form or long form customer survey. This doesn't mean they can't be successful. However, it definitely makes their chances for learning a lot more about their customers and applying that knowledge to finding "home run" locations more difficult.

If you ever decide to open additional retail or restaurant locations, or grow your business through franchising, my advice is to hire a company or a person who brings both expertise and experience to the table. Hopefully one of your hires will be a person who thoroughly understands site selection and can help you pick locations which are "winners" while avoiding locations which turn out to be "losers."

Incidentally, I always encourage business owners to "swing for the fences" when it comes to gathering information in their effort to secure a "home run" location. After all, you'll never be able to grow your business footprint geographically if you end up with a location which turns out to be nothing more than a "single" or a "double."

With the right system and personnel in place, you should be well positioned to consistently choosing either an outstanding or good *site* in what turns out to be either an outstanding or good *area*.

With **winners** and **losers** in mind, I would like to urge you to build your company around **two towers of strength**: great operations and profitable site selection. With regards to the former, you need to understand the psyche of customers since they have so many choices of where to shop or eat. Turning their visits into enjoyable as well as memorable experiences needs to become your goal, or perhaps your next passion.

To paraphrase a sage person, **"If you don't know a lot about your customers you don't really know your business."**

If you do as I suggest with respect to operations and site selection and later on decide to become a franchisor, you will put yourself in the enviable position of hopefully earning continuing royalties in addition to periodic franchise fees. While royalties can become a long-term profit center for you and your company, please be careful about who you select as franchisees. The wrong franchisees - those who are so anxious to open for business that they overlook important retail and/or restaurant site selection considerations - can end up not only hurting your brand, but disrupting your plans for further expansion.

In conclusion, as I was going through my files in preparation for writing my book, I came across some information about customers I decided needed to be shared with you. This important information originated with a friend of mine, since deceased, who owned a small multi-unit, family style pizza restaurant.

His commitment to taking good care of his customers reminded me of my father. Growing up, he told us that we should always "Treat his customers like family because they pay for our mortgage, they pay for your college, they pay for...." You get the idea.

Anyway, here are some of the "words of wisdom" that my friend wanted his franchisees and managers to not only understand, but take to heart and make the foundation for building **strong, long-term customer relationships**. He wisely understood that his was a business where you don't get many second chances.

I'll start off by telling you what my friend thought about one of the keys to success - **CUSTOMER SERVICE.**

- **SERVICE** is your invisible product.

- Good **SERVICE** is more often felt than seen.

51

- **SERVICE** is the most important thing we sell.

- Good **SERVICE** today means better business tomorrow.

- Customers vote with their feet. If **SERVICE** is bad, they'll go somewhere else.

- If you try hard, **SERVICE** is the one thing you can do better than your competition.

- If customer **SERVICE** is really poor, 91% of customers won't go back to a restaurant. That means you'll never have the opportunity to make them repeat customers.

Now, it's time to tell you why my friend valued **SMILES.** I hope his "words of wisdom" will remain with you as you serve your customers, regardless of whether they are first time visitors or repeat customers.

- Greet customers with a **SMILE**. It fosters goodwill and pays long-term dividends

- While a **SMILE** happens in a flash, the memory of it can last forever.

- A **SMILE** costs nothing, but creates much.

The next time you conduct customer surveys I hope you'll consider asking one or more questions about the level of service your customers received as well as whether or not they remember being served with a smile. If you do, "for better or worse," I think you'll put yourself in a position to learn a lot.

Chapter Six
Site Selection Tools

Every person who is engaged in retail and restaurant site selection is advised to utilize a series of standardized tools which can not only help direct their searches for "home run" locations, but either eliminate or minimize doing what, regrettably, too many businesspeople end up doing - relying on their "gut" in order to make important decisions.

Some of the most important site selection tools you should consider using are as follows:

- A Site Selection **Checklist**

- Site Selection **Criteria/Standards**

- Site Selection **Guidelines**

- A Site Selection **Strategy**

In the following pages I will discuss each of the aforementioned site selection tools. While some will be described in more detail than others, they are all essential components for making "smart" location decisions - the kind which will help your business not only succeed, but potentially flourish.

The **SITE SELECTION CHECKLIST** which follows introduces you to a host of important location related factors which I consider to be "foundational." While gathering the information which they identify promises to be time consuming, you need to understand that **there are**

no "shortcuts" when it comes to site selection.

As you begin your site selection search, you should focus your attention on not only the amount, but the composition of the **critical mass** within ¼ - ½ mile of the particular location you like.

Next, determine approximately how much of the surrounding area's **square footage** is devoted to retail, to restaurants, to office, to hotels/ motels, to industrial, to medical, to entertainment. And, be sure to get a good handle on not only the types, but the extent of **housing** in the surrounding residential area.

Is the location you like located in what could be considered a **12-15 hour activity area**?

From a **connectivity** perspective, is the location you like on a major road or street which is easily accessed by one or more intersecting streets? Please keep in mind, that **connectivity** drives customer **convenience** - something which enhances the opportunity for customer **patronage**.

Is the space you like an **end cap**, **inline**, or a **freestanding** building?

Does the space you are considering sit **parallel** or **perpendicular** to the street?

Regardless of the type of space you are considering, would you rate your immediate neighbors as being either **compatible** or **synergistic**?

Approximately how many **parking spaces** are located within 100 feet of your front door? How many are located within 150 feet?

What are the **lighting levels** like within 300 feet of the space or building you are considering?

Will the space or building which you are evaluating provide you with adequate **identification signing**?

Can future customers make easy/convenient/safe **turning movements** into and out of the property you are considering?

What is the approximate average daily **traffic count** on the street where you hope to open your business?

Do any trees or buildings either block or partially block **visibility** to your building signing and/or storefront?

Is the space or building you are considering located in a fast growing, modest growing, or slow growth **business corridor**? The same questions apply to the **surrounding residential area**.

List the individual **strengths** and **weaknesses** of the Area, Site, and Space (or building) you are thinking about for your business.

As you are finalizing the answers to the aforementioned information, please don't let high rents be a deterrent. Instead, **focus your time and energy on locations which are capable of generating the highest sales levels**.

SITE SELECTION CRITERIA/STANDARDS are differentiated by being quantifiable. Typically, they consist of fifteen (15) or fewer critically important measurable variables which determine whether or not the retail or restaurant space or building you are considering meets or exceeds certain minimum requirements. In no particular order, the following are representative examples.

Minimum lot and **space sizes** - i.e. 40,000 square feet and 3,000 square feet.

In the case of restaurants, a minimum **lot frontage** of 125-150 feet.

A minimum of **one seat per** 50 square feet of floor area for restaurants.

A minimum **Average Daily Traffic (ADT) count** on the street where your business will be located of 20,000 vehicles.

A location where the **speed limit** does not exceed 45 miles per hour.

A **building setback** which does not exceed 150 feet.

Thirty (30) or more feet of **window frontage.** (Note: glass wrap should be considered a "bonus" type of amenity.)

A **building depth** of ninety (90) feet or less.

A building **depth to width ratio** which does not exceed 3:1.

A minimum 10 minute drive time **daytime population** of 20,000, 30,000 or 40,000, etc.

A minimum 10 minute drive time **nighttime population** of 50,000, 75,000 or 100,000, etc.

A minimum **median household income** of $50,000, $60,000 or $70,000, etc. within a 10 minute drive time.

SITE SELECTION GUIDELINES are similar to site selection criteria/standards. The difference is that guidelines consist of *preferred* variables while criteria/standards consist of *required* variables.

Site selection guidelines identify what should be *priority* location options. The list can be long as opposed to short. As such, don't feel compelled to limit them to just 5 or 7 or even 10 variables.

What follows is a comprehensive list of what I like to think of as important site selection **benchmarks**. When considering a particular location, it is up to you to select the guideline variables which you deem to be the most important.

The presence of both a nearby **daytime population** and a nearby **nighttime population**.

The opportunity to display both freestanding and building **signing** consistent with your businesses' minimum requirements.

The opportunity to locate within a **business cluster** where one or more of your competitors is present.

The opportunity for uninterrupted **visibility** from all angles on the street where your business will be located.

The opportunity to **differentiate** your store facade. The opportunity to feature window **awnings**.

The opportunity to occupy space which is not negatively impacted by either incompatible or parking intensive **neighboring or nearby businesses**.

The opportunity to feature outdoor seating - especially covered **outdoor seating** (if your plans are to open a restaurant.)

The opportunity to occupy space which ideally reflects or approximates a **3:1 ratio** – 3 feet of depth per 1 foot of frontage.

A location which is not negatively impacted by (a) being on a **one-way street**, or (b) the presence of a **median**.

The presence of one or more **synergistic neighbors**.

The presence of one or more **shadow businesses**.

The presence of one or more nearby **anchor stores**.

The presence of a **mix** of retail as well as a **variety** of restaurants (fast food, fast casual, and table service) in the nearby area.

The appearance of a **well-maintained** property as opposed to one where property maintenance has been deferred.

The presence of **vacant space.**

The existence of **curb appeal.**

The ability to add a **drive thru or pick up window** as well as a bypass lane. (Note: Applying this "benchmark" is optional.)

A location in a **pedestrian friendly** or **amenity rich** shopping center where either a "Third Place" or "Experiential" opportunity exists. (Note: Applying this "benchmark" is optional.)

Depending on the type of business you plan on opening, do you need to be on the **going to work** or **going home** side of the street?

*****

One of my favorite site selection **memories** comes from a consulting trip I made to a large metropolitan community where my job was to determine if the area's franchisee and the commercial realtor he had hired were on the right track.

I wasn't impressed with an empty space we looked at near a university which was located in a dense urban area. As a result, over lunch I took the opportunity to communicate exactly what I was looking for to both the franchisee and his commercial realtor.

Afterwards, we headed out to look at a suburban location the commercial realtor was high on. When we drove up, I saw my **first "red" flag**. The small retail center he was going to show the franchisee and me space in was located behind a busy McDonald's restaurant. Right off the bat it was apparent that the building suffered from a lack of clear and unobstructed visibility.

As we approached the building, I saw my **second "red" flag**. The three of us needed to climb five steps in order to look at the subject space. That represented a limitation - a "big" barrier if you will, for some people.

After climbing the steps, I noticed my **third "red" flag**. The walkway in front of the door was only 4 feet wide. While this was a tight corridor, its narrow width eliminated the opportunity to add any outdoor seating.

When we walked through the subject space, I immediately saw **"red" flags number four and five**. The subject space was smaller - 1,200 square feet - than what was acceptable. Plus, it was only 15 feet wide - 5 feet less than the absolute minimum requirement.

When I expressed my disappointment to the commercial realtor about the site as well as the space we looked at (a former Subway sandwich shop) he got a puzzled look on his face. Then he became annoyed when I used a baseball analogy to inform him that what we saw was the equivalent of a "single" and nothing close to the "home run" location I was looking for.

This is when he told me something that only reinforced what I was thinking. He said, "But this is the best suburb in the entire metropolitan area!" What he had forgotten about was something I'm sure some commercial realtors and some prospective businesspeople either forget about, or perhaps don't really know about.

As you've learned by now, Location, Location, Location consists of three important variables. A good **AREA** without a good **SITE** and a good **SPACE** is a *loser*, not a *winner*. That's obviously something this under-educated, chauffeur-type realtor obviously knew little about. Just because a particular location is in a good area doesn't mean a site or a space are ready for "prime time."

Why have I chosen to tell this story now? My answer encompasses both the franchisee and the commercial realtor. As for the franchisee, he appears to have done a poor job of mastering his franchisor's site selection requirements. Furthermore, he more than likely failed to communicate this very important information to the commercial realtor who he chose to work with.

You may be interested to know that I sometimes refer to Location, Location, Location as my *ASS Principle* - something that gets everyone's attention right off the bat! Even though I thought it was memorable, one publication I wrote an article for thought it was offensive and wouldn't print it.

It's important that you know that I was a member of the commercial real estate community for thirty plus years. Coming from the public sector - I worked as a city planning director for 10 years - I earned a steady paycheck. However, there's no weekly paycheck when you decide to pursue a career as a commercial realtor. That's why I decided I needed to work with a mentor - someone who could put me on the *fast track* to earning money. Fortunately, I found that person and was subsequently *off to the races.*

Regarding the fact that retail and restaurant site selection requires doing lots and lots of "homework," I want to remind you of a quote I think is instructive. It's one of my all-time favorite quotes - one which is attributed to the late, great, legendary UCLA basketball coach John Wooden. He was fond of reminding his NCAA national championship basketball players that "failure to prepare is preparing to fail." My advice to you is to <u>never</u>, ever, downplay or dismiss what coach Wooden said. Always be prepared! Always do your "homework!"

In the long-term, the **real estate strategy** you choose to adopt and implement will play a key role in the success of your retail or restaurant business. If you think like the "Big Boys" - the national and regional players - you can rest assured that you'll have outstanding role models. When it comes to site selection, these are the companies who continue to hit "home run" after "home run." With few exceptions, they know how to pick WINNERS and avoid LOSERS.

The **site selection tools** previously described in this chapter, along with the **Site Selection Scorecard** which is profiled in Chapter Eight, constitute your *blueprint* for making "smart" location decisions.

While there is no substitute for conducting fieldwork, be sure to supplement your efforts by using Google Street View. It offers a compilation of panoramic photos which provide users with the opportunity to see a 360 degree view of the property (or properties) they are considering as well as other area properties.

Set your goals high. If you don't, you could easily be stuck with a mediocre or poor location - something that could end up testing your survival skills. With regards to doing your "homework," you are absolutely correct to liken it to having "a gun to your head." While that may sound harsh, it's a simple fact of life. Remember that old adage - "you get what you pay for."

In the absence of having a *mentor* to help you with site selection, please don't hesitate to work with either a commercial realtor who *specializes* in retail and restaurant site selection, or a site selection consultant, or both. In the long run, *they can help put money in your pockets*. Remember, they can also help introduce you to two very important parties: landlords and developers. Think of these two parties as *"partners."* Once you've established a relationship with either or both of these important players you can not only expect them to help guide you, but potentially bring you future "home run" opportunities.

In closing, I hope you recognize by now that people who are **patient**, **disciplined**, and **knowledgeable** are the ones who are the most likely to open more than one "home run" retail or restaurant locations - especially if they possess **good operations skills**. Indeed, these are the people whose respective businesses are the most likely to produce the kinds of robust sales and profits which will enable them to periodically open additional profitable locations.

Chapter Seven
Walking and Talking

Walking and Talking - known to many as "cold calling" - is an exercise you need to not only familiarize yourself with, but get used to - the sooner the better. During my thirty plus year real estate career, I found it to be not only an immensely informative tool, but immensely enjoyable. I regard it as an exercise which, more than any other, separates "the men from the boys."

I can't count how many times I've put on a smile and walked into a business when they aren't busy (i.e. early morning or 2-4 pm on weekdays) and asked to speak with either the owner or the manager of a retail store or restaurant. After introducing myself, giving them my business card, and advising them about the purpose of my visit, I've been able to learn lots of important information. What follows is a list of questions which, depending on time and priorities, I'm likely to ask.

*Approximately how many **years** have you been in business at this location*? Whether a business has been open for months or years doesn't matter to me. Anything ownership or management tells me is potentially important information.

*About how many **square feet** does your business occupy*? The benefit of knowing the answer to this question is that I can now begin thinking about sales productivity.

*When during the day or evening is your **busiest sales period?*** For some breakfast/brunch/lunch restaurants, the answer is early morning, midmorning, and early afternoon. Other restaurants will be busiest over the lunch and/or dinner periods. Some will do more business during weekends rather than during weekdays. For most retailers, weekends - especially Saturdays - is "prime time" for customer visits.

*Who are your **primary customers**?* Some restaurants and retail businesses cater primarily to men, while others have a predominantly female base. Some depend primarily on Millennials while others serve mostly Generation Xers. Many rely on a broad mix of customers. While some businesses appeal to value-oriented customers, others serve a less price sensitive customer. Some have built their success around serving primarily businesspeople and/or families.

*What do you consider to be **the strengths and weaknesses** of this particular location?* Here, my primary interest is learning insights which are based upon my **PASTA V** variables. For instance, I want to know if adequately as well as conveniently situated **P**arking exists? I want to know if **A**ccess allows customers to get in and out of a site easily? Is their sufficient **S**igning? Is the amount of **T**raffic driving or walking by a store or restaurant's front door a lot or moderate? Is it free flowing or is it congested? Is it two way or one way? Is **A**ctivity and critical mass in the nearby area - generally defined as being within a quarter of a mile of the subject business either growing, stable, or experiencing decline? And last, but by no means least, is storefront **V**isibility excellent, good, or in need of improvement?

By far the hardest question to get a straight or honest answer to is *Generally speaking, what are your annual sales?* This is typically confidential "market intelligence" information, and something I have to be careful doesn't end our conversation. Since I oftentimes already have some insight to this question from publicly reported sales data for most national and regional chains, I might preface my question by saying "Are you doing approximately $30,000 (or $40,000 or $50,000, or $60,000) per week in sales? You'd be surprised at how many of the people I talk to are willing to "spill the beans" and identify specific figures. That's what makes this important exercise so valuable!

In addition, I'm also going to ask a series of questions about the **Space** individual businesses occupy. Does your space have sufficient frontage? Is the amount of glass adequate? Do you have adequate room for display purposes? Are any of your neighbors synergistic? Do any of them provide you with additional customer traffic? Do you regard any of your immediate or nearby neighbors as incompatible? In addition, I like to make "mental" notes of any site amenities I see, such as awnings, bay windows, outdoor seating, LED facia/side/rear lighting, and/or a differentiated storefront.

On a scale of 1-10, how would you rank the appeal of the surrounding business area? What you are looking for is a score of **8** or more. A "bubble" score is 7. Any other score I regard as a negative - a potential warning sign. Afterwards, I typically like to ask the person I'm speaking with to elaborate on his/her impressions about the dynamics of the nearby area. Here, my goal is to learn as much as possible about which businesses are or aren't prospering/thriving.

I always like to ask *who do you regard as your major competitor(s)?* This is almost always an easy question for people to answer. It allows me to begin assessing competitor locations. Are they as good, superior, or inferior locations in comparison with the specific business I'm inquiring about.

I also want to know something which I regard as very important: *From a sales perspective, how does your business compare with others in your system?* What I want to learn is whether the subject business is performing at a high, average, or below average sales level. Specifically, I'm looking forward to doing something very important - begin separating the "winners" from the "losers."

If, during your questioning, you find that lots of retail stores and restaurants which are located in close proximity to the location you are considering are performing well, you should be very encouraged. On the other hand, if you find that it's a mixed bag - some places are doing good while others aren't - then you know to be a bit more cautious as you continue conducting area, site, and space visits.

When I'm through asking a series of questions I always thank the person I've been speaking with, whether our conversation lasted for 2 minutes, 5 minutes, 10 minutes, or longer.

Please note that throughout this important process the only notes I'm making are in my head. As you can appreciate, if I started writing everything down or recording answers, I'm pretty sure my visit wouldn't last very long, or be as productive as hoped.

Over my many years in commercial real estate and retail and restaurant site selection I've learned that "walking and talking" is not an activity that the majority of people charged with conducting detailed fieldwork and information gathering are willing to do on a comprehensive level, in part because it's not only challenging, but time-consuming. Most commercial realtors, start-up business owners, and first-time franchisees are intimidated by the process. I regard this as unfortunate since it ends up robbing them of something which is of immense importance - firsthand information. As a result, their knowledge base is, you guessed it, negatively impacted.

One of my favorite means of gaining a better understanding of a particular location is to conduct what I call "patio research." I'm betting most people don't have a clue about what I'm talking about.

That's ok. It's pretty simple. During a lunch hour, you sit outside on the patio of a fast food or fast casual restaurant and count and then record how many vehicles came through the drive thru. In the process, you record one or more observations such as: is the driver alone or with other people; are they male or female; are they old, older, youthful, or young; and, what do they end up ordering?

Fred Burkhardt, the President and CEO of Geneva Analytics noted that "small businesses are often constrained by not only capital, but expertise." Don't let this be you! I'm counting on you to always do your "homework."

Whether you realize it or not, **site selection is all about being able to accurately estimate sales** - a skill set which is lost on far too many people. If you can't wrap your arms around potential sales, you won't have a good handle on how much you can afford to pay in rent, or land acquisition, or building construction. Indeed, it is the equivalent of "rolling the dice!"

If you happen to earn your living working as the Real Estate Director for a growing multi-unit company or franchise restaurant or retail company, you no doubt understand the importance of cold calling via "walking and talking." As a result, you may already require each and every real estate broker or salesperson who represents your company to engage in this critical means of gathering "market intelligence." The same standard should also apply to franchisees - especially new franchisees. Accordingly, you need to not only arm them with "how to" information, but also train as well as mentor them to perform what I am convinced needs to become a "go to" means of learning important and helpful factual information.

Something else you can do as a Real Estate Director, business owner, or manager of a retail store or restaurant is to impress upon people you work with the importance of the quality of a customer's "experience." Doing so can make a significant difference when it comes to achieving business success, or experiencing business failure.

People today have unlimited choices when it comes to shopping and eating out. Some will be price sensitive while others will be brand sensitive. For still others, convenience is king. However, what will motivate all of them to "talk up" a particular retail store or restaurant is really quite simple: the quality or lack thereof, of the "experience" they had.

The quality of a person's "experience" is very likely to make a difference in not only how often he or she returns to eat or shop at a particular business, but how much money he or she decides to spend. Keep in mind that a person's impressions can extend well beyond the service they receive to such important influences as available seating, cleanliness, lighting levels, noise, wait times, odors and smells, merchandise selection, flooring, wall colors, decorations, and music.

It is absolutely paramount that every business owner, every manager, and each and every employee understand that the absence of a series of positive impressions can, regrettably, have a negative impact on the overall success of a particular retail or restaurant location. What may have originally been regarded as a "home run" location could potentially end up becoming a less productive, less profitable location - perhaps a "triple" or a "double" - if their customers "experiences" aren't consistently positive. In today's competitive environment, businesses which don't deliver a quality customer "experience" risk losing their most valuable asset - you and me!

In an article Matthew Dollinger wrote for **Fast Company**, he recounted a 15 minute conversation he had with the manager of a Starbucks store. He learned that "The idea behind customer service here is to make it one that isn't just good, we want to make it great. If people have a bad experience, they tell 7 people. If they have an average experience, they'll tell no one. If they have a great experience, they'll tell 23." This example illustrates why it's essential to "raise the bar" if you want to create a positive customer "experience."

You may be interested in learning that former Dallas Cowboys five-time Super Bowl champion quarterback Roger Staubach, affectionately known as "Captain America," upon retiring from football and on his way to building a fortune in real estate, was fond of saying something everyone in the business world needs to take to heart: **"It takes a lot of unspectacular preparation to have spectacular results…"**

Simply put, a good, average, or bad "experience" can become a "game changer." I hope you understand and will never, ever, forget, that an excellent or good location - one which passes not only my **Area, Site & Space** requirements but my **PASTA V** test - but is plagued by so-so or subpar management, and/or high prices, and/or low quality, and/or a poor customer "experience" can, quite simply, negatively impact the longevity of a business. Too often, when a store or restaurant fails and subsequently closes, guess which one of the aforementioned factors typically gets blamed more than any other? If you said **location**, you are, unfortunately, correct!

As you think more about the value of conducting fieldwork, I hope you'll remember what Yogi Berra the famous New York Yankees catcher and manager said. **"You can observe a lot by watching."** The only thing I'd add to the advice he offered is: (a) get in the habit of recording what you see for later reference, and, (b) don't forget to take pictures. They can be a vital, long-lasting source of information.

There's one more piece of advice I'd like to offer. Treat the selection of a retail or restaurant location much like choosing a wife or a husband; you need to be "picky." Please don't think that you can be the exception - you can't!!!

Chapter Eight
Creating A Site Selection Scorecard

For the uninitiated, site selection is similar to *rolling the dice* at a gambling table: sometimes you are going to win and sometimes you are going to lose. Therefore, I strongly recommend you complete a Site Selection Scorecard.

A Site Selection Scorecard is a tool which is based upon rating a series of variables as opposed to relying on your "gut" or some other overly simplistic reason(s) when it comes to making location decisions. Examples of the "wrong" reasons for selecting a particular location include: (a) cheap rent, (b) you live nearby or fairly close, (c) the space you are considering is vacant, and, (d) the subject space already has the upgrades and/or FF&E package (furniture, fixtures, and equipment) you need.

A Site Selection Scorecard is part of a *system of tools* which, when applied, will provide you with the confidence and assurance that you have not only done a significant amount of "homework," but will be able to "Sleep Well At Night" – otherwise known as **SWAN.**

Sadly, other than major and mid-size multi-unit retail and restaurant companies my experience has taught me that employing a **systematic** means for making location decisions is rare. The reasons for this boil down to one or more of the following: (a) an owner who insists on being solely responsible for deciding the fate of a location, (b) the lack of in-house real estate staff, (c) the lack of a Site Selection Checklist, SS Criteria, and/or SS Guidelines, and (d) a reluctance to work with either a commercial realtor or site selection consultant who has a track record of success.

The Site Selection Scorecard which follows is meant to be an **illustration** only. It employs a simple, easy to understand and easy to use point-based scoring system - one that can be tweaked as needed. You'll see that the most positive impression values are worth the most points. Relatively positive impression values are given the next highest number of points. The least impressive values are assigned the least number of points.

What I have identified below is a RESTAURANT Site Selection Scorecard. It is best used in a suburban setting rather than in a downtown, older business district, or dense urban neighborhood setting. For each and all of the latter, you'll need to make a series of modifications.

STEP ONE: "AREA" Specific POSITIVE Criteria

<u>Points Added</u> = 4, 3, or 2

<u>Factor</u>

The presence of one or more nearby retail **Anchors** _____

The amount of nearby **Critical Mass** _____

Nearby **Connectivity** to the surrounding area _____

Nearby **Daytime** traffic generators _____

Nighttime traffic generators _____

Desirable Nearby **Traffic Count** levels _____

Nearby **Synergy** opportunities _____

The nearby presence of *desirable* **Land Uses** _____

The nearby presence of *desirable* levels of
Nighttime Population _____

The nearby presence of *desirable* **Income** levels _____

The nearby presence of *desirable* **Education** levels _____

The nearby presence of *desirable* levels of
Daytime Employment   _____

The nearby presence of *desirable* **Age Groups**   _____

The nearby presence of *desirable* **Housing Values**   _____

Total Number of Positive Points out of 56   _____

At this point, it is important to clarify what is meant by **nearby**, both from a demographics and a site perspective. There is some latitude here depending upon the type of business you have.

With respect to demographics, nearby for a destination type business may either be a 3 mile radius or a 10 minute drive time. For convenience-oriented business, nearby can mean as little as a 1 mile radius or a 3 minute drive time.

Regarding site, nearby means very close. Typically, this means you should be looking at between ¼ and ½ mile.

When it comes to drive times and radii, I strongly prefer drive times for the simple reason that people's everyday actions are based more on drive times than on miles. While many people can easily recall that it took them 5 minutes to get to a particular location, they often struggle when determining how many miles they drove.

STEP TWO: "AREA" Specific NEGATIVE Criteria

Points Subtracted = 2 or 1 or 0

Factor

Area **Image**   _____

Corridor **Dynamics**   _____

Excessive **Competition**   _____

High **Speed Limit**   _____

71

Nearby Incompatible **Land Uses**   _____

Median Presence   _____

One Way Street   _____

Physical or Perceived **Barriers**   _____

Traffic **Congestion**   _____

     Total Number of Negative Points out of 18   _____

Now you need to <u>subtract</u> the Negative Influence score from the Area Specific score in order to arrive at a Total Score. **If the Total Score ends up being 46 or higher, then the AREA you have selected can be regarded as either a good or outstanding area**. *However, if the revised score doesn't meet this minimum acceptable point total, you need to begin looking at other areas for your business.*

While finding the right area should not be a significant challenge, finding the right site within said area will definitely prove to be more time consuming as well as more difficult. This is where the hard work begins. Remember to be patient. You may be interested to know that, over many years, I have found that too many people are in a hurry. As such, they are oftentimes willing to settle for a secondary **AREA** location. The sad truth of the matter is they just want to get open for business. You can bet this type of mindset would <u>not</u> be tolerated by the multi-unit companies who should serve as your role models.

STEP THREE: "SITE" Specific Key POSITIVE Criteria
                                     Points Added = 5, 4 or 3

<u>Factor</u>

Sufficient On-Site **Parking**   _____

Good **Accessibility** (Ingress and Egress)   _____

Adequate **Signing** (Building + Freestanding)   _____

Acceptable Levels of **Traffic**   _____

Good Level of Nearby **Activity**   _____

Good/High Levels of **Visibility**
(from East, West, Nouth & South)   _____

Total Number of Positive Points out of 30   _____

STEP FOUR: Other "SITE" Specific POSITIVE Criteria

Points Added = 3, 2 or 1

Factor

Anchor Presence   _____

Building **Setback** Distance   _____

Lighting Levels   _____

Tenant **Mix**   _____

Tenant **Synergy**   _____

Curb **Appeal**   _____

Total Number of Positive Points out of 18   _____

STEP FIVE: "SITE" Specific NEGATIVE Criteria

Points Subtracted = 2 or 1 or 0

Factor

Dated **Appearance**   _____

Excessive **Occupancy** Costs   _____

Excessive Building **Depth**   _____

Vacancy/Vacancies   _____

Undesirable Neighbors   _____

Deferred Property **Maintenance**   _____

73

Total Number of Negative Points out of 12 _____

The <u>next step</u> is to <u>subtract</u> the Negative Influence Score from the combined total of the STEP THREE and Secondary STEP FOUR Positive Scores. **If the Total Score is 44 or higher, then the SITE you have selected can be regarded as either good or outstanding.** *However, if the revised score doesn't meet this minimum acceptable point total, then you are advised to begin looking for another site.*

The following ***"bonus" points*** are only applicable IF the point totals for the AREA and SITE you have selected are rated as either Good or Outstanding.

STEP SIX: "SPACE" Specific POSITIVE Criteria

<u>Points Added</u> = 5 or 4

<u>Factor</u>

Adequacy of Store **Frontage** _____

Adequacy of **Front Window** Space _____

Presence of **Side Windows** (glass wrap} _____

Presence of Outdoor **Patio** _____

Presence of <u>or</u> Opportunity for **Neon Light Band** _____

Dimensions <u>not</u> exceeding 3:1 ratio _____

Total Number of Positive Points out of 30 _____

What you are looking for here is a score of 24 or more. Consider these points to be "icing on the cake" if you already have selected a Good or Outstanding Area which is coupled with a Good or Outstanding Site. On the other hand, **you might think twice about a SPACE score of less than 24** unless you can secure the kind of enhancements which can lead to a higher customer count and increased sales.

When it comes time to totaling up the combination of your **AREA** and

SITE scores here is the direction you should be looking for:

"Grand Slam" Locations	= 100+ points	= **Highest $ Potential**
"Home Run" Locations	= 90 - 99 points	= **Very Good $ Potential**
"Triple" Locations	= 85 - 89 points	= **Good $ Potential**

Remember, these are the only types of locations you should be paying attention to! When these locations signal a **GREEN LIGHT**, your next task is to make sure that the score total for the SPACE you are considering is sufficient to merit leasing.

The Six Step Approach which has been described is often overlooked by (a) most start-up, (b) lots of mom & pop operators, and (c) many small multi-unit operators as well as emerging franchisors because, in part, it spells out a laborious means for analyzing potential locations. I hope you won't be guilty of taking the easy way out as you embark upon finding a "home run" location.

The truth of the matter, as I've tried to illustrate, is that you need to not only find a good or outstanding **AREA**, but you need to also secure either an outstanding or good **SITE** if you are going to be taking the next step - finding a good or outstanding **SPACE**. This is how you compete! This is how you succeed!

The following Site Selection Scorecard evaluation shows how three competing suburban sites - (a) an amenity rich, pedestrian friendly mini lifestyle center compares with (b) a conventional strip shopping center and (c) a lifestyle center. Each of them is home to market leading restaurant and retail tenants, are located on busy multi-lane streets, and are located within ¼ mile or less of an interstate highway. In addition to rooftops, each of them benefits from having lots of nearby offices. Furthermore, each is located close to both grocery stores and drugstores.

Age wise, they were all built within 10 years of one another. Besides a difference in square footage, the most notable difference is that the lifestyle center features a regional as opposed to community trade area. After going through this comprehensive evaluation process, you should be in a good position to determine which one or two sites to prioritize and subsequently pursue.

STEP ONE: <u>Area Positives</u>

Factor	The Pointe	Buttermilk	Crestview
Anchors	4	2	3
Critical Mass	4	2	4
Connectivity	3	3	4
Daytime	3	4	4
Nighttime	4	4	4
Traffic Counts	3	4	4
Synergy	4	4	4
Land Uses	4	4	4
Population	3	3	4
Income	4	3	3
Education	4	3	3
Employment	3	4	4
Age Groups	4	3	3
Housing	4	3	3
TOTAL POSITIVE POINTS	+51	+46	+51

STEP TWO: <u>Area Negatives</u>

Factor	The Pointe	Buttermilk	Crestview
Image	0	-1	0
Dynamics	0	-1	0
Competition	0	0	0
Speed Limit	0	0	0
Land Uses	0	0	0
Median	0	0	0
One Way	0	0	0
Barriers	0	0	0
Traffic Congestion	0	-1	0
Street Repairs	0	0	0
TOTAL NEGATIVE POINTS	0	3	0
STEP #1 *Minus* **STEP #2** =	+51	+43	+51

AREA CONCLUSION: OUSTANDING GOOD OUTSTANDING

STEP THREE: <u>Primary Site Positives</u>

PASTA V

Factor	The Pointe	Buttermilk	Crestview
Parking	5	4	5
Accessibility	5	4	5
Signing	5	4	5

Traffic	4	5	5
Activity	5	5	5
Visibility	4	4	5
TOTAL POSITIVES POINTS	+28	+26	+30

STEP FOUR: <u>Secondary Site Positives</u>

Factor	The Pointe	Buttermilk	Crestview
Frontage	3	3	3
Windows	2	2	3
Anchor	3	3	3
Setback	3	2	3
Lighting	3	3	3
Synergy	3	2	3
Pedestrian	3	2	3
Appeal	3	2	3
TOTAL POSITIVE POINTS	+23	+19	+24
STEP #3 *Plus* STEP #4 =	+51	+45	+54

STEP FIVE: <u>Site Negatives</u>

Factor	The Pointe	Buttermilk	Crestview
Appearance	0	-1	0
Costs	0	0	-1

78

Building Depth	-1	0	0
Space Shape	-1	-1	0
Neighboring Uses	0	0	0
Maintenance	0	-1	0
Vacancy	-1	0	0
TOTAL NEGATIVE POINTS	-3	-3	-1
STEPS #3 & #4 Minus STEP #5	+48	+42	+53
SITE CONLUSION:	**OUTSTANDING**	**GOOD**	**OUSTANDING**
AREA + SITE SCORE:	**+99**	**+85**	**+104**
CONCLUSION:	**"Home Run"**	**"Triple"**	**"Grand Slam"**

Each of the aforementioned locations are WINNERS. Now your task is to make sure that this classification also describes your SPACE. **The total SPACE points you've identified will either qualify or disqualify the location you have been evaluating!**

The evaluation system which has been described permits a certain level of subjectivity. However, what is important is that you don't allow emotion to replace objectivity. You need to complete your evaluations with a level head. Sometimes getting a second opinion is the best thing you can do in order to remain objective.

When making evaluations you might consider looking at **aerial photographs** in order to get a heightened overview of the site as well as the surrounding area. In addition, you should be talking with area businesspeople in order to gain a better understanding of both the site and the area that you are contemplating making an investment in.

Commercial realtors who are not directly involved in listing a subject property represent another potential information resource. And, if you feel compelled to discuss your interest with more resource people, you might consider talking with a **site selection consultant** who has many years of experience working with retail and restaurant owners both in and outside of the location where you are contemplating making a major investment.

By employing the scoring system which has been identified a person will be able to more easily determine what constitutes a "Home Run" location as well as what can be classified as a "Triple" location. In rare instances, you may even come across a "Grand Slam" location. They are very special types of opportunities. They consist of not only an outstanding site but an outstanding area. For classification purposes, these are the A+ types of locations - the kind which not only represent a very strong and enviable foundation for future growth, but which have the capability of preventing your competition from locking up superior sites.

"Triple" locations consist of good sites in what can be classified as either good or outstanding areas. They should, along with "Home Run" and "Grand Slam" locations be the only types of locations that you move forward with. In order to avoid almost certain failure, you should look past what constitutes the great majority of retail and restaurant locations that periodically become available - the so called "double" and "single" locations. Even if the rent is cheap, the opportunity for immediate occupancy exists, and/or the site is close to where you live, please do not keep any subpar locations under consideration. If you do, you will be guilty of ignoring the substantial amount of advice which this guidebook provides.

In conclusion, if you feel that the **Site Selection Scorecard** information which has been described is somewhat overwhelming, please don't panic. It is, indeed, a lot of information to absorb - something that very few people will fully comprehend the first time they read through it. As a result, don't shy away from rereading this important information over again, or, perhaps even over and over again!

_____

While this chapter showcases a *Suburban Site Selection Scorecard,* similar scorecards can and should be developed when evaluating *Older Business District, Dense Neighborhood and Downtown locations.* While the scorecard format will remain the same, some new variables should be added while some previously identified variables need to be deleted.

Perhaps the most challenging scorecard to create is one which I haven't mentioned yet; the *Mixed-Use Site Selection Scorecard.* Given the increasing popularity and pronounced growth of mixed-use development, creating such a scorecard should become a priority.

Many large urban mixed-use developments feature pedestrian friendly environments and public open space - places where people can gather for a wide variety of purposes. Here, amenities such as water, outdoor seating, park-like settings, wi-fi, and programmed activities which promote venues ranging from concerts to farmers markets, are counted on to attract people as well as add a little "sizzle."

Chapter Nine
Estimating Retail and Restaurant Sales

Developing a system for accurately estimating future sales is not an easy task. Like site selection, it is part art and part science. It is, however, an extremely important step and something which needs to be completed prior to opening a new business.

Two longstanding and highly reliable methodologies exist for forecasting sales. The first of these is called the **analog** system. It was developed by the Kroger Company many, many years ago and relies exclusively on past sales from stores possessing a series of similar characteristics as well as exit surveys to accurately forecast new store sales volumes.

The other forecasting method is even older. It is known as the **gravity** system. It looks at the size and composition of an area's critical mass to forecast customer sales from the surrounding trade area. Hypothetically, the bigger a geographic area's critical mass the bigger its trade area draw, and, the greater its overall sales. In addition, the gravity model established one of the guiding principles of location analysis: **sales decline with distance**.

Rather than rely exclusively on one or the other of these proven systems the author typically likes to borrow from each of them. In addition, he likes to interject a third consideration - significant amounts of customer information coupled with growth related information - whenever he is involved in projecting retail or restaurant sales.

A reliable sales forecasting system will take many variables, rather than only a few variables, into consideration. Each variable has the potential to influence projected sales - some more than others. Two often overlooked variables are advertising and marketing.

Knowing as much as possible about your customers is an essential first step. In particular, **you want to learn everything you can about your best and most loyal customers.** While your best (repeat) customers may only account for a minority of your overall customer traffic counts, they are traditionally responsible for a significant amount of your sales.

Important questions you want to learn the answers to include: who are your customers, where are they coming from, how many minutes did it take them to get to your place of business, what did they end up buying, how much money did they spend, how often do they visit, etc., etc.

Demographic and lifestyle factors, along with information obtained as a result of conducting Area, Site, and Space related field visits, are especially critical components for developing reliable sales forecasts. Once such variables have been identified the real challenge becomes how much weight should be assigned to each of them.

Consider, for instance, which of the following demographic factors should be the most heavily weighted in determining future retail or restaurant sales. Total population (total *number* of people), the *number* of college educated households, the number of households with incomes of $75,000 or more, the *number* of homes valued at $250,000 or more, or the *number* of people employed in professional/business/financial and related jobs. By now it should be clear that you need to focus on numbers as opposed to percentages!

What you also need to do is **begin looking at which factors are correlated with sales**. Some will be highly correlated while others will have little or no correlation. **Your job is to learn which factors have the most important influence on sales.** Only after you complete this very important exercise can you begin building your site selection model.

One of the first things you need to do is determine whether there is a correlation between sales and trade area population. Similarly, you need to evaluate whether a correlation between trade area households and sales exists.

Next, you need to determine if any correlation exists between sales and a number of important variables. Examples might include (a) the number of people possessing a Bachelor's, a Master's, and/or a Professional School Degree, (b) the number of people twenty-five to fifty-four years of age, and (c) the number of people who are employed in white collar jobs - especially in the professional/business/financial sector.

You will also need to determine if any correlation exists between sales and the number of trade area households in certain income ranges such as $75,000 - $99,999 or $100,000 - $149,999. Other sales correlations might be related to the value of home owner occupied housing (such as those costing $300,000 or more) and the number of daytime employees who work in an area – people who may become customers.

It is also essential to determine what impact both area and site factors have on retail and/or restaurant sales. With respect to the former, you need to determine if any correlation with sales exists for variables such as the size of the nearby critical mass, the number and size of nearby anchor stores, the number of shadow businesses, the amount of competition, and, the type of land use mix in the nearby area.

Be sure to look at activity generators when estimating sales. Office buildings typically provide a boost to breakfast and brunch restaurants. On the other hand, cinemas enhance evening and weekend sales. While shopping malls generally generate customer traffic throughout the day, evenings and weekends are their busiest times.

In addition to determining the correlation between sales and the number of parking spaces serving your business, some secondary site variables which you might add to your evaluation list include: the amount of lot frontage, the amount of store frontage, the amount of building setback, and the amount of synergy with both nearby and adjacent uses.

For those of you who want to delve into micro analysis you might consider such correlation to sales variables as the presence or lack of connectivity to the surrounding area, the local speed limit, the number of moving lanes of traffic, the presence or absence of a nearby traffic signal, and the hours during which significant business activity occurs.

Whether a business is freestanding, in an end cap, or is classified as inline space, the type of space your business occupies will have an impact on sales. In most instances, sales correlations are highest for freestanding buildings and decline for both end cap and inline building locations. For evidence of this all you need to do is visit your corner drugstore. Over the last decade drugstores have made a "big" time switch from occupying end cap building space to locating into freestanding buildings. While a freestanding location, especially one which is situated at a corner and is served by a traffic signal, is going to be expensive, the bottom line is that the substantial increase in sales justifies why drugstores have been sold on relocation.

Both a series of nontraditional and easily overlooked factors can also influence sales estimates. Gathering information which details the number of new residential lots which have been approved and/or platted, building permits which have been issued, the number of new postal drops, projected increases in school enrollment, new job growth, and attendance at large seasonal attractions such as amusement parks and major sporting events can help explain why you should count on a boost in sales revenues.

Whereas the owner of multiple retail stores or restaurants can reference sales at existing locations in order to project sales for a new location, the start-up businessperson has no choice but to make a series of assumptions - something which can be a daunting exercise to say the least. Furthermore, estimating sales for a start-up business can be difficult because a new business owner must take into account a factor which is frequently overlooked - a start-up period during which sales may not get off to a fast start. Given these obstacles, the first-time business owner has no choice but to be as thorough and realistic as possible.

When making retail sales forecasts, **sales per square foot** is the best and most common standard for measuring business success. While sales per square foot are also important in the restaurant industry, another important variable - **sales per seat** - should also be considered. Furthermore, whether applied to retail stores or to restaurants, another very credible performance measure is **sales per parking space**.

If you want to consider more sales barometers, some of which are more meritorious than others, you should look to your trade area with respect to sales per resident, sales per household, sales per family, sales based upon the number of people with BA, MA, PhD, and professional school degrees (primarily doctors, dentists, and attorneys), sales based upon certain age groups, sales based on certain income levels, sales based on certain home values, and sales based on the number of persons employed in white collar jobs. The take away here is that **the more ways you have to evaluate sales performance the better.**

If your business locations include a series of drive thru or pick up windows, by all means use sales attributable to such an amenity to help forecast future sales at locations you are considering for expansion.

Based upon my experience, it's beneficial to incorporate as many benchmarks (analogs) as possible when putting together sales forecasts. Unfortunately, this important performance-based information is not available for either start-up retail and restaurant businesses or first-time franchisees - something which puts them at a distinct disadvantage when trying to arrive at a reliable sales forecast figure.

When doing your "homework," please don't overlook **POS** (Point of Sales) data. It will tell you when, what, and how much money a customer spent while visiting your retail store or restaurant. It's absolutely imperative that you have the most sophisticated equipment possible in order to capture detailed customer related information.

It's time to look at some examples of how you might determine future sales for a potential "home run" location. The seven (7) benchmark sales forecast data illustrations which follow project sales for a New Store Location which is based upon (a) two carefully selected strong performing existing stores and (b) their most recent annual sales. Here, the focus is exclusively on **nighttime population.**

For illustration purposes, I'm labeling them as Locations **K** and **B**. Within a **3 mile radius**, Location **K**'s most recent annual sales reached $1,449,507, while the annual sales for Location **B** were $988,068.

Benchmark #1 = **SALES PER PERRSON**

Location **K sales** divided by 67,229	$21.56
Location **B sales** divided by 49,623	$19.91
Average sales of stores K & B	$20.75
New Store Location = 60,118 people	
New Store Location Sales Forecast	**$1,247,450**

Benchmark #2 = **SALES PER HOUSEHOLD**

Location **K** sales divided by 28,830	$50.28
Location **B** sales divided by 20,172	$48.98
Average sales of stores K & B	$49.63
New Store Location = 22,326 households	
New Store Location Sales Forecast	**$1,108,039**

Benchmark #3 = **SALES Based Upon** # of B.A., M.A. & Professional School **College Degrees**

Location **K** sales divided by 14,070	$91.33
Location **B** sales divided by 11,842	$83.44
Average sales of stores K & B	$87.39
New Store Location = 18,146 people	
New Store Location Sales Forecast	**$1,585,779**

Benchmark #4 = **SALES Based Upon** # of People Age 25 - 64

Location **K** sales divided by 34,233	$42.34
Location **B** sales divided by 27,540	$35.88
Average sales of stores K & B	$39.11
New Store Location = 33,177 people	
New Store Location Sales Forecast	**$1,297,552**

Benchmark #5 = **SALES Based Upon # of Household Incomes of $75,000+**

Location **K** sales divided by 9,545	$151.86
Location **B** sales divided by 8,467	$116.61
Average sales of stores K & B	$134.28
New Store Location = 10,638 people	
New Store Location Sales Forecast	**$1,428,471**

Benchmark #6 = **SALES Based Upon # of Homes Valued at $200,000+**

Location **K** sales divided by 6,144	$235.92
Location **B** sales divided by 4,266	$231.61
Average sales of stores K & B	$233.77

New Store Location = 7,751 homes
New Store Location Sales Forecast   **$1,811,951**

Benchmark #7 = **SALES Based Upon** # of Residents Employed in Professional/Business/Financial & Related **White Collar Jobs**

Location **K** sales divided by 14,152	$102.42
Location **B** sales divided by 11,763	$85.00
Average sales of stores K & B	$93.71

New Store Location = 16,398
New Store Location Sales Forecast   **$1,536,657**

The next sales forecasting step is to determine whether to use some or all of the seven (7) previously identified benchmark factors in order to make a final estimate of future sales for the new store location.

EXAMPLE #1. The easiest thing for the person making a sales forecast would be to equally "weight" each of the aforementioned seven sales forecast figures. Doing so produces a new store location sales estimate of $1,252,636.

EXAMPLE #2. Since my sales forecast is based upon working with an "upscale" retail store, another option would be to determine which 4 benchmark factors are deemed to be the most relevant for driving sales. Doing so might result in the following: Sales per Person, Sales per

Household, Sales per Educational Achievement, and Sales per White Collar Jobs. If each of these were to be weighted equally, estimated new store location sales would be $1,369,481.

EXAMPLE #3. Note, if one additional benchmark factor – **Household Incomes of $75,000 or more** - was added to the 4 benchmark factors mentioned above, the new store location sales estimate would change only slightly to $1,381,279.

At this point, one might ask if the three sales forecast averages which have been identified are sufficient to make a location decision? My answer would be "maybe." **I say this only because I think assigning a "weighting" factor is a plausible option. The takeaway here should be that not all sales factors, like not all location factors, are created equal.**

Below, is an illustration of a "weighted" forecast methodology which depends entirely upon the "studied" opinion of the person making the sales forecast. In this case, I have only included what I think are the 4 most relevant benchmark factors which should be employed when deciding whether or not to open a new store location.

Benchmark #1 = $1,247,450 x .20 = $249,490

Benchmark #5 = $1,428,471 x .25 = $357,118

Benchmark #7 = $1,536,657 x .25 = $384,164

Benchmark #3 = $1,585,779 x .30 = $475,734

Collectively, the aforementioned benchmark figures add up to estimated sales of $1,466,506. Note: Daytime population and Visitor data can also be used to forecast new store location sales, albeit primarily on a secondary basis.

_____

Armed with comparative sales data, you now have an invaluable knowledge base which can be used to create a sales forecasting model. Doing so will provide you with a powerful new tool which is capable of helping you separate the *winners* from the *losers*.

Importantly, a sales forecasting model or system will enable you to determine if you can afford to buy or rent a property. For your information, most businesses can afford to pay 7-8% of their sales in rent. Where a land purchase is being pursued, things can become more complicated. For example, are you looking at buying a raw piece of ground, or one which has been graded and has all the utilities on site? Depending on your answer, what you can afford to pay will vary.

I hope you won't forget that the most overlooked influence on sales is day-to-day management/operations. A good manager or owner, along with a well-trained work force, can make a huge difference in determining the success of a retail store or restaurant. A skilled manager/operator is certain to make sure that things "fire on all four cylinders," whether it be service, value, price, cleanliness, and/or quality. Sadly, too many businesses fail, not from an inability to meet my **Location, Location, Location** and **PASTA V** tests, but, from none other than poor management/operations.

Speaking of the value of having good or great operations, you may be surprised to learn that, in some instances, the person who either manages or operates a retail or restaurant business will be the person who has a lot to say about whether a particular real estate location gets "green lighted" or "red lighted." Personally, I favor such input.

One other very important consideration I think is worth mentioning is the need to determine whether or not it's important for your retail or restaurant business to be located on the going to work or going home side of the street.

With regards to knowing which side of the street to be on, I want to recount two examples that have stuck with me for a long time. Years ago, McDonald's had good locations in two fast growing suburban corridors and one in a busy older part of town on what constituted the going home side of the street. However, when breakfast sales became an increasingly larger component of overall business revenues, it was a "no brainer" that moving across the street would boost sales. This is exactly what they did - something which resulted in each location being not only busier, but able to record substantial increases in sales.

Given the above example of McDonald's, it's pretty clear that, if you are in the bakery, coffee, or donut business, you should pursue locations which are primarily on the going to work side of the street. In select instances, locating on the going home side of the street either at or near a traffic signal represents a potential, but secondary, alternative.

No discussion of sales would be complete without mentioning the "danger from within" - cannibalization. When decision-makers decide to expand, they need to be very careful about approving any new locations which have the potential to overlap an existing retail or restaurant's trade area.

My own belief is that, unless a new location has the potential to become a big/huge winner, it would be sheer folly to authorize opening a new retail store or restaurant if it stands a good chance of eroding sales at an already existing location by more than approximately 3-5% unless, of course, said location is already a big/huge winner. The potential for any larger loss of sales is the equivalent of "playing with fire." It would be like inviting the fox into the henhouse.

Sales cannibalization, is something which, regrettably, happens from time to time. Most often, it is due to business leadership's being in a hurry to roll out new locations without first completing exhaustive "homework." What's the best way to avoid potentially cannibalizing sales? The answer is simple: make sure that you understand the extent of your existing store or restaurant's trade area.

I want to take this opportunity to tell you what fast food restaurant behemoth Chick-fil-A considers to be the <u>4 most important factors for building customer loyalty</u>. They are: Taste, Speed, Attentiveness/ Courteousness, and Cleanliness. Why am I mentioning this information here? The answer is, because if you are in the restaurant business you might consider incorporating some or all of these important factors in the form of one or more questions the next time you decide to conduct a customer survey.

While impossible to quantify, there's no doubt in my mind that all of these important factors are capable of boosting customer sales. As such, you might want to take each of these "icing on the cake" factors into consideration the next time you need to estimate future sales.

FYI, Chick-fil-A generates more sales per restaurant than any other fast food restaurant! Furthermore, they accomplish this by being open only six days a week! I don't mind telling you that if Chick-fil-A were a publicly traded company I wouldn't hesitate to own its stock!

Chapter Ten

The Role of Commercial Realtors
and Consultants

It's extremely important for you to understand that there are two types of commercial realtors. The first, and by far the most prevalent, are what are referred to as Listing Agents. These are people who specialize in listing retail and restaurant properties. You'll know them by the freestanding signs they post on properties and/or in windows of the retail and restaurant buildings they are seeking to either lease or sell.

The second type of commercial realtor is a person who specializes in retail and restaurant site selection, and, is someone who oftentimes is knowledgeable about as well as involved in some manner of commercial development.

Listing agents initially spend a lot of their time on developing marketing brochures and marketing properties - whether it be land, an existing or to-be constructed retail or restaurant building, or, vacant or soon to be available space - to other realtors as well as potential end users and investors.

Realtors specializing in retail and restaurant site selection represent a "minor" percentage of all commercial realtors. They are field driven, meaning that they focus their time, energy, and expertise on working with end users as well as developers. They are relationship as well as performance driven people. They are people who prioritize building the types of relationships which lead to repeat business.

Listing agents typically have upwards of a dozen listings at any one time. Indeed, some have more than two dozen listings as a result of their experience, track record, and name recognition. These are people who, for the most part, have a steady or fairly steady income stream.

Unlike listing agents, commercial realtors specializing in retail and restaurant site selection don't have dozens of "irons in the fire" at any one time. That's because they are busy building relationships, "knocking on doors," conducting demographic and psychographics research, and visiting public offices in an effort to learn about existing zoning, comprehensive plans, traffic counts, and utilities. They look at themselves as analysts who are capable of creating opportunities.

Working as a commercial real estate agent licensed to do business in two states, I've worked on both the listing and site selection sides. I've made a good living from both. However, I've enjoyed the site selection side of the coin much more than the listing side - not only because I became adept at identifying "home run" locations, but because I also enjoyed working with retail and restaurant developers.

One thing I can tell you that separates listing agents from people working in the field of site selection is that the latter can't afford to juggle more than 2-3 listings at a time. Why? Simply because, in order to represent the people who hired them, listing agents need to **market, market, market** - something a site selection specialist cannot afford to spend lots of time on because he or she typically spends a great deal of time outside of the office as opposed to being in the office. For many site selection specialists, their car is their office, the road their "home away from home."

One attribute both retail and restaurant listing agents and site selection specialists have in common is a deep knowledge/good understanding of Letters of Intent, Leases, and Purchase Agreements. In addition, both parties are veterans when it comes to negotiating. and creating "win-win" opportunities. While no doubt challenging, they typically excel at both.

If you are interested in hiring a listing agent, you'll have a different set of interview criteria than you would if you were going to interview someone with a background in retail and restaurant site selection. However, in either case, you should look for someone who possesses a track record of success - preferably for more than just 2-3 years. Afterall, the skills you are looking for are learned and employed over the long-term as opposed to the short-term.

While I refrain from calling listing agents "order takers," I don't mind telling you that's somewhat descriptive of their jobs. While referrals are always welcome and are important to building every commercial realtor's business, they may or may not constitute a significant portion of an agent's listing portfolio. From my perspective, listing agents might be looked upon as "Farmers."

People specializing in retail and restaurant site selection, on the other hand, are oftentimes thought of as "Hunters." That's because they aren't shy about "hunting" in order to find new business. Thinking of them as "hustlers" would not be insulting. These are people who don't worry about rejection; they have thick skins and can be very persistent.

In the world of real estate brokerage, neither listing agents nor site selection specialists are typically paid a base salary. Instead, they earn commissions. This is because "staying hungry" is viewed as an essential part of their motivation to succeed.

You may be interested to know that I never got offended when the owner of the commercial real estate brokerage company that I worked for initially would knock on my door (as well as others) and ask "What have you done for me today?"

Both listing agents and site selection specialists need to be disciplined when it comes to time management. Being a member of the real estate profession is not an easy job. Accordingly, the old expression "If you snooze you lose" is very appropriate.

While it's wise for both listing agents and site selection specialists to be a member of a **TEAM - T**ogether **E**verybody **A**chieves **M**ore - site selection specialists are typically very comfortable being "Lone Wolves."

No offense to listing agents, but it's people with a site selection skill set who, because they are aggressive, confident, and employ a "never give up" attitude, that business owners and decision-makers are advised to recruit if they want to work with people who are dedicated to consistently bringing them "home run" locations.

When you are out scouting locations for your business, don't overlook potential resources like commercial realtors and site selection consultants. Consider adding one or both of these resource groups to your **TEAM**, much like you would your banker, your accountant, and your attorney. In the long run, you'll be thankful because these are parties who can help prevent mistakes, especially "big" time mistakes - the kind that can significantly shorten the duration as well as quality of your business career.

Retail and restaurant site selection consulting is a profession I have periodically engaged in during my real estate career. It is a field of expertise which newer as well as multi - unit companies and franchise organizations are strongly encouraged to contract with in order to minimize mistakes and accelerate the growth of "home run" locations.

Like myself, real estate site selection consultants have years and years of valuable experience assisting retail and restaurant businesses. While consultants charge by the hour for their services, they are only expensive if you focus on the cost of the services provided rather than on the value of the returns.

At this point, I'd like to introduce you to a term which consists of 4 highly important factors. I "coined" the acronym **RORR** as a result of trying to get a better handle on the principal drivers of retail and restaurant sales.

The first **R**, with the exception of downtown areas, stands for what is widely acknowledged to be the single most important source of customer traffic - **ROOFTOPS**.

The letter **O** stands for **Offices**. They are a meaningful source of business, not only in many downtowns, but in many suburban areas.

The second **R** stands for **Retail**. In this case, I'm talking about other retail stores in the area where your business is located, or where you are considering opening a new retail store location.

The third **R** stands for **Restaurants**. Again, I'm talking about other restaurants in the area where your business is located, or where you are considering opening a new restaurant location.

Collectively, these 4 types of land use generate lots of consistent, as opposed to periodic, vehicular traffic - something which other businesses such as entertainment and sporting events can't match.

Thus, all of the **RORR** factors need to be incorporated into not only the site selection process, but the sales forecasting process.

For your information, commercial realtors don't make sales forecasts. While their opinions and best guesstimates are certainly welcome, sales forecasting is a key service best left to long established retail and restaurant site selection consultants. That's because they understand that sales forecasts are the core, the foundation, for making "smart" location decisions.

This important group of "data hounds" and location analysts can be a key resource for not only small multi-unit companies, but emerging multi-unit franchise organizations. Without a doubt, employing the services of site selection consultants is a great way to continue growing your retail or restaurant business.

Conversely, too little "homework" can result in businesses which don't have a long shelf life. Having "Hit and Miss" businesses in your real estate portfolio is a guaranteed way to cripple your company's future growth and profitability - something which, no doubt, is a major factor in why so many businesses tend to "come and go."

Today, mobile data is becoming an increasingly popular tool in forecasting customer sales. With mobile data, you can track a customer's travel path - where they started their trip, how they ended up at your retail store or restaurant, and where they went afterwards. Mobile data is increasingly being used as a supplement to customer surveys.

Generally speaking, it's important to note that the combination of the **RORR** land use factors account for a substantial percentage of all customer visits.

If you consider the long-lived 80-20 rule to be being relevant - that 80% of your business sales are generated by 20% of your customers - then it's imperative that you understand as much as possible about who your best customers, your "regulars" are. The real payoff from "mining" the data derived from knowing customer profiles is attaining a better match when researching future retail store and restaurant locations.

Data collection and analysis - or "data mining" - is fast becoming the "wave of the future." If you don't understand it or employ it you risk being "left behind" in the highly competitive retail and restaurant landscape. Indeed, this is one of the reasons why the "Big Boys" get bigger. Think McDonald's. Think Starbucks. Think Chipotle. Think Chick-fil-A. Think Target.

Nonetheless, you can't afford to become over reliant on predictive data. You still need to make fieldwork and being "out and about" a high, high priority. In the long run, fieldwork, including "walking and talking," is absolutely key to your ability to make "smart" location decisions.

With fieldwork in mind, I'd like to relate something I learned from working with McDonald's. When conducting a site selection search, they expected me as well as other commercial realtors to know as much as possible about a prospective location as well as the dynamics of the nearby and surrounding areas. If that meant working mornings, lunch hours, and evenings seven days a week that's what you did. As a result of doing the "homework" that was expected, they hoped that you'd become an expert - someone who earned their respect.

Getting back to predictive data, while it can provide you with great trade <u>area</u> information, it is less effective at the <u>site</u> level. And, when you drill down to the <u>space</u> level, it's all about (a) conducting customer surveys, (b) analyzing POS and customer loyalty information, and, (c) mobile data if you decided to "go the extra mile." Collectively, the aforementioned "trio" are guaranteed to provide you with a wealth of very helpful, very useful, very valuable information.

If you decide to initiate a working relationship with a commercial realtor, consider screening them by asking either some, most, or all of the following questions.

How many years have you been directly involved in retail and restaurant site selection? (You are looking for someone with a minimum of 5-7 years of "hands on" experience.)

Do you actively seek out listings? If the answer is yes, ask them about how many listings do you currently have? (If their answer is more than 2-3, note this as a potential "red flag.")

How would you describe the difference(s) between tenant representation and site selection? (You are looking for someone without a "chauffer mentality" - defined as someone who is primarily focused on showing you vacant space. Instead, you want to work with a resource person who understands the retail and restaurant marketplace in terms of current availability, space which is turning over in either the short-term or near-term future, and space which is either under construction or about to be built.)

Ask the commercial realtor(s) you are considering to explain the meaning of **Location, Location, Location**. (What you are looking for is someone who understands the difference between **Area, Site**, and **Space**. Remember, picking out the right **Area** is fairly simple compared to finding the right **Site** and the right **Space**.)

Also, don't be shy about asking the commercial realtor(s) you are interviewing how comfortable they are waiting for 6 or more months to finalize a lease agreement or purchase agreement. (You are looking for someone whose focus is on your future success as opposed to gaining a quick pay day.)

Ask if, during your career in commercial real estate, they have either periodically or actively been involved in new retail and/or restaurant development. (You want to prioritize working with someone who has a good working relationship with developers. Furthermore, pay particular attention to the resource person who has a track record of not only bringing end users to the table but facilitating the development of retail centers and/or mixed-use developments.)

Ask the commercial realtors you talk to what their thoughts are regarding width-to-depth space ratios. (Remember, 3:1 works best.)

Ask who are some of your current clients? Also, ask who are some of your previous clients. (You are looking for someone who has established businesses relationships with multiple clients - whether they are local, have a regional presence, or have a national footprint. Pay special attention to their having assisted market leading retail and/or restaurant companies.)

Ask the person or people you are interviewing to tell you a little something about their company and the types of clients the company has served. (What you are looking to learn about is long-term relationships, the kind that result in repeat business.)

Ask the individual(s) you are considering working with if they typically review and offer comments on leases and purchase agreements. (You are looking for someone who sees his or her job including a variety of advisory services. If they say that's not my job, you are advised/urged to look for someone else.)

Ask the person(s) you are interviewing how familiar they are with drive time and radius-based demographics. (Here, you want to have access to daytime and nighttime data as well as psychographics. You want to make sure they have experience reviewing, summarizing, and offering comments on these very important sources of information.)

Ask the person(s) you are talking to if they are familiar with spotting maps. (You want to work with someone who can map the locations of businesses you like to "shadow." At TOM + CHEE, we especially liked being near Chipotle. Other businesses we liked to "shadow" included such retail and restaurant stars as Starbucks, Panera, and TJ Maxx. FYI, all site searches need to use this mapping technique as a starting point. Otherwise, the tendency for brokers is to chase mostly vacant spaces.)

Ask the person(s) you are working with the following question: About what percentage of sales do retailers and restaurants in this market typically pay in base rent? (Hopefully, they'll tell you 7-8% is typical.)

Ask the person(s) you are interviewing what their motivation is for working with your company. (You be the judge of whether or not the answer they provide is adequate.)

Ask the person(s) you are interviewing to name 2-3 building amenities which they think would help attract more customer traffic. (You are looking for answers like a storefront which is differentiated from its neighbors by design/colors/building materials, the ability to display LED lighting, the opportunity to use awnings, and the right to provide outdoor seating.)

Ask the commercial realtor you are contemplating working with to name several site factors which are capable of contributing to a high level of sales. (Specifically, the answers you're looking for will mirror **PASTA V - P**arking, **A**ccess, **S**igning, **T**raffic (on the street where you are), **A**ctivity (in the nearby and surrounding area), and **V**isibility.

Be cautious if a commercial realtor you are talking with wants you to sign an exclusive representation agreement. (Advise him/her that the right time to talk about such representation is <u>after</u> they have not only brought you a "home run" location, but helped you secure it.)

You may be interested to know that during my real estate career I NEVER asked any retail or restaurant company for exclusive representation. Why? Because I was confident that if I could bring them a "home run" location they would realize that I wouldn't be wasting their time, and that I was capable of bringing them a second and a third "home run" location. I want you to know that my philosophy, coupled with my skill set, resulted in numerous repeat business opportunities - something I'm not only extremely proud of, but something that helped set me apart from "the crowd." Accordingly, I don't take offense being called a Site Selection Snob!

Whether you are looking at working with a commercial realtor or a retail and restaurant site selection consultant, here is a checklist you might consider using early in the communications process. In no particular order of importance, the person you are going to potentially work with/hire should:

Be **Energetic** - Be **Focused** - Be **Dedicated** - Be **Trustworthy**

Be **Connected** - Be a **Good Communicator** - Be **Responsible**

Be **Responsive -** Be Committed to Conducting **Fieldwork**

Be Knowledgeable about **Demographics** & **Psychographics**

Be Knowledgeable about **Zoning** - Be a skilled **Negotiator**

Have a Track Record of **Success** - Have a Good **Reputation**

Have a Good Understanding **of Commercial Development**

Have a Good Understanding of **Trade Areas**, and, very importantly, **not** be on a **Learning Curve**

Commercial realtors and site selection consultants can be worth their "weight in gold" not only during site selection, but during both (a) lease/purchase negotiations and (b) the zoning process. As such, you should look at them not only as a valued member of your team, but as a valued "partner."

Chapter Eleven
Working With the Public Sector

I'm excited to write this chapter, in part because I worked as a City Planning Director for two small communities - one in Southwest Ohio and the other along the Central Coast of California.

Besides advising City Managers and City Councils, Planning Commissions, and Boards of Architectural Review, I had the opportunity to work with engineering and building department staffs. I'm very proud to have been a City Planning Director for ten years.

During my time as a City Planning Director, I was fortunate to also work with the local business and development communities, the California Coastal Commission, local property owners, and, of course, local residents.

One of my most important takeaways from working in the public sector was that I periodically had the opportunity to ask businesspeople, or prospective businesspeople, why they picked a particular location for their business. Indeed, beginning with my parents' restaurant in Upstate New York, I've always been interested in learning what drove customers to a particular location.

As a trusted advisor to local elected and appointed officials, I was very fortunate to have developed many wonderful working relationships. With very few exceptions, they were always supportive of the recommendations I made. I attribute this to the fact that I was always well prepared. In other words, I always did my "homework." By doing so, I earned something priceless - both their trust and respect.

It was in Ohio that I enrolled in my first real estate class. Why? Because I thought it would provide me with a better insight into what was happening around me. Ours was a community which had recently annexed a regional mall. In addition, we were fortunate to have a fairly large-scale residential project underway.

I am happy to say that I'm still a member of the American Planning Association (APA). I've been a presenter at one of their national conferences as well as the featured speaker at an educational session at their headquarters office in Chicago.

During my planning career I wrote zoning ordinances, sign ordinances, a land use plan, subdivision regulations, a comprehensive plan, and even a vision plan - all of which I continue to have in my home library.

Let's look at some of the above briefly, starting with comprehensive plans, also known as Master Plans. They are official public documents which are adopted by local legislative bodies as a policy guide to making future decisions about the physical development of a community. The minimum time horizon they address is usually ten (10) years. These plans are comprehensive in scope as well as general and futuristic. They primarily address housing growth, commercial and industrial development, open space needs, and both infrastructure and transportation improvements.

Comprehensive Plans provide local elected and appointed officials, as well as community residents, businesspeople, developers, lenders, and realtors, among others, with important insights into how public and private property is proposed to be used in the future.

Zoning and subdivision regulations are intended to implement the proposals and recommendations identified in the Comprehensive Plan. Zoning divides the land in a community into a variety of districts such as Single Family Residential, Multi-Family Residential, Office and Industrial, Neighborhood, Community, and Regional Commercial

Districts, etc. Furthermore, zoning identifies standards for important improvements such as parking, signing, and landscaping. Subdivision Regulations, on the other hand, are primarily concerned with development standards for new streets and essential utilities.

Inviting citizen participation at the start of the planning and development process, rather than waiting until the end, is an important component of the comprehensive planning and zoning processes. It is very important that local property owners and businesspeople, developers and realtors, and a variety of other stakeholders have the opportunity to become involved as well as provide comments and insights prior to the adoption of comprehensive plans and zoning regulations. This is where the "partnering" process begins. The goal of such participation is to build consensus - the kind which will lead to something I feel strongly about - public and private sector partnering.

As a former City Planning Director I can say, without any hesitation, that my city managers, planning commissions, architectural review boards, and city councils looked to me for direction and advice, in part because of my habit of always making sure that I was well prepared. I'm certain being well prepared is also characteristic of lots of other planning directors. In my mind, it's the "secret" to winning support, and to getting lots of important things done.

Over the years, I've witnessed that some permit applicants bypass preliminary meetings with staff by putting their faith in hiring an attorney to speak on their behalf. While doing so isn't objectionable, attorneys can sometimes be adversarial - something which can turn out to be a big mistake. They should, in my opinion, make a habit of touching base as early as possible with planning and zoning staff prior to making any presentations to local boards, commissions, and elected officials.

If you are in the commercial retail and restaurant development business, please consider inviting planning and zoning staff, as well as commission and board members, out to your site so they can become familiar with what you are proposing to do. Doing so will provide you with an opportunity to not only educate them, but to respond to their questions and concerns. This is how you can begin to bond with them while learning whether they have any doubts or objections about your project.

In California, I'm happy to say I always brought members of my Planning Commission on site visits to make sure they were well informed about what was on our monthly agendas. It gave us an opportunity to get to know one another better as well as set the expectation that they also needed to do their "homework." If you don't realize it, this is a great way to begin building important relationships.

Whether working in Ohio or California, my philosophy was that it was essential for the public and private sectors to reflect a "we" attitude as opposed to a "me" attitude. As such, you can imagine my being shocked when a member of my planning staff told me that "developers are our enemy." Needless to say, he and I had a lot to talk about.

Unfortunately, the person I just spoke about is not alone in his attitude when it comes to working with developers. Having worked in the private sector for most of my career, I've seen my fair share of public employees who are suspicious of developers and commercial realtors. They sometimes think that all we care about is making money. In an effort to minimize this type of attitude, realtors and developers need to be willing to build bridges - something I'll admit is oftentimes not an easy task. That's why getting to know people in the public sector "one on one" is an essential first step in being able to build better working relationships.

When I chose to leave the planning profession for the commercial real estate profession it wasn't because I didn't enjoy my job. Indeed, nothing could be further from the truth. I relished my job. Nonetheless, being a new father without any family - no grandparents, brothers or sisters - living nearby made my wife and I realize that relocation was imminent.

When my wife and I relocated back to the Midwest with our son, I did a little bit of consulting before passing the licensing exam which enabled me to subsequently join a well-respected commercial real estate brokerage firm. During my interview process I emphasized that I was looking for a mentor to assist me while I transitioned into a new career. Fortunately, working with a mentor became a reality.

Early on in my commercial real estate career I established site selection relationships with the real estate representatives for two market leading national retail companies - Pier 1 Imports and Blockbuster Video. I'm happy to say that working with them resulted in multiple deals over a several year period. In particular, I was extremely proud of the fact that I brought Blockbuster what turned out to become their number one company and number one franchise locations in the state of Ohio.

Another fond early memory involves Buffalo Wild Wings. I introduced them to a newly built shopping center opportunity which, I'm happy to say, has ended up being a 30 year occupancy - pretty amazing when you look at the significant turnover that occurs in today's retail and restaurant industry. It also represented a big first for me – negotiating a percentage rent clause which enabled Buffalo Wild Wings to open for business at a slight rental discount in exchange for later paying their landlord a percentage of annual sales in additional rent beyond an agreed upon breakpoint. I continue to smile every time I drive by this location and proudly recall being a part of what turned out to be a win-win for both parties.

I'm proud to say I built a successful career in commercial real estate not because of the money I made, but because I consistently brought the parties I worked with "home runs." For me, it was never about the money. Instead, it was all about seeing them *succeed*.

Incidentally, I'll be sharing more of my **site selection memories** later on in my book.

Having worked primarily on new development opportunities, I eventually decided to go to work for two diversified developers. Not too long afterwards, I became actively involved in the community where I lived. I chaired a downtown revitalization committee - something which led to my appointment to our local Board of Architectural Review. Several years later I joined our local preservation organization and ended up becoming the principal author of our community's vision plan.

In addition, I started teaching a retail and restaurant site selection continuing education course for commercial realtors at not only the local, but state levels. Ultimately, I was able to do the same at the university level.

Right about now you're probably asking yourself, why have I chosen to go into all of this detail about my background? Well, the answer is twofold. First, I continue to subscribe to the premise that the public and private sectors need to work together to not only build the local tax base, but to enhance local quality of life. That starts with me.

Second, I believe there are too many commercial realtors out there who are not very knowledgeable about retail and restaurant site selection. These are people who also need to be better educated about how the public approval process works if they are to become more valuable resources for the businesses they are working with.

I think I have a unique set of credentials - something which instantly gives me credibility with both the public and private sectors. Indeed, throughout my career in commercial real estate I've felt very comfortable talking to and working with members of the public sector almost always starting at the beginning stages of completing either a site selection assignment or a development-related opportunity. As you can appreciate, developing good working relationships with local planning and zoning staffs as early as possible is something I wish more people would do. For what it's worth, my advice to you is to be proactive as opposed to reactive. Don't wait until the last minute to become involved.

Parking, **signing**, and **trees** - especially parking lot trees - are three "hot button" issues which planning and zoning staff, as well as commercial developers and tenants/prospective tenants, need to be discussing on an ongoing basis.

My experience has been that too many small, multi-tenant shopping centers suffer from a lack of parking. On the other end of the spectrum are the big box stores. They oftentimes have way too many vacant parking spaces. Finding an acceptable balance is difficult, especially given the periodic turnover which regularly occurs in the shopping center and commercial real estate business.

Most retail and restaurant businesses, including multi-unit national and regional chains, have a very good understanding of exactly how many customer and employee parking spaces they need. They fully understand that each parking space generates X number of dollars in customer sales, and, that insufficient parking will "rob" them of customer sales. As a result, they won't hesitate when it comes to providing more parking than local zoning requires.

Unfortunately, most start-up as well as many small retail and restaurant businesses prioritize the availability of vacant space and cheap rent over the adequacy of parking. While this is common, it is, in my opinion, regrettable. If their learning curves are short, it can, unfortunately, result in their never achieving the kinds of sales they need to not only stay in business, but generate the kinds of profits which will enable them to eventually expand. As such, the risk of "one and done" for many small businesses is very real.

Of special concern is the lack of on-site parking in older neighborhood business districts. While many of these business districts are walkable, they don't typically have the luxury of having more than a few off- street parking spaces - whether serving ownership, employees, or customers.

As a result, sales can be negatively impacted. One solution to this very common problem is to create some type of municipal parking - preferably at no or minimal expense to customers. Successful businesses attract more businesses - something which not only adds money to the local tax base but helps improve local quality of life.

In many neighborhood business districts, only a relatively small amount of on-street parking is available. While such parking can be free, in most instances it is regulated by parking meters or pay stations. This can be a huge deterrent to driving customer traffic and achieving small business success. On the other hand, whenever free on-street parking is available it can potentially make the difference between failure and some level of success. Nonetheless, providing free on-street parking is not, by itself, going to substantially boost customer traffic counts or retail and restaurant sales.

Because of the small size of neighborhood business districts, building garage parking is not a realistic option. It becomes more viable at the community and regional business district levels, as well as in busy downtowns. Here, the community, local business owners and property owners oftentimes work together to create an amenity which has the capability of paying long-term dividends via increased customer counts and increased sales revenues.

If you are a developer, commercial realtor, or small business owner, you need to be knowledgeable about such things as handicap parking, temporary parking for pick up, carryout, and delivery purposes, shared parking, total number of required parking spaces, and the size requirements for individual parking spaces.

Here's something you may not know: if zoning permits, developers will typically build to a *minimum* required standard. This can lead to several undesirable consequences. For instance, unless you drive a compact or a "smart" car, eight and a half (81/2) foot wide by eighteen (18) foot long parking spaces no longer make sense. The tremendous growth in the sale of vans, SUVs, and trucks have made them increasingly obsolete. In my opinion, today's parking spaces need to be ten (10) feet wide by twenty (20) feet long at a minimum. Where possible, I believe underutilized parking areas should be studied to see about their accommodating the construction of larger parking spaces.

Parking which is unusually tight (short and narrow) may potentially cost a business repeat customer visit. Who wants to have to struggle to get in and out of their vehicles because someone has parked too close to them? Or, who wants to discover that they have a dent on the side of their vehicle because someone was careless opening a door?

Quite frankly, this is where it would be beneficial for shopping center owners and planners to work together to create larger parking spaces.

If you don't already know it, be forewarned that many small business owners and managers and their employees like to park directly in front of their restaurants or retail stores. While they may feel a sense of privilege, it's inexcusable. This is where owners, managers, and employees need to park in one or more designated areas.

If I were a developer or shopping center owner, I'd recommend doing what I saw and marveled at during one of my out-of-town site selection visits. First, I'd separate *customer parking* from *employee parking*. Second, I'd stripe employee parking a different color than what was used to identify customer parking. While white lines might continue to be the color of choice for individual customer parking spaces, I'd paint employee parking spaces a color that really stands out like green, red, or even yellow.

There is one last thing I'd like to mention regarding parking. I'd like to recommend that planners look seriously at minimizing areas where an "ocean" of unused blacktop parking exists or is likely to occur as a result of what I like to call overzealous parking requirements.

The "extra" land which would be created by reducing the number of

113

required parking spaces could easily be used for a number of other purposes, one of which might be facilitating the creation of one or more outlot opportunities. In my opinion, city planners and shopping center owners should consider studying this "problem" and identify a series of acceptable options

---

With the exception of the seasonal proliferation of temporary political signs that appear "here, there, and everywhere" during election cycles, expect jurisdictions to limit as well as vigorously enforce the amount and type of signing a business is permitted to display - something which is completely reasonable. On the other hand, sign regulations should periodically be revisited as well as updated.

Potential concerns such as (a) limited storefront signing, (b) multi-tenant signing, and (c) limited storefront visibility should be studied, perhaps by a task force comprised of property owners, business owners, planners, and local residents. There's no denying that creating such a task force would enable the public and private sectors to "join hands/lock arms" and work together to resolve such important issues. This, in my opinion, would be a great opportunity for commercial realtors to become involved.

Where resolving potential signing issues is a high priority, be sure to also involve local sign companies. This isn't their first rodeo. Chances are good that they will be able to identify a series of options which can be evaluated by the appointed task force. During your discussions, be sure to create an opportunity for everyone to meet one or more times on site as opposed to holding your meetings somewhere else - i.e. city hall.

In addition to enhancing opportunities for maximizing storefront signing and visibility, you might consider asking planning staff about other possible sign issues. For instance, can the size of freestanding signs be increased? If projecting building signs and neon signs aren't currently allowed, can they become options? How about the option to display "coming soon" signs? What about window signs? Also, are you permitted to punch-up storefront and business visibility by flying a flag?

Besides signing, three excellent ways to attract attention to your business are (a) to display awnings - either with stripes or solid colors, (b) feature building materials which will set you apart from your immediate and nearby neighbors, and (c) use one or more attention getting building colors.

Two other items you might also consider adding to enhance storefront visibility are (a) shade umbrellas for your outdoor dining tables, and, (b) colorful annual plants which can be displayed in either window boxes or containers in order to help frame entryways in addition to making your outdoor dining area more inviting. Hopefully planning staff won't object to these attractive attention getting options.

There's one other meaningful but potentially controversial change which I'd like to see communities embrace in order to help improve building visibility. I'm talking about public decision-makers being a lot less zealous about requiring the planting of what might be argued are too many trees in parking lots which are located (a) in front of large, single user and multi-tenant retail buildings and (b) along the streets and drives which provide customer access.

I'm confident that the great majority of local residents as well as daytime employees and visitors to the area don't want to be welcomed by an ocean of empty parking lot spaces filled with lots of "lonely" trees - some of which struggle to thrive let alone survive. In addition, lots of trees will be negatively impacted not only by high reflective heat levels, but by inadequate rainfall/watering.

I believe it would be wise to plant the same number of parking lot trees as is currently required. However, I would suggest the option to allocate them to different areas of multi-tenant and large single user commercial properties. If the same number of trees were permitted to be planted in small clusters not only in parking lots, but in front of, in back of, and alongside buildings, I'm convinced they can become attractive landscape features. I also believe that, collectively they can help return the same or even higher levels of oxygen to the environment while creating greater storefront visibility. Indeed, I'm convinced that making these types of changes would result in a huge win-win opportunity that everyone in the public and private sectors could be proud of.

Most planners I know are people who enjoy doing research, gathering information, meeting with stakeholders, promoting public discussions, and, welcoming citizen, property owner, and business owner participation. Hopefully, they can be a resource for developers and commercial realtors working to promote business development as well as tax base enhancement.

If you are considering developing a new shopping center, one of the first things you and members of your team - such as architects, landscape architects, commercial realtors, and/or engineers - should consider doing is schedule a meeting with planning staff. There, you can share your plans/vision and learn what requirements need to be satisfied. Hopefully, when you walk away, you'll have not only learned more about the permit and approval processes, but initiated what hopefully is perceived to be a collaborative working relationship - something which could end up being extremely helpful.

In addition, when you meet, ask the Planning Director or one of his/her staff members, if there are any new residential and/or other commercial developments in the pipeline, especially anything that might get underway in the next year or so - something that could potentially bring new customers to the project you are working on.

Always remember that local planning and zoning staffs have credible relationships with local decision-makers. In many instances they have been advising city managers, planning commissioners, architectural review boards, and other influential decision-making and advisory bodies for years. This means they have not only valued relationships, but a significant level of credibility that very few developers and commercial realtors have. As a result, they need to become your *allies* as opposed to your *adversaries*.

With building relationships in mind, commercial realtors might consider becoming an appointed member of their community's Planning Commission or Architectural Review Board. These important decision-making groups need to have a broad-based membership which includes people with a business background and expertise. You may be interested to know that in my first City Planning Director job, I felt very fortunate to have the president of the local bank, the owner of a large auto dealership, and a homebuilder on my planning commission.

If you are a commercial realtor or commercial developer, you understand better than most the importance of networking. One of the best ways to achieve this is to join your local Chamber of Commerce. These are people who welcome growth and tend to have lots of relationships. Here, you might consider adding a local elected official or perhaps the Planning Director to your list of potential event speakers and/or future guests.

If you join your local Chamber of Commerce, be sure to become active on a committee - perhaps one dealing with economic development.

In the future, there may be another "hot button" issue that more city planners will be addressing. I'm talking about the possibility for communities **to ban restaurants with drive thrus**. This is the type of divisive issue which commercial realtors all over the United States are bound to see surface.

I was shocked to learn that way back in 1982, San Luis Obispo, California, citing concerns about traffic and community character, banned fast food drive thrus. Due to a perceived "obesity epidemic," in 2008 Los Angeles passed an ordinance prohibiting the construction of fast food restaurants in several low-income neighborhoods.

A recent University of Alberta study found 27 communities across Canada have, for a variety of reasons, implemented either a partial or full ban on the future construction of fast food drive thrus. And, in 2019 Minneapolis voted to ban the construction of new fast food restaurants with drive thrus out of a concern for reducing air pollution specifically greenhouse gas emissions.

Incidentally, it was interesting to read in Restaurant News that the typical drive thru experience (pull up, select/choose, order, pay, pull away) lasts, on average, almost 4 minutes. That's a lot longer than I expected. (Customers visiting restaurants and coffee shops whose menu boards don't list a significant number of purchase options can place their orders and drive away faster - something which may account for why some customers decide to shift their business to other restaurants and/or coffee shops.)

Hopefully banning restaurants with drive thrus won't become an issue in your community. But, if it does, commercial developers and commercial realtors need to be prepared to participate in what promises to be not one, but a series of potentially contentious public meetings.

Chapter Twelve

Types of Retail and Restaurant Location Options

By now you probably realize that **there's a building hierarchy when it comes to business locations**. It should come as no surprise that freestanding buildings occupy the number one position in this hierarchy. In the number two and three positions are end cap and inline locations.

Freestanding Building Locations. Coupled with good visibility, good ingress and egress, good signing, and sufficient parking, freestanding buildings have advantages that end cap and inline locations don't.

Freestanding buildings are typically more expensive to own and/or rent than either end cap or inline locations. However, the extra costs associated with occupying such buildings can be justified by the fact that, in most instances, they will generate higher or substantially more sales. In the long run, spending a little extra money in order to provide your business with a freestanding building address should end up being a wise investment.

The ultimate freestanding location is one which features a **drive thru** - something I want to talk just a little bit about. A huge driver of satisfying consumers' ever-increasing demand for convenience, drive thus have helped businesses - especially fast food restaurants and coffee shops - not only grow their sales, but expand the number of locations they have.

Today's suburban landscape is increasingly dotted with drive thrus (think banks and fast food restaurants in particular) which feature not just one, but multiple drive thru lanes. While some restaurants are experimenting with drive thru only formats, others have dedicated drive thru lanes to accommodate customers who have pre ordered meals and drinks on their mobile apps.

If you're interested in learning a little bit of history, Adam Chandler, the author of "*Drive Thru Dreams*," says that Red's Giant Hamburg, "a now defunct Route 66 burger joint in Missouri that opened in 1947, is credited by some with being the first drive thru in the world." Meanwhile, a Wikipedia search gives this honor to In and Out Burger.

End Cap Building Locations. Businesses which occupy the end (corner) space in a building are not only more visible, but offer a number of other advantages. These range from increased signing opportunities to the potential for not only more parking, but more convenient parking, increased window area, outdoor seating, and even the potential to add landscaping on the side of the building.

End cap locations are much in demand, especially by anchor tenants. However, they remain a less attractive option than freestanding buildings. Drugstores are a great example of businesses which have previously occupied lots of end cap locations and have subsequently transitioned into freestanding buildings. In the process, they added prescription pick up windows – an amenity which has enabled them to generate higher sales levels.

End cap locations aren't cheap. So, expect to pay a premium price. As you can appreciate, whenever an end cap location is able to feature the addition of a drive thru or pick up window, it will increase customer traffic as well as customer sales.

Inline Building Locations. Not every business wants or can afford a freestanding or an end cap location. Plenty of successful retail and restaurant businesses occupy inline space. The challenge for a new business is determining which inline space best meets their needs. In order to make not only an informed but a "smart" location and "smart" site selection decision the best thing you can do is to (a) look for a prominent building feature which differentiates your business from its neighbors and (b) incorporate one or more of the many ideas listed under the heading Dense Urban and Dense Neighborhood Locations into the design of your space.

The following narrative identifies many different types of business locations - some of which may be of interest to you as you embark or continue on your site selection journey.

Airport Locations. Catering strictly to the convenience needs of passengers, the only kinds of businesses with a history of succeeding in airports are those selling food, drinks, and convenience items such as magazines, books, and newspapers.

Like other business areas, airports have "home run" locations as well as their fair share of lesser performing locations. Finding traditional or kiosk space in a busy central as opposed to modestly trafficked "edge" location will cost you more but is your best bet for driving higher sales volumes and generating higher profits.

Because the peak travel times at airports are in the morning between 5 and 7, be prepared to serve breakfast - even if it is not one of your traditional menu items. If you're in the fast food business your best bet is to rent space in a centrally located cluster of businesses much like you'd find in a food court at a mall. You don't want to be in a secondary location where traffic counts are low.

When making your location evaluation, don't be shy about talking to the managers of the individual businesses which are located within the business cluster you are considering. In addition, be prepared to observe as well as record customer traffic levels on both weekdays and weekends.

The advantage of renting space in a business cluster is that it will enable you to benefit from the significant customer traffic that the more well-known businesses generate - something which will initially help you build customer visits. From there, how good an operator you are will end up determining whether your business succeeds or fails.

Cluster Locations. Food and retail clusters (groupings) are wonderful for not only creating synergy among various businesses, but for creating unique destinations which have a significant amount of drawing power. Here the emphasis is on lots of choices - a factor which helps explain their popularity.

Businesses which are in a food or retail cluster needn't be located side by side like you would expect to find in a mall. Rather, they can be concentrated in a particular area or along both sides of a street. While some businesses may end up competing with one another for customers, for the most part, they actually end up expanding one another's respective trade areas.

Food and retail clusters bring to mind the old saying "where there's smoke there's fire." When scouting for potential locations they should be high on your radar screen.

College & University Locations. While these types of locations feature a "captive" student audience you need to understand that the great majority of students are on campus for only about nine months a year. As such, your business will experience peaks and valleys with respect to annual sales.

With few exceptions, college and university locations are all about convenience. For fast food and casual dining restaurants, locating either on campus in a food court, or, along the "main drag" is very important. In the case of the former you can expect your business to occur primarily over a two-hour (11:30 am to 1:30 pm) lunch period. No such limitation exists, however, for off campus restaurants, in part because they also serve residents who live and work in the nearby area.

122

Ideally, you should strive to find a location which is in the heart of a commercial strip rather than on its edge. Also, don't lose sight of the fact that being located just one block off the "main drag" can mean that a substantial amount of student traffic will likely be intercepted by your competition before it ever makes it inside your front door.

Pizza and sub sandwiches are by far the two most popular types of food that college students consume on a regular basis. If you are in a different type of restaurant business, then locating either near or in a cluster of pizza and sub restaurants will help you gain valuable exposure as well as increase customer traffic counts.

While there is definitely a place for retail stores near college and university campuses, they represent a higher risk than restaurants, in part because they are much more of a luxury rather than a necessity. As such, you should expect to spend more money marketing your business if you are going to build name recognition and attract customers from non-campus neighborhoods.

Corner Lot Locations. This type of property is always in high demand - especially when convenience is a primary site selection factor. Because corner lot locations are typically expensive to acquire or rent, they need to generate high sales volumes.

Corner lot locations provide businesses with enhanced visibility and signing opportunities. Hopefully, they'll also feature lots of parking. In addition, they are typically characterized by an increased number of curb cuts as well as higher traffic counts. Collectively, these factors help explain why corner locations are coveted by banks, coffee shops, convenience stores, drugstores, gas stations, and fast food and casual dining restaurants.

If you have the resources to purchase a corner lot, you are advised to focus your efforts on acquiring a far corner. Look for sites which are served by traffic signalization. Avoid locations which sit opposite a median and be careful about committing to sites which are impacted by traffic stacking - something which can not only inhibit safe and convenient customer ingress and egress, but negatively impact future sales.

Crossroads Locations. Similar to locating your business at a major street intersection, opening your business close to where two major highways or roads meet can be a big positive. Here your business will benefit from not only increased traffic, but increased exposure. And, hopefully, it will enjoy easy ingress and egress.

Dense Urban and Dense Neighborhood Locations. Every big city exhibits these types of locations. One way to differentiate dense urban and dense neighborhood locations from other types of business locations is their strong reliance on higher levels of pedestrian traffic. These types of locations, however, can present a major challenge - making your retail store or restaurant stand out in a crowd. Think about how it not only needs to differentiate itself from adjoining and nearby businesses, but how it can become more memorable.

Dense urban and dense neighborhood locations need to create a unique identity for themselves by doing one or more of the following: feature a recessed entryway, using a variety of colors, incorporating a variety of building materials, and, making use of awnings and entry canopies.

Other ways to stand out include: installing one or more bay windows, adding sidewalk and/or patio seating, displaying flower boxes, adding projecting signing, displaying banners and/or flags, and, like Google, using two or more colors in the name of your business.

More ways to distinguish your business include: featuring neon window signs, providing special lighting, using symbols to heighten sign awareness, displaying an oversized or colorful clock, showing the current temperature, and adding a window television - especially if it provides sports scores or stock market pricing.

Several other means of distinguishing your place of business include:

sidewalks which feature brick edging or incorporate a paver pattern, displaying an attention getting mannequin or statue, adding gooseneck building lighting, decorating building columns, and featuring clever window signing like "Free Smells."

Businesses wishing to locate in dense urban and dense neighborhood locations should emphasize being within easy walking distance of one or more major traffic generators such as offices, retail anchor and specialty stores, hotels, restaurants, major tourist attractions, train and/or subway stations, performing arts centers, large parks, open space facilities like plazas and squares, and rooftops. Securing a location which relies on more than one of these types of land uses to generate customer traffic is highly desirable.

Finding space in an area with some immediate or nearby on street parking should be regarded as a bonus. In addition to locating your business in a busy, safe, and well-lit area, being able to secure a site which is characterized by lots of pedestrian traffic throughout the daytime and evening hours should be a high priority.

Downtown Locations. In the past, every city's downtown was where both retail and restaurants liked to cluster. However, the expansion of suburban malls coupled with the introduction of suburban power centers and lifestyle centers have substantially weakened the attractiveness of downtowns when it comes to operating successful retail businesses.

Cities have increasingly been willing to diversify their business mix beyond offices, hotels, retail stores and restaurants. By relying upon programming as well as one of a kind uses such as convention centers, performing arts centers, libraries, museums, cinemas, theatres, plazas and squares, and sports facilities, coupled with the addition of new rooftops, cities have been able to attract more people downtown more frequently and for lengthier periods of time.

These days, cities are seeing a residential revival as condominiums punctuate the skyline. People relocating to large and mid-size downtowns covet not only being where the "action" is, but having lots of good service focused as well as experiential choices - especially when it comes to restaurants. Speaking of restaurants, downtowns are increasingly becoming great places to find growing clusters of locally owned, nonchain restaurant businesses. Furthermore, the quantity, quality, and diversity of start-up as well as mom and pop restaurants and bars which are concentrated in downtowns have helped create 18 hour long, as opposed to 12 hour long, environments.

While downtowns are full of "B" and "C" locations, "A" locations will likely cost you "a pretty penny." Therefore, it is essential to focus your site search efforts on locations with high nighttime lighting levels, lots of slower moving traffic, and lots of pedestrian activity - preferably areas where specialty retail stores and restaurants are clustered, and where other nearby major traffic generators, especially offices (daytime traffic) and hotels (nighttime traffic), are located. Being near or inclose proximity to major transportation hubs as well as large concentrations of surface parking and parking garages can be attractive attributes.

In conclusion, unless you are near a major activity generator such as a sports arena or stadium, you are advised to concentrate your site search in areas which are either close to or in the center of activity as opposed to being located on the edge of the central business district. In addition, be careful that you don't underestimate the importance of locating in areas which are perceived as being not only safe but clean. Furthermore, if you want to maximize customer opportunities, always prioritize street level as opposed to second floor or lower-level retail and restaurant spaces.

Food Court Locations. Malls have long known how to create activity. Mall food courts are one of their success stories. Food courts create the ultimate convenience, not only for people visiting a mall but also for the hundreds of employees who work there on a daily basis.

While rents can be high and the hours can be demanding, food court locations are a great place for national, regional, and sometimes local businesses to rent space. While finding a seat is sometimes a slight negative, it is also a wonderful testimonial to the popularity of food courts. The synergy and choices which food courts provide are also significant and serve as a model for developers and landlords in other types of venues such as outlet centers and lifestyle centers. Besides rent, there's a very good chance that your lease here will include a percentage rent clause.

Food Hall Locations. Food halls have emerged as an attractive amenity for mixed use, office, and multifamily projects. Food halls often serve as "incubator" spaces They offer not only convenience, but destination dining options. They are similar to food courts in malls. But, unlike their mall cousins, they almost exclusively feature local start-up and independent businesses which offer a variety of popular as well as unique cuisines. Food halls provide counter as opposed to table service, and are busy primarily during lunch and dinner. Some food hall businesses also sell alcoholic beverages. Common seating is available, including lots of communal dining.

Food Truck Locations. Commercial landscapes increasingly reflect the presence of food trucks. They are convenience as opposed to destination types of businesses. Their trade areas tend to be tiny. They are increasingly located in the parking lots of gas stations. They serve walk up customers a wide range of freshly prepared food, especially ethnic food, at very affordable prices. Males age 25 - 44 are their predominant customers.

Highway Interchange Locations. While not always welcomed by local residents, highway interchanges have become ubiquitous across the United States. In particular, they have become popular locations for fast food and quick service restaurants, the sale of gas and convenience items, and motels. The busiest highway interchange locations generate customer traffic morning, noon, and night.

127

If you are in the fast food and fast casual restaurant business, you want to be as close as possible to gas stations. Similarly, if you are in the gas business you want to be next to or near a variety of restaurants. More and more often, you'll see gas stations leasing small amounts of space to nationally recognized restaurants such as McDonald's, Taco Bell, Arby's, KFC, and Subway. Together, these two types of businesses illustrate how the power of synergy and the power of convenience combine to boost customer traffic counts and sales.

If you are contemplating opening a business at a highway interchange location, be careful not to locate too far from one or more of the area's major traffic generators. Furthermore, don't be fooled into thinking that you can sacrifice any of the **six keys** which are described in Chapter Two and end up being a success story. Unfortunately, this is a mistake that some small businesspeople who are in a hurry to open their doors to customers tend to make.

Iconic Locations. Fifth Avenue, Madison Avenue, and Times Square in New York City, Union Square in San Francisco, North Michigan Avenue in Chicago, and Rodeo Drive in Beverly Hills, California are examples of Iconic locations. They are destination retail locations which are known nationally and internationally for high end clothing, jewelry, and shoes. Here, you can expect to find expensive rents. (FYI, Fifth Avenue has the highest retail rents in the world!)

Iconic locations are high profile locations. They have lots of eye appeal. Because they project a positive image they tend to be in strong demand. Iconic locations establish the impression that what a particular business represents and what they are selling is something special, something unique, something which might even be regarded as "the best of the best."

It is not uncommon for national retail and restaurant companies to seek out iconic building locations in iconic areas and/or in iconic business districts because they are the types of locations which help them differentiate themselves from their competitors. Starbucks is a good example of a company which likes to rent space in iconic locations.

Industrial Park Locations. With few exceptions, industrial parks are hard pressed to generate any significant amount of restaurant and/or retail business given the limited amount of daily traffic they generate. As a result, their trade areas are relatively small.

Prospective businesses owners - those catering to the convenience needs of customers - are better off locating on the perimeter of these types of locations. Here they are much more likely to serve customers coming from nearby industrial employers, offices, and motels than from surrounding rooftops or retail.

Infill Locations. Land which remains undeveloped and properties which are ripe for redevelopment represent significant opportunities for accommodating new retail and restaurant projects in both older urban and suburban areas. While often expensive to acquire and time consuming to assemble, they typically possess two very important building blocks for success: convenience to nearby rooftops and proximity to commercial critical mass.

In the future, interest in infill locations will become more prevalent, whether for small, medium, or large commercial and/or mixed-use projects. If you have an interest in opening a business in such an area your best bet is to stay in touch with three parties: City Hall, area developers, and commercial realtors.

Intercept Locations. Gas stations, coffee shops, and convenience stores are examples of businesses which covet the types of locations where customers will think twice about driving past them in order to spend money at a competitor location. The real key to consistently intercepting customer traffic is knowing which side of the street your business should be located on - the going to work side or the going home side.

Interstate Locations. The first two businesses that come to mind when the word interstate is mentioned are gas and food. Not only are they by far and away the two most popular land uses to be found at or near interstate highway interchanges, but two highly synergistic uses. As I've mentioned before, McDonald's absolutely loves being paired with gas and vice versa.

Highway interchange locations differ significantly from one place to the next and, by themselves, are no guarantee of success. If you are considering opening up a business at or near a highway interchange the first thing that you want to do is find out daily traffic counts. High is good. Low is bad. The second thing you want to do is measure the amount of critical mass. More is better. Like food and gas, traffic counts and critical mass in these locations are highly correlated.

One word of caution: don't expect to benefit from a highway interchange presence unless you are no more than approximately a quarter of a mile from an exit ramp. Otherwise, the strong likelihood exists that your competition will end up intercepting potential customers and your business will likely lose out on potential sales. On the other hand, don't make the mistake of picking a site which, because it is closer to the interstate, suffers from such stumbling blocks as a lack of visibility and/ or poor ingress and egress.

Lifestyle Center Locations. Lifestyle centers have become the new focus for retail and casual dining restaurant activity. Typically anchored by a department store, they are a popular attraction for some of America's most visible businesses. FYI, Chain Store Age ranks the Easton Town Center outside of Columbus, Ohio number one for retail experience. It annually attracts more than 30,000,000 people!

Speaking of Easton, 80% of its corner locations are occupied by restaurants! Are you paying attention developers?

Lifestyle centers are like all other shopping centers - they offer a variety of location types to prospective businesses. However, the simple truth of the matter is that some locations are destined to be better than other locations. In other words, not all lifestyle center locations have the potential to become "home run" locations.

All things being equal, the best locations within lifestyle centers are likely to be those which enjoy outstanding visibility, have one or more anchors as well as lots of parking nearby, and are located in areas with lots of pedestrian traffic.

Lower Level and **Basement Locations.** Unless you locate your business in a mall or area where other retail and restaurants are consistently found below street level, you are advised to avoid lower level and basement locations. These are highly suspect locations, primarily because of limitations on signing, windows, natural light, and an overall lack of visibility. In addition, most shoppers and people who are looking to eat don't like walking up and down stairs or taking a potentially crowded elevator or escalator - especially if they are carrying shopping bags or are accompanied by small children.

Main & Main Locations. When two major streets or highways intersect, you can typically expect to find a small, medium, or large cluster of retail and restaurant businesses. Such clustering is explained, in part, by not only the added convenience which major intersections provide, but the increased traffic count and activity which they generate.

In addition to benefiting from heightened awareness, most urban as well as some older suburban Main & Main locations are characterized by another important advantage: they typically provide people with more than two means of access. For example, in addition to being able to drive there, customers oftentimes have the choice of either being able to walk or take the bus. And, in certain high-density communities, the ability to ride some form of rapid transit can play a major role in boosting customer counts.

Locating your business at or near a Main & Main location is something you should explore. Nonetheless, you need to make sure that sufficient customer parking exists, that neighboring businesses offer some level of synergy, that adequate signing exists, and that the demographics and psychographics in the immediate area match or have a high degree of correlation with your customer profile.

Mixed Use Building Locations. Mixed use buildings consist of a dominant use as well as one or more secondary business uses. In many instances, the dominant use will be either office or hotel and the secondary uses will consist of ground floor retail and/or restaurants. In certain instances, however, the dominant use will be residential condominiums and the secondary uses will be ground floor retail and/or restaurants.

Generating street level customer traffic for a business which is located inside a low rise, mid-rise, or high rise building with a mix uses can be tricky. Your immediate challenge will be to create easy access as well as a strong identity. Regardless of the amount of building frontage you have, your best bet for maximizing storefront visibility is to feature large windows which are framed by awnings - especially colorful awnings. Paired with memorable facade and window signing, awnings can help your business do something very important: stand out.

A word of caution is in order. While some prospective businesspeople may think that they will have a built-in or captive audience because of the people who either live or work in a mixed-use building, you can't count on these groups to provide you with the majority of your customer traffic. Indeed, you need to prioritize attracting street level customer traffic as well. Doing so should increase customer traffic and sales.

All things being equal, I would not make locating a business inside a building with a mix of uses a high priority - especially if it will have not only limited windows, but limited sign exposure to the street.

Mixed Land Use Locations. What I am referring to here is a mix of land uses as opposed to a mix of uses within a building. Besides offices and **the three R's** - residential, retail, and restaurant - mixed use locations typically feature a visitor lodging facility (hotel/motel), and/or an entertainment (cinema/theatre/museum) component. Here, cafes, bars, and pubs not only provide outdoor dining opportunities, but encourage people watching. A complimentary mix of retail stores is a bonus. Collectively, these elements can make mixed use locations vibrant, memorable, and special places to visit.

What the small businessperson looking for a location in a mixed-use development should prioritize is a pedestrian friendly environment, a complimentary mix of uses, a high level of synergy between user types, and lots of curb appeal. Extended hours of operation beyond 8:00 or 9:00 pm are sure to be a bonus. In addition, mixed use locations should also pass the **PASTA V** test. You can count on these influences to help attract customer visits, and boost customer sales.

Office Building Locations. Opening either a retail store or a restaurant inside an office building not only limits your exposure, but also isolates you from other businesses. This, in turn, significantly reduces your ability to draw customer traffic from other areas. While having a monopoly may sound appealing, you can't afford to overlook the fact that you need to count on more than just office workers if you are going to maximize sales. Look what happened during covid.

Office Park Locations. Too many people think that locating their business in an office park is going to enable them to generate high sales volumes. Wrong! Like industrial parks, you want to consider sites which are located on the edge of an office park - locations which can take advantage of higher traffic counts and are more capable of capturing business from other nearby uses, especially nearby rooftops.

Older Business District Locations. Older business district locations, in part because of their affordable rents, are especially popular places for new start-up businesses. However, you need to look carefully at the availability and adequacy of off-street parking for your customers and

133

your employees.

One Hundred Percent (100%) Locations. These are the "home run" locations that every company is looking for and wants to own or lease a lot of. For the small businessperson such locations are usually very difficult to secure because the cost of owning or renting them isn't cheap. Unfortunately, what I have learned over many years is that cheap is usually at the forefront of too many small business owners site selection criteria.

One hundred percent (100%) locations are worth their weight in gold. Not only do they pass the **PASTA V** test with flying colors, but they end up consistently producing the kind of high customer traffic counts which result in outstanding profit opportunities. In the world of site selection, it doesn't get any better than that.

Outlet Mall Locations. Outside of an occasional small food court space, very few start-up and/or small business owners will ever have the opportunity to locate in these types of interstate highway and vacation dependent destination focused locations. This is the domain of mostly national chain stores. Even without a major anchor store, outlet mall locations have become very popular. They attract not only residents living within an approximately one-hour drive, but travelers and even buses that are filled with tourists.

Outlot Locations. Also known as pad sites, these locations typically offer excellent visibility from the street for either a single user, a co-branded building, or a small retail strip center with a limited number of tenants. They are a staple in front of larger shopping centers with one or more anchor tenants. Examples of such centers include regional malls, power centers, lifestyle centers, and discount centers.

Outlots may have indirect as opposed to direct access to the street on which they are located. While they aren't the cheapest places to own or rent, outlot locations are in great demand, primarily because the businesses which like to call them home generate sales which are consistently well above average.

Pedestrian Friendly Business Locations. Older business districts and older neighborhoods are typically pedestrian friendly. This is because they weren't built to attract primarily customers who are almost exclusively dependent upon cars, SUVs, mini vans, and trucks to get around.

Pedestrian friendly locations are typically found in areas with moderate to high residential densities, a mix of surrounding or nearby land uses, few parking lots of any real size, wide sidewalks, blocks with few if any curb cuts, on-street parking opportunities, a network of nearby interconnecting streets, one lane of traffic moving in either direction, some form of mass transit, tree lined streets, and, streets with low posted speed limits.

Lifestyle centers are relatively recent examples of shopping center dominated developments which are designed to be more pedestrian friendly than almost all other types of shopping centers. They have been patterned after successful older business districts in order to create a more appealing and more vibrant pedestrian scene. In doing so, they have captured the middle ground between yesterday's older areas and today's growing areas.

Pedestrian friendly business areas offer a mix of retail, restaurant, and service type businesses. In today's convenience dominated society, very few businesses can survive, let alone thrive, if they are dependent solely upon pedestrian traffic. Ironically, the availability of nearby parking opportunities, even if relatively limited, is absolutely essential to the success and longevity of the different types of businesses which are located in pedestrian friendly environments.

Large businesses such as grocery stores, modest size businesses such as drugstores, and smaller businesses such as fast food restaurants are likely, for any number of reasons, to typically be absent from or avoid pedestrian friendly locations. Conversely, many types of small businesses fit easily into this once prevalent type of location. Bakeries, casual dining restaurants, specialty retail stores, sandwich shops, ice cream stores, jewelers, art galleries, frame shops, gift shops, florists, used bookstores, and coffee shops are some of the better-known types of businesses which can commonly be found in pedestrian friendly locations.

Plaza & Square Locations. These are sought-after locations - that is if they are in the right area. Typically, the right area means one which is pedestrian friendly, a location which not only welcomes but is capable of accommodating crowds of people, and one which is surrounded by a synergistic mix of uses such as retail, restaurants, entertainment, offices, and hotels.

In all instances, some form of common fixed seating is featured - an amenity which helps create the ideal place for people to be able to relax, eat, drink, and periodically engage in people watching throughout much of the day and early evening.

Plazas and squares are usually characterized by attractions such as a fountain, a grassy park, a staging or display area, and statuary. They are fun places to be as well as wonderful places to gather with friends and family, or for events and special occasions.

Businesses serving food and drinks are good bets for locating either on or opposite plazas and squares. Restaurants, bars, coffee shops, bakery shops, and ice cream shops are just a few of the businesses which these types of special places frequently attract.

You can expect to pay a little more in rent for the privilege of opening a location in a plaza or square area. However, since you will be where the action is, chances are extremely good that you can count on lots of people stopping into your business establishment.

Pop Up Locations. These are temporary places for start-up businesses to gain exposure and determine if there is, indeed, a market for their products. Typically, high pedestrian traffic areas such as a plazas and squares are most suitable for these types of aspirational businesses. In other instances, they set up shop in large, underutilized parking lots located on busy streets.

The grilled cheese and tomato soup restaurant **TOM+CHEE** is an example of a pop-up. It traces its origins to Fountain Square in Cincinnati where the founders began selling a variety of grilled cheese sandwiches and soup to people during the late mornings and early afternoons. After achieving a high level of sales, the founders opened two company owned restaurants - both of which became popular destinations. Together, they served as the impetus for the founders' appearance on the popular television show Shark Tank. Here, they made a funding pitch which impressed Shark Barbara Corcoran. She subsequently became a "junior" investor and **TOM+CHEE** was "off to the races."

It wasn't too long before **TOM+CHEE** began selling franchise opportunities. It eventually expanded into a dozen states. Unfortunately, within several years, the restaurant's star faded and most of its locations closed. Sadly, such a scenario is not uncommon.

Power Center Locations. Power centers are among the least pedestrian friendly of all shopping centers. Aesthetically, what is most memorable about them is a combination of blank walls, deep building setbacks, and large underutilized parking lots.

Because they are the province of big and mid-size box stores, the typical power center tenant mix is often devoid of small businesses. In such centers, the best locations for small businesses are out front on pads (outlots) where building and sign visibility can be maximized. They are the type of locations which enable a mix of freestanding retail and restaurant uses to intercept street traffic as well as cater to the customer traffic which either shops at, or works at one or more power center stores.

Street & Sidewalk Vendor Locations. Most big cities have a variety of vendors who sell from street as well as sidewalk locations. Many of them sell freshly prepared food like hot dogs, pizza, and burritos in high pedestrian gathering places which are either surrounded by, or near office buildings, retail clusters, convention centers, stadiums, hotels, and plazas and squares.

Strip Locations. Strip locations are ubiquitous across the United States. They are home to a vast array of fast food restaurants, convenience stores, gas stations, grocery and drugstores, all kinds and sizes of shopping centers, big box stores, motels, tire stores, auto parts stores, automobile dealers, and the list goes on and on.

Mostly a result of the automobile friendly growth which took place in America's post-World War II suburbs, strip locations can go on for miles and miles. They are often laced with curb cut after curb cut, lots of traffic lights, telephone poles galore, uninspiring buildings, half empty parking lots, and sign after sign. Collectively, these characteristics help explain why some people consider strip locations to be unsightly.

Strip locations are characterized by high traffic counts - something which helps explain their popularity. However, heavy traffic volumes and seemingly endless roadside clutter also contribute to the difficulty that many motorists experience when it comes to easily spotting individual retail and restaurant destinations. Therein lies the challenge for many small businesses: how to maximize visibility. Your location either has visibility or it doesn't - there really is no in between.

Do you remember in Chapter Two that I identified visibility as one of the *six keys* to site selection? If you want to stay in business the biggest favor you can do for yourself is to make sure that your sign(s) as well as your storefront or building have good visibility, not just from straight ahead (head on), but from a distance of 100-300 or more feet. The further away your business can be seen the better for both you and your customers.

Strip Shopping Center Locations. Whether big, small, or medium in size, these are, on a daily basis, the most popular types of locations for local, regional, and national retail and restaurant companies.

It is important to remember that not all strip shopping centers are created equal. Some enjoy better visibility, more parking, and easier access than others. Similarly, some can point to more activity, higher traffic counts, and better signing than other nearby strip shopping centers. Your job is to determine which locations maximize your ability to generate a high level of customer sales.

Also, be aware of the hierarchy that exists within a strip shopping center. End caps typically offer more glass, more parking, and more signing than inline spaces. This is one of the reasons why they are favored by many restaurants and many retailers.

Subway and Train Locations. A number of big cities are served by subways and trains. This can result in people who live and work in the surrounding area periodically making trips back and forth to a subway or train station. These are people who are a good bet to periodically make one or more convenience or impulse oriented purchases. They represent what is known in the business as "captive" audience sales.

Some transit-oriented locations have heavy concentrations of office around them. Some are surrounded by a mix of residential types. Others may feature retail. In any case, a variety of retail and restaurant businesses are likely to be found either inside, next door to, or across or down the street from subway and train facilities.

Don't assume that your business can thrive solely off the customer traffic which is generated by subways and trains. Instead, think about the "capture rate" - the percentage of people who ride these alternative forms of transportation and are likely to spend money either prior to boarding, or upon exiting them. The answer typically is not very much. Indeed, only a fairly low percentage are likely to spend money.

The most common types of businesses which are found either in or near subway and train stations include, in no particular order, bagel shops, carryout restaurants, coffee shops, convenience stores, fast food restaurants, liquor and tobacco stores, newsstands, and sandwich shops.

Tourist Area Locations. Because they tend to be seasonal, prospective businesspeople need to do lots of "homework" before locating in tourist areas. If you are considering renting or buying space in an urban tourist location you should look for a significant cluster as well as a good variety of busy, successful businesses. A good example of a busy and very successful urban tourist attraction is Navy Pier in Chicago. It is a great model for attracting lots of people for many different reasons, not only during warm weather months, but year-round.

Non-urban locations can also be successful. However, without critical mass and a variety of synergistic attractions they are riskier places to make a major investment in, especially if they are located in an area where tourist traffic tends to be seasonal and is subject to large fluctuations of visitors. In these types of areas an emphasis needs to be placed on not only differentiating yourself from your competition, but in selecting a location which is either in or near the heart of activity as opposed to being located on the edges - places where little or a small fraction of tourist traffic is found.

Truck Stop Locations. Located at highway interchanges, newer truck stop locations offer customers a synergistic combination of gas, snack foods, beverages, fast food, and even pizza. In almost every instance, the names of the businesses who are located here are easily recognized, mostly national brands such as McDonald's, Subway, Wendy's, etc. Consequently, you will find very few mom and pop businesses at truck stop locations. Sadly, very few next door or nearby businesses are likely to benefit from the types and levels of traffic which truck stops generate.

Upper Level Space. Like lower-level space, upper-level space should be off limits unless the space you are considering is located in a vertical mall like Water Tower Place in Chicago.

About the only reason for justifying renting this kind of space is if you are in either the service retail or novelty retail business, and, you operate what can be classified as a destination type business. For instance, a good beauty salon or a busy palates studio can succeed in upper-level space if they are well signed, offer lots of natural light, and provide customers with an alternative means of access such as an elevator or an escalator.

In most situations the only three words you need to remember with respect to opening your business in an upper-level location are "no way, Jose."

You're no doubt exhausted after reading about the many different types of location options which exist. However, I want you to remember that they all have a common denominator - "turnover." I hope you won't be surprised to learn that today's diverse marketplace is characterized by retail and businesses that, sadly, come and go on a regular basis. In the future, I sure hope your business won't be one of them!

Chapter Thirteen
Certified Site Selection
Specialist Designation

I debated long and hard about where to include the information which follows. I ultimately decided that if I was going to build support for what I am recommending, that it would be best if I could give it a visible, prominent, front and center position as a stand-alone chapter.

Certified Site Selection Specialist. Currently no such designation exists for professionals who assist small business owners, newer retail and restaurant franchisors, and start-ups with site selection. This is an unfortunate oversight - something I strongly feel needs to be corrected. It's very important to know that not everyone who is a commercial realtor is a site selection specialist. Most are not. Indeed, being a site selection specialist means being a member of a small select group.

Just as the shopping center industry benefits from having Certified Shopping Center Managers and Certified Leasing Specialists, so would the commercial real estate community if certification of site selection specialists were an option. In particular, more business owners, franchisors, and start-ups would recognize the benefit of working with a trained and highly skilled professional whose focus was on consistently finding "home run" locations for his or her clients.

Whether at the undergraduate or graduate school level, it's rare for real estate programs at major colleges and universities in the United States to offer students any type of comprehensive coursework on site selection. On the other hand, based upon my personal experience, I know that practicing real estate professionals, myself included, have from time-to-time been invited to give classroom presentations to introduce students to site selection.

Furthermore, I know from first-hand experience, that a course on retail and restaurant site selection is seldom available to realtors who need to periodically satisfy their state mandated continuing education requirements. That's the primary reason why I decided to develop a three (3) hour long continuing education course on retail and restaurant site selection - something I'm proud to say I've been teaching for more than twenty years.

Obtaining a Certificate in Site Selection, whether it is in retail and restaurant site selection, industrial site selection, or office site selection, is a great way for major colleges and universities to not only differentiate themselves amongst their peers, but add a new source of reoccurring revenues to their programs.

Furthermore, this is a professional credential which I believe will be quickly embraced by commercial real estate practitioners because it enables them to not only learn about, but subsequently market a newly acquired specialty expertise. Having a good understanding of site selection will also help them build customer relationships while enabling them to simultaneously increase their incomes.

Two long lasting mutual benefits of seeing colleges and universities offer Certificates in Retail and Restaurant Site Selection to individuals who possess a minimum of 5 years of commercial real estate experience is the opportunity to also provide something invaluable to their undergraduate and graduate level students: work-study programs and internships with local, regional, and/or national commercial real estate and development companies.

Earning a professional designation in commercial real estate is nothing new, as evidenced by practitioners sporting such longstanding prestigious credentials as CCIM, SIOR, and CRE after their names.

Certificates in retail and restaurant site selection can be earned through a combination of coursework focused on reading, reviewing, and discussion of real estate books, articles, and experiences via (a) lectures, (b) seminars, (c) case studies, and (d) fieldwork - something which should be a key component in every institution of higher learning's real estate curriculums.

While offering daytime classes might be attractive to college and university students, being able to offer a combination of evening, weekend, and online courses in retail and restaurant site selection is much more likely to attract people who are active in the commercial real estate profession.

Offering one or more Certificates in Site Selection will also be a great opportunity for real estate practitioners with significant experience to network with colleagues and share valuable information. And, in select instances, it could potentially enable them to join the ranks of a school's Adjunct faculty on a part-time basis. Talk about a win win!

How many hours of classroom and online coursework should be required before a person is able to obtain a Certificate in Site Selection will vary from school to school. Generally speaking, I'm recommending that 18-30 hours be required to earn such a specialized certificate. This would result in enrollees taking as few as six (6) three (3) hour courses or as many as ten (10) three (3) hour courses.

Examples of courses that could potentially be incorporated into a curriculum leading to earning a real estate Certificate in Retail and Restaurant Site Selection include the following: (a) Market Analysis, (b) Demographics and Psychographics, (c) Walking, Talking, and Information Gathering, (d) Zoning and Related Government Approvals, (f) Site Planning, (g) Retail and Restaurant Building Design, (h) Retail and Restaurant Site Development, (i) Build to Suits and Land Leases, (j)

Sales Boosting Site Amenities, (k) Structuring Letters of Intent, (l) Leases and Purchase Agreements, and (m) Win Win Negotiations. Incidentally, you'll find **The ABC's of Retail and Restaurant Site Selection** touches on many of the aforementioned topics in varying degrees.

Establishing a Site Selection Certificate program could also potentially lead to colleges and universities becoming invaluable repositories for a broad range of real estate information from commercial real estate brokers and commercial real estate developers.

While certain types of "deal" related information will need to remain confidential, commercial real estate brokers and commercial real estate developers are very capable of contributing a wide variety of valuable information, from elevation and architecture drawings to site plans to permit applications to marketing literature to correspondence to build out exhibits to details identified in Letters of Intent and Lease Agreements, and, to public presentations before elected and appointed officials. Acting in an Adjunct capacity, they are the perfect choice to teach one or more or all of the proposed courses.

Chapter Fourteen
Meaningful Career Experiences

Writing this book has been a joy. Furthermore, writing this chapter has been one of my very favorite experiences. Why? Because I get the opportunity to share a series of wonderful memories - some that taught me a lot and others which describe experiences I hope other people will learn from.

Where possible, I promise to keep my walk down "memory lane" brief. In no particular order, here's what I hope you find interesting, starting with some fond memories I have from my experience working at **TOM + CHEE**.

Working as a site selection consultant before becoming the Real Estate Director for Shark Tank restaurant favorite **TOM + CHEE**, I had the opportunity to travel a lot. One of my fondest memories was boarding a 4-passenger airplane with the president of **TOM + CHEE**. (In case you're wondering, hearty grilled cheese sandwiches, tomato soup, and grilled cheese donuts were the primary reasons why people chose to dine here.) We flew from a small airport in Cincinnati, Ohio to Evansville, Indiana. The pilot had recently been awarded the franchise rights for southwest Indiana. With him was a friend - someone who owned a popular family style restaurant and bar business. While the "roar" of the engines periodically interrupted our conversations, we managed to talk all the way there and back. It was exciting to not only talk business, but to see a lot of pretty country - mostly flying below or not too far above the clouds.

For the uninitiated, **TOM + CHEE** became an overnight sensation after attracting an investment from long-time Shark Barbara Corcoran. Demand was high, and the company awarded franchises throughout the country, mostly to what I liked to call first-timers - people who were new to the restaurant business but were "intrigued" by the opportunity to serve delicious food to hungry customers, mostly over the lunch hour. However, we were fortunate to also attract people with lots of restaurant experience, including franchisees from McDonald's, Buffalo Wild Wings, Five Guys, the Bonefish Grill, and the Outback Steakhouse.

*****

During a site selection visit to Denver to meet our Front Range franchisee, I had the opportunity to visit the original Chipotle restaurant - a former Dolly Madison Ice Cream shop. It was located on the edge of the University of Denver campus next to a "smoke" shop. It was tiny by today's standards, and had very little off-street parking. It was set up for carry out as opposed to dine in. I introduced myself, the president of **TOM + CHEE**, and our franchisee to Billy, the manager. He was kind enough to spend 20 minutes with us, and even posed for a couple of pictures. I'm proud to say I still have one of those pictures displayed on a shelf in my home office.

*****

When I was in Shreveport, Louisiana to meet with two **TOM + CHEE** franchisees we toured several locations - one of which fit our site selection guidelines. After meeting the landlord and learning more about the opportunity to lease space, the franchisees took me to a small, fast growing chicken finger restaurant. I was impressed with the food. I was also intrigued by its very simple menu - a welcome departure from the many fast food restaurants with many, many menu items. I support the KISS principle: Keep It Simple Stupid. Today, Raising Canes has become a major player in the fast food industry – a restaurant I'm happy to say my wife and I like to frequent.

147

*****

Back home in Cincinnati, I wondered if **TOM + CHEE** would be an attractive tenant for the region's premier mall. As a result, I contacted and later met with the mall manager. Because of the "hype" and "buzz" surrounding **TOM + CHEE**, we found ourselves in the enviable position of looking at a premier corner space across from a busy Starbucks and only one hundred or so feet from the mall's food court. The mall owners were even willing to encroach into a commons area to provide us with some customer seating. It wasn't too long before we had a proposal to pour through. In spite of this big-time opportunity, the more our leadership team analyzed things the more we realized that the high cost of build out, coupled with high rents plus a percentage rent requirement, was a deal breaker. So, we decided to pass - something I thought was the right decision.

*****

Having worked for a couple of diversified developers, I knew that building long-term relationships with good tenants was a win win outcome for everyone. Accordingly, I placed a call to Simon Properties in Indianapolis - the largest owner of top performing malls in the country. From our perspective, we thought **TOM + CHEE** would be a good tenant for some of their off-mall retail locations. As a result, our company's president and I drove two hours to Indiana's capital city to meet with Simon Properties' Vice President. Afterwards, he agreed we might be a good fit at any number of their properties. While things, unfortunately, never materialized, what we had hoped would happen was confirmed. If we leased a "home run" location which generated a high level of sales, Simon would be willing to "partner" with us at properties they owned all over the country.

*****

On a visit to a suburban Akron, Ohio location which **TOM + CHEE** franchisees ended up leasing, I was introduced to the owner/developer of their grocery anchored shopping center. Concerned about the tendency of both grocery store and shopping center employees to compete with shoppers for conveniently situated parking, he decided to identify separate areas for each party to park in. Accordingly, he painted customer parking spaces white and employee parking spaces green. I thought his decision to do this was pure genius - something I mentioned elsewhere in my book.

*****

"Site selection is not a democratic process." These are the words I unhesitatingly spoke to a developer of a mixed-use project in a "home run" *area*. He and his team were hoping to persuade our leadership team to open a **TOM + CHEE** restaurant in what was a small, irregular shaped end cap space in a busy mixed use suburban center where convenient parking was, because of the existing cluster of nearby restaurants, already at a premium. Fortunately, our leadership team voted unanimously in support of my position. While complimented, they realized that the proposed end cap had some limitations which could, potentially, end up making it either a "double" or "triple" location rather than the "home run" location we needed. Since it would be a company operated, as opposed to franchisee location, they also realized that an underperforming restaurant could slow down internal growth.

*****

In its early stages of growth, **TOM + CHEE** had an opportunity to lease inline ground floor retail space in a three-story office building located in Cincinnati's premier mixed use lifestyle center. Two busy table service restaurants at opposite ends of the building anchored the first floor. Across the parking lot were two freestanding table service restaurants and a fast casual dining restaurant. We all liked the idea of

149

being a part of a busy restaurant cluster. On the other hand, surface parking, as opposed to garage parking, was at a real premium. Being primarily a lunch restaurant, our leadership team had some doubts about whether we could thrive here.

This is when the company looked to me for direction. The President of **TOM + CHEE** told me the decision was in my hands. Wow! Thank heavens I had done my "homework." While I was complimented, I didn't want anything to do with giving the "green light" to a potential failure. When I called the landlord and told him our decision, he was disappointed. To this day, I'm very comfortable with the decision I made. Restaurants are expensive to build out, and this would have been a company owned store whose failure would have not only tarnished our image and slowed down the company's future growth, but would have greatly diminished their faith in me and my site selection skills.

Not all of my stories are about **TOM + CHEE**. I've got a few others I'd like to tell you about.

Early in my real estate career I called the area real estate representative for McDonald's. He told me bluntly that "realtors are a waste of our time." Hearing that impression, I quickly and confidently responded "I've got a master's degree in urban geography and I promise you that I won't waste any of your valuable time if you are willing to share your site selection requirements with me - something he decided to do after paying a visit to my company's office and getting to know me. Needless to say, I was a very "happy camper."

Here's another story which is related to McDonald's, but not about this fast food giant. A couple of years into my commercial real estate career Blockbuster Video had opened for business along a busy, busy commercial strip in suburban Cincinnati. I decided to call their real estate representative and advise him about a shopping center expansion opportunity in a heavily populated, higher income area in Cincinnati. When he told me their interest was going into regional locations, I let him know the location I was promoting was anchored by two grocery stores - one of whom had the highest square foot sales of any of their stores in the United States. This statement caught his attention. He told me to give him a few days and he would be back in touch.

I'm glad I talked about sales productivity to Blockbuster's real estate rep - something I learned as a result of doing my "homework."

When I heard back from Blockbuster's real estate representative, he told me he had passed my information along to the company's new real estate director. Lucky for me, this person had formerly been the real estate director for none other than McDonald's. He was aware of the location I had identified as a result of looking for "home run" opportunities in the same area, including at the same community shopping center.

Imagine my thrill in learning that Blockbuster was interested in leasing 6,000 square feet of space in an inline location which, you guessed it, was adjacent to an end cap space that McDonald's decided to lease. This story only gets better. Not only did McDonald's open a "home run" location - one which featured a drive thru - but the space Blockbuster ended up leasing became their #1 company owned location in the state of Ohio. This led to a relationship which enabled me to bring Blockbuster a location on the other side of town - one which became their #1 franchisee owned store in Ohio!

*****

As a commercial realtor, I decided to contact a hometown favorite - a company with a long-established reputation for serving premium dessert products. I made phone call after phone call - none of which were ever returned. Being the persistent person that I was, I decided one day to make a "cold call" visit hoping to catch the president of the company. It turned out to be my lucky day! The president and I spent a few minutes getting to know one another as well as get comfortable with one another.

I told him about a suburban location that had the potential to become not only a top performing store, but his #1 location. I told him that the location I liked was located (a) across the street from a 400,000 square foot office complex, (b) had two new motels for neighbors, (c) was very close to a number of busy dine in and fast food restaurants, (d) was near lots of retail shopping, (e) was in an "upscale" growth corridor, and, (f) was located within a couple of miles of a large amusement park. I got his attention. As a result, he decided he wanted to visit the subject property and the surrounding area.

His company ended up buying an acre of retail zoned property and soon opened what quickly proved to be a "grand slam" location. Fortunately for me, this very positive experience led to other opportunities - one of which was writing his company's site selection manual. In addition, within a short period of time, I brought him two other locations - both of which quickly turned out to be "home runs."

*****

I grew up in the restaurant business back home in western New York. My parents had bought a shell of a freestanding building located at a signalized intersection in a busy employment area and opened a mom and pop restaurant - one which generated a lot of lunch business. It was a demanding business, but one my father loved. It became his passion and ended up becoming a "home run."

I never had the luxury of going on vacation until I graduated from college because the "Alibi" was open for business 7 days a week. If we went to Buffalo or Niagara Falls it was always a quick out-of-town trip because my father wanted to be home in time to serve his "regulars."

Besides cleaning tables and stocking beer coolers, I got the opportunity to help bartend when I would come home from college. My father impressed upon me something I never forgot. He told me "Treat my customers like family." That's how he thought of them. He reminded me that his customers were the ones who paid for our mortgage as well as my college tuition and room and board. His success left a lasting impression on me. His values became my values. They resulted in my being "service minded" - something which has allowed me to build many meaningful long-term relationships.

*****

I had the opportunity to work with the owner of a local "upscale" pizza restaurant after having conducted a series of revealing customer surveys for another business. When we asked survey participants where they liked to go for pizza, we learned his restaurant was at the top of the list. Impressed with the opportunity to pair with such a synergistic business, we approached the pizza owner about opening a suburban location. He was quick to inform us that he wasn't thrilled about expanding out into the suburbs. However, when we told him our game plan was to create a "Third Place" environment he was "all ears."

The owner of the dessert business I previously talked about and I took the owner of the small pizza chain out to see the site we thought had the potential to become a "home run." On our ride, we described our vision to him. After visiting and walking the site, we drove around to familiarize him with the surrounding "upscale," fast growing family area. He was impressed. This was the start of a business relationship which took off as a result of our focusing on the development of what I like to refer to as a pedestrian friendly, amenity rich, mini-lifestyle center.

*****

Speaking about pedestrian friendly, amenity rich, mini-lifestyle centers, I'm proud to say I facilitated the development of two of these popular destinations in suburban Cincinnati. In both cases, the people I worked with prioritized (a) the construction of two small (10,000 square feet each) brick buildings, (b) the creation of a plaza for gathering purposes, (c) small clusters of outdoor seating, (d) the addition of either a water fountain or water jets, (e) individualized storefronts, (f) parking spaces located in not only the front, but the back as well as on the sides of each of the small tenant occupied buildings, and last but not least, (g) four end caps spaces featuring glass wrap. Two end cap spaces, incidentally, were separated by a fifteen foot wide landscaped connector corridor built with pavers in order to facilitate people walking back and forth between the front and rear parking areas.

*****

On a vacation in Vermont, my wife and I visited the Ben & Jerry's store in downtown Burlington, Vermont. It was located on an inviting pedestrian friendly street. It was midday when we walked in to buy a sweet treat for ourselves. As we entered, I was struck by the presence of a plastic cow - something which had several kids petting it and wanting to climb on it. Nearby were happy parents taking pictures with their phones and cameras. I marveled at the smiles and joy on their kids' faces. If displaying a plastic cow was meant to create a memorable, happy experience, Ben & Jerry's "gimmick" worked. It was a winner - something I found myself telling a number of "experiential" business owners about once I returned home.

*****

I joined the staff of a diversified developer just in time to make an important contribution to the design of a new 34,000 square foot drugstore anchored retail center they were in the process of building. This was their second shopping center. As a result, there was still a bit of a learning curve.

The larger portion of the retail center sat parallel to a heavily trafficked street. However, given the slope of the site, the other portion was being built at an angle to the street. Between the two attached buildings under construction, two small "recessed" tenant spaces were going to be created. Looking at the architect's drawings, I realized these spaces would not have any street facing signing - a big turn off to potential lessees in my estimation. As a result, I suggested that one of the building columns not only be "fattened," but project above the roofline to enable additional signing. While this meant spending more money, the company I was the commercial sales and leasing manager for realized that my suggestion would not only help speed up the lease process, but would boost pro forma rents. As a result, our collaborative efforts ended up creating a win-win opportunity.

*****

Lots of small, independent retailers and restaurants know very little about the extent of their respective trade areas. I found this especially irritating when I proposed a new location to a multi-unit retail company and was told it was too close to one of their existing locations. As a result, I embarked on some important fieldwork, starting with driving the area separating the two locations. Given the drive time, number of traffic signals and stop signs that I encountered, I concluded that people living in the general vicinity of the property I was proposing would not likely drive the distance (time + miles) between the two sites except perhaps on weekends. Not too long after meeting with ownership and sharing my thoughts, I was elated when they called to tell me that they were willing to move forward. Within less than a year they opened a new "home run" location.

*****

I asked one business owner I provided site selection and development guidance to if they were going to add a drive thru at their new location. His answer was "no, that doesn't fit our image." Quite frankly, I was surprised, stunned, and disappointed - you name it. I was absolutely convinced that he would be taking money out of his pocket. As a commercial realtor looking to establish a long-term relationship, I didn't feel it was in my best interest to argue with him even though I knew a drive thru would be "icing on the cake" for what ended up becoming a "home run" location.

Every time I stop at this location for a delicious treat, I like to ask the manager or person who waited on me why they didn't have a drive thru? The answer I've heard over and over again is "because the owner decided to put the utility room and restrooms on that side of the building." Oh well.

*****

I once received a phone call from an out-of-town prospective franchisee with an impressive restaurant background. He wanted me to do something very simple: drive him around Greater Cincinnati in order to evaluate the quality of Chipotle's locations. He was considering opening multiple locations over several years in order to compete with Chipotle. After spending most of the day with him, he thanked me and said he had a lot to think about. When he called me back several days later, he told me that Chipotle had "locked up" some very good locations. As such, he thought it would be risky to bring a rival franchise into the local marketplace. Accordingly, he said he was going to look at opening restaurants in another market.

The aforementioned points out the importance of securing "home run" locations when entering a new market. In this case, "home run" locations are what served as a deterrent to a would-be competitor. You may be interested to know that a couple of years later another person representing the same franchisor decided to enter the Cincinnati market. Maybe it's the food or maybe it's the pricing, or, maybe it's even the locations. However, this rival restaurant chain today has, sad to say, only a tiny presence in Cincinnati.

What I'm about to tell you really doesn't qualify as a memory. Rather, it illustrates just how valuable an amenity a drive thru can be.

Several years ago, Howard Schultz, the founder of Starbucks, was quoted as saying: "Drive thrus create incremental revenues and profits compared to traditional stores, and represent a fast growing and highly profitable format for Starbucks. They comprise just over one third of our U.S. company operated stores but contribute nearly 45% of our U.S. retail profit."

Today, Starbucks is closing locations without a drive thru and opening new locations a short distance away. Meanwhile, Panera and a number of other well-respected companies are doing the exact same thing.

Further evidence of the importance of having a drive thru is illustrated by the fact that market leading companies such ss Chick-fil-A, Taco Bell, and Dunkin Donuts are now building multi-lane drive thrus.

Incidentally, I was surprised to learn that McDonald's opened its first drive thru restaurant way back in 1975! Think about it; that's 50 years ago! Needless to say, today, drive thrus have become a dominant feature in America's roadside landscape.

Closing Thoughts

If you do your "homework," chances are very good that you will put yourself in a position to make "smart" site selection decisions. A very important part of doing your "homework" is reading, as opposed to skimming, through the pages of "The ABC's of Retail and Restaurant Site Selection."

Another part of doing your "homework" is being well organized. With this in mind, I would like to conclude my guidebook by providing you with a summary description of what I like to refer to as **The Ten Preliminary Steps to Site Selection Success**.

Number One. Have you taken the time to prepare a **business plan**? If the answer is no, then you need to delay the start of your site search.

Number Two. Have you put together a list of **site selection criteria**? If not, you need to determine which factors are the most important to the future success of your business or business concept. In other words, which factors are absolutely essential to being able to identify a "home run" location? This is a good time to revisit the Site Selection Scorecard information which is described in Chapter Eight.

Number Three. Have you determined who your primary **customers** are? Have you created a customer profile? Do you have a customer loyalty program? If you're contemplating going the franchise route, your franchisor should be a big help to you. If you have an existing business but haven't yet either conducted or analyzed any customer surveys or established a customer loyalty program then you need to do so as soon as possible. To have "market intelligence" information at your fingertips and not utilize it is inexcusable.

If you are a start-up business then you are at a bit of a disadvantage. However, knowing as much as possible about your **competition** and who their customers are can prove to be a good starting point.

Number Four. Have you decided where you will begin your site search? Will you be looking for a regional location or a community or neighborhood location? Will you be looking for a location with lots of nearby **rooftops** or one which is surrounded by a significant number of daytime **employees**? Will you be looking for a location in a fast growth suburban area or will you concentrate your time and energies on finding a location in an older, underserved urban area?

Number Five. You need to think about how you are going to proceed. Will you go through the site selection search alone, or, will you develop a **working relationship** with one or more of the following: a commercial realtor, a site selection consultant, a prospective landlord, a property owner, or a commercial developer?

Number Six. Obtaining demographic and psychographic information is important. What is even more important, however, is that you know what specific information to look for and analyze when you read thru **demographic and psychographic reports**. Remember to focus on numbers as opposed to concentrating on percentages. If you need to, revisit and reread the contents of Chapter Four.

Number Seven. Once you have identified a particular location that you want to be in you need to conduct **surrounding area research**. It is critically important that you understand as much as possible about zoning, traffic counts, critical mass, anchors, competition, shadow businesses, subdivision activity, hours of operation, etc., etc.

Number Eight. At the same time, you are conducting surrounding area research, you should begin narrowing your list of **site options**. In determining which sites have the potential for becoming "home run" locations don't forget to revisit Chapter Two - The Six Keys To Making

"Smart" Site Selection Decisions. You'll recall that this is where you were introduced to the very important **PASTA V** method of site analysis.

Number Nine. Once you have narrowed your list of candidate sites down to one or two, your next task will be to (a) begin **estimating sales** and (b) get a good handle on potential **costs**. It's very important that your emphasis be placed primarily on future sales. This, unfortunately, is where too many new or small businesspeople get it wrong.

Number Ten. If you have completed the many different types of "homework" which have been described in Steps 1 - 9 you should not only be well positioned to make a series of "smart" location decisions, but, be able to negotiate either the purchase or the lease of **prime real estate** - the proverbial "home run" location. Once you have accomplished this important milestone you will, hopefully, be on the road to consistently being able to **pick winners and avoid losers**.

About the Author

Frank Raeon has been helping clients find high volume retail and restaurant locations for more than thirty years. He prides himself on doing comprehensive, in depth "homework," and is very careful when it comes to determining which retail and restaurant locations qualify as "home runs."

Within months of entering the real estate profession Frank quickly observed that not all locations are created equal. His "hands on" experience has taught him that there are a lot more "singles" and "doubles" types of locations out there than "triples," "home runs," and "Grand Slams."

Understanding why one location is superior to another has long been his foremost goal, and is what set him on the path to becoming a retail and restaurant site selection specialist.

During his real estate career, Frank focused his efforts primarily in the areas of site selection, tenant representation, and the promotion of new, small scale commercial development. Besides leasing and selling real estate he has periodically advised the commercial development community on market opportunities, site planning, tenant mix strategies, building design enhancements, and zoning. In addition, he has periodically taught a course on retail and restaurant site selection at the local, college, and state levels.

Working in the exciting field of retail and restaurant site selection, Frank has facilitated transactions which have resulted in the execution of numerous lease and purchase agreements. His advice to people who are interested in joining the ranks of the site selection profession is to find a mentor, someone who has significant experience helping national, regional, and local companies identify as well as secure "home run" locations.

Frank recently retired from being a licensed commercial real estate agent so he could focus his efforts on spending more time traveling, writing another book - tentatively titled *"Inside Site Selection"* - and becoming engaged in a few select site selection consulting assignments.

Frank is the principal of *Location Decision Advisors*, a Cincinnati based real estate advisory company which helps retail and restaurant companies not only identify, but better understand how to find "home run" locations. In this capacity, he primarily (a) writes site selection success manuals, (b) provides demographics and psychographics analysis and assistance, (c) designs, administers, and evaluates customer surveys, (d) creates customer spotting maps, (e) provides sales forecasts, and (f) provides clients with site selection advice.

Frank's real estate background includes working for several commercial real estate brokerage companies. Here, he developed the types of relationships which resulted in repeat business opportunities. He achieved success working with market leading national, regional, and local retail and restaurant companies. In addition, he's been the Leasing and Sales Director for two Cincinnati area commercial developers.

Prior to becoming active in commercial real estate, Frank worked as a City Planning Director for two small communities - one in southwest Ohio and the other on the central coast of California.

Frank's undergraduate degree is from the State University of New York at Albany. Here he majored in both History and Geography.

Frank earned his Master's degree in Urban Geography from the University of Cincinnati where he was a Graduate Teaching Assistant.

Given his many years of experience and his ability to consistently produce "home run" locations, Frank is fond of telling people that he will never waste their time. He relishes the opportunity to play a leadership role and considers himself to be a strategic partner in the site selection process - especially when assisting companies who, for one reason or another, do not employ the services of a person whose full-time job responsibility is (a) locating, (b) negotiating, and (c) securing prime real estate - the proverbial "home run" location.

If your retail or restaurant company ever needs a second opinion as to whether or not a particular location qualifies as a "Home Run" location, you are encouraged to contact Frank Raeon.

You might be interested to learn that **fewer than 1 in 10 people who work in commercial real estate are classified as site selection specialists.** Therefore, when it comes to making retail and restaurant location decisions be "extra" careful about who you choose to work with. Make sure that he or she isn't on any type of "learning curve."

Book Audience

"The ABC's of Retail and Restaurant Site Selection" has been written for a broad and diverse audience. At one end of the spectrum are the many *entrepreneurs* who are hoping that "the more they dream the more they will achieve."

As I was politely reminded more than a decade ago by a well- respected restaurant site selection consultant and author, most *entrepreneurs* tend to be "emotional" thinkers. As such, it may prove challenging to convince them that (a) doing a significant amount of "homework" is mandatory, and (b) that their best interests are served by working with a trusted real estate advisor. This is the one group who, more than any other, is likely to be characterized as "lone wolves."

The next group I'm hoping to reach are *businesspeople with a single location*. These are people who have "tasted success" and are motivated to expand their business footprint. While they may not have a large war chest to spend, they are convinced that the local marketplace is ready to support a second and maybe even a third location. This group is more likely than the first group to realize the importance of engaging outside expertise. Their biggest challenge is to avoid what I've heard too often in the past: "find me a kitchen." As you know by now, site selection is much more than simply finding space. It's about making sure your location satisfies not only my **Area**, **Site**, and **Space** requirements, but all of my **PASTA V** requirements.

The next group who stands to learn something valuable from reading my book are the *owners of retail and restaurant businesses with multiple locations*. While most of their locations serve the local market, some are likely to be in nearby markets. One characteristic of this group is that, even though they could, they've chosen not to employ a staff person who is capable of providing them with site selection expertise. This may be due to the fact that they aren't comfortable having someone in-house share responsibility for making location decisions. As a result, they may not have a lot of "home run" locations in their portfolio. Rather, it's much more likely that they have primarily "triples" and maybe even a few "doubles" in their inventory.

You may be intrigued to learn that small businesses make up approximately 90% of all businesses in the United States, and, that they also account for the majority of new jobs which are created.

The fourth business group I want to speak briefly about is *emerging franchise organizations*. They can learn a lot from my book if they are careful and deliberate as opposed to being in a "rush" to sell franchises, something which is often a major motivator due to the fact that it will provide franchisors with not only fees, but future royalties. On a positive note, more than any of the aforementioned parties, franchise organizations have a variety of dedicated staff, including real estate, in place to help facilitate not only growth but needed support services.

You may be surprised to learn that my list of potential beneficiaries continues. In this case, I'm talking about serving the "educational" needs of *commercial realtors* - primarily those who are just entering the profession and are in need of structured professional guidance. These are people who are paid via commissions and need to start making money relatively soon. I've been in their shoes. I understand what they're going through. In case no one is there to "mentor" them, I can say, without any hesitation, that these "newbies" will be on a steep "learning curve." Hopefully, they will become members of a collaborative team which consists of at least one or two people who possess an expertise in retail and restaurant site selection. Otherwise, the opportunity to develop meaningful site selection skills will, unfortunately, be postponed.

The next group who stands to benefit from reading my book are ***college and university real estate, geography, and business faculty***. While this group is admittedly widely respected, many, if not most, are not well versed in retail and restaurant site selection. Reading my book will put them on the "fast track" to better serve the students who enroll in their classes.

I also think that ***small commercial developers*** represent a potential audience for my book. Before they can establish meaningful end user relationships, they need to have a good understanding of the principles of retail and restaurant site selection.

Others who will find "The ABC's of Retail and Restaurant Site Selection" instructive include ***directors of Small Business Development Centers (SBDCs), SCORE counselors/mentors, Chamber of Commerce officials and their members, City Planners, Community and Economic Development officials, and Redevelopment Corporation staff***.

While my book is capable of becoming an invaluable resource for all of the aforementioned groups, **readers who apply its wisdom will find themselves well positioned to make the move/leap from the "minor" leagues to the "major" leagues.**

Appendix A
Site Selection Influences

The following alphabetical list of important influences further points to the comprehensive nature of retail and restaurant site selection. For anybody who decides to forego the recommendations identified in this book in favor of taking the easy/lazy way out, all I can say is you're "playing with fire." Taking such action would be the equivalent of trusting your "gut" and/or "winging it," instead of taking the advice of your financial advisor when it comes to making an investment decision. DON'T DO IT is the best advice I can provide.

Adjacencies. Not enough businesspeople pay attention to who their next-door neighbors are. This can be a serious oversight and can result in not only lost revenues, but business failure. If you are contemplating opening a restaurant next door to a beauty salon you could be making a terrible mistake. This is because both businesses will likely be competing for the same valuable customer parking spaces.

Other potential adjacency problems can arise if two neighboring businesses aren't compatible. For instance, someone who is contemplating opening up a restaurant should avoid a location which is next door to a pet store. Similarly, if you are thinking about opening up a children's boutique you should be careful about choosing a location next to a bar or tavern.

Anchors. These are the businesses which not only drive customer traffic to a particular location, but also help attract other businesses. They can be big box stores, mall stores, grocery stores, drugstores, bookstores, toy stores, discount clothing and shoe stores, and even destination

167

restaurants.

Some anchors, like grocery stores and drugstores, will generate weekly customer traffic. Others, like malls, will generate less frequent customer visits. Regardless of how often a customer is likely to visit a retail or restaurant anchor the bottom line is that their ability to increase customer traffic counts will positively impact customer counts for your business.

Area Hours of Operation. When conducting your fieldwork make sure that you know which area businesses are open early and which remain open late. If you are counting on evening traffic to generate customer traffic and you are the only retailer in the area who is open during the evening then you can count on attracting fewer shoppers to your store.

Understanding when prospective customers are in the area where you are located will enable you to not only make more informed site selection decisions, but allow you to get a better handle on estimating future sales.

Barriers, Physical & Psychological. From a physical standpoint, interstate highways, hills, rivers, and large expanses of undeveloped land often negatively impact both the size and shape of customer trade areas. Whether individually or collectively, they create a real divide. As a result, any businessperson or prospective businessperson should be aware of their presence and their ability to inhibit both customer traffic and sales.

Many "psychological" barriers, such as different levels of street lighting, a change in the character and/or physical condition of the buildings lining a street, racial composition, income levels, lack of conveniently situated parking, the high cost of parking, and crime levels are individually as well as collectively potential impediments to the success of a business.

Be forewarned that potential barriers can, unfortunately, sometimes be overshadowed by an over reliance on statistical data.

Building Setback. With the exception of large retail anchor stores, the closer a business is located to the street the better. This is especially true of businesses which cater to the convenience crowd. Good examples of such businesses are bakeries, coffee shops, dry cleaners, and sandwich shops.

Too often businesspeople fail to take into consideration the fact that prospective customers are depending on signs as their primary way of finding a particular business. If you were to put yourself in the shoes of a prospective customer which of the following building sign distances would end up being the most visible to you: those which are located one hundred, two hundred, or three hundred feet off the road?

Common Area. This is the portion of a shopping center which is located immediately outside both the front and back doors of space which is occupied by individual tenants. It is the area which includes entryways, driveways, parking lots, sidewalks, storefront and parking lot lighting, common seating, the dumpster pad, common signing, landscaping, and water features.

Common Area Charges. In addition to paying your pro rata share of common area maintenance costs, pass through expenses typically include your pro rata share of real estate taxes and insurance. Collectively, these costs are commonly referred to as CAM charges.

These costs are above and beyond the cost of your monthly rent and typically should only increase a little every year.

Compatibility. When making a location decision, please make sure that your business fits in well with neighboring businesses. What you want to strive to be a part of is a good tenant mix, one where businesses can easily coexist and no business is detrimental to its neighbors or to nearby businesses.

Hours of operation, parking, and types of businesses are all important components of compatibility. In certain instances, compatibility will lead to one or more businesses sharing customers. This, in turn, will result in increased sales revenues for each business.

Competition. Knowing who your competition is, what their price points are, what they have to offer, how their site stacks up, and why they are successful is important information. Even more important, however, is knowing who their customers are and what their sales volumes are.

Remember that while it is easy to identify who your competition is, it is much more difficult to understand what impact they will have on your sales. Since the opportunity exists to share some of the same customers make sure that you periodically monitor your competition.

Connectivity. The more ways there are for customers to reach your retail store or restaurant the easier and more convenient it will be for you to capture their business. While locating your business on a busy commercial corridor is desirable, the ideal is to find a site on a busy street which is served by two or more nearby intersecting streets. This is what will potentially provide you with a competitive advantage.

If your business is located too far off the street, typically more than approximately one hundred and fifty feet, or, is located in either a large multi-tenant shopping center or a long row of businesses where little or no storefront differentiation occurs, being either close to or near a street intersection will not be of any real benefit. Indeed, excessive setbacks and getting lost in a crowd are two factors which can lead to an increased risk of business failure.

Co Tenancy. This important term refers to a lease clause which can be very influential with respect to sustaining customer traffic and preventing a decline in your sales revenues. This is one instance where you are definitely advised to seek legal counsel.

The longevity and prosperity of one or more anchors or major tenants in the shopping center or building where your business is located is also crucial to the longevity and prosperity of your business. As such, you want to make sure that if an anchor or major tenant leaves, otherwise known as "going dark," or occupancy levels fall below a certain level, that you are entitled to some form of rent relief, or, are able to either scale back your hours of operation or break your lease.

Critical Mass. The overall size and extent of the business district which surrounds your site is important. Typically, you want to locate your business in an area where there are two or more reasons for people to be out and around. Being able to go to the drugstore and the dry cleaner, or perhaps the car wash, the gas station, the bank, or your favorite pizza carry out in one trip represents a huge savings of time.

In order to increase your chances for business success look for locations in areas which are surrounded by not only a mix of business types and land uses, but which include one or more retail or restaurant anchors. The benefits which are attributable to such locations include increased name recognition as well as increased customer traffic. Unless you are contemplating opening either a convenience store or a gasoline business you should definitely avoid being a pioneer – the first business to open in an area.

Curb Appeal. Simply stated, most people will recognize it when they see it. If curb appeal exists count yourself fortunate. If it doesn't, you are automatically positioning yourself behind "the eight ball." From attractive entryways to appealing landscaping to easy-to-read signing to functional windows to colorful awnings, curb appeal is one of the most overlooked and least understood criteria in the site selection decision-making process.

Business owners spend the great majority of their time inside their stores and restaurants. As a result, making outdoor related observations can sometimes be overlooked. However, the opposite is true of prospective customers. They are more than willing to "judge a book by its cover." If your business has some, little, or no curb appeal you are restricting opportunities for building customer traffic. Consequently, you need to spend more time thinking about ways to enhance your curb appeal in order to do the most fundamental thing of all - attracting both first time and repeat customers.

Customer Profile Information. When you are searching for a location, you should have a thorough understanding of who your customers are and where they will be coming from. If you are the operator of an existing business, you should already possess this important information. In instances where you are contemplating buying a franchise make sure that the prospective franchisor provides you with this type of site selection information. If the franchisor can't, then you are advised to find out why not?

If you are opening a start-up business as opposed to taking over an existing business you have the disadvantage of not having any customer profile information. In such instances, it would be helpful to know as much information as possible about the customers who are buying from your primary competitor(s).

Without having some knowledge of either existing or future customers you need to understand that you will be assuming a greater degree of risk with respect to the future success of your business location.

Daytime Population. The focus here is on understanding as much as possible about the population which works within the trade area serving your business as opposed to the population which lives in the surrounding trade area. Daytime demographics play a very important role in supporting certain types of businesses. For example, convenience-oriented businesses such as fast food and fast casual restaurants, gas stations, and banks are good candidates to attract steady business from daytime workers in the nearby area.

Keep in mind that different types of employers will have different hours of operation. Furthermore, some businesses might restrict the amount of time which is available for employee lunches to thirty minutes while other businesses may allow an hour.

While some employers will have low pay levels others may provide higher paying jobs. Some businesses may employ more women than men. The point is, don't assume that every nearby daytime worker is alike and represents the same "capture" opportunity for your business.

Obtaining current as well as reliable daytime information can prove to be challenging. This is why talking to commercial realtors, landlords, and commercial developers is very important. Similarly, you should count on making visits to individual businesses, to City Hall, and to your local Chamber of Commerce. And, don't overlook the need to conduct fieldwork. It is an absolutely vital exercise.

Density. The more people who live and work in a particular area the greater the likelihood that your business will be able to capture increased customer traffic. Higher density areas - whether they are comprised of residential, retail, restaurant, and/or office - can definitely be a boost to customer sales. Consequently, density should be taken into consideration during the early stages as opposed to the later stages of the site selection process.

Differences in density are most apparent as you transition from urban to suburban to rural areas. In urban environments people may have many, many choices within a five-minute walk or drive time. In suburban areas they may have lots of choices within a ten-minute drive time. In rural areas they may have only a few choices and may need to drive fifteen or more minutes in order to visit stores, restaurants, banks, etc. As such, it is important to remember that as density increases the size of individual trade areas typically shrink.

Depth of Space. Ideally, for every three feet of depth, a store or a restaurant should have one foot of frontage. Thus, a twenty-foot-wide storefront should have a maximum depth of sixty feet. Achieving a 3:1 ratio is important because narrow, deep space is not only less functional for most businesses, but is less appealing from a customer perspective.

I hope you'll never embrace "the bowling alley look" when evaluating retail or restaurant space. In particular, you want to avoid space which exceeds a ratio of approximately four feet of depth for every one foot of frontage. While the rent for such elongated space will be less per square foot than the rent for conventionally shaped space, the bottom line is that it risks being less functional, less productive lease space.

Design Enhancements. These are the "extras" that can help differentiate your location and its surrounding area from your competitor's place of business. Examples include outdoor seating, fountains and water features, upgraded landscaping, differentiated storefronts, pedestrian scale lighting, and shopping center entryways which make a positive first impression.

Drive Thru. They have become ubiquitous. A drive thru allows customers at fast food restaurants to place their food and drink orders without the need to leave their cars. Orders are placed using a built-in microphone at food menu boards. As customers drive forward, they typically pay for their purchase at a drive thru window which may or may not be separate from the drive thru window where they pick up their food and drinks. Due to the huge convenience which they offer, wait times are becoming increasingly longer. FYI, the typical drive thru experience lasts approximately 4 minutes.

Drive Times. It is very important that you know about and understand the extent of both your primary and secondary customer trade areas. Driving times measured in "minutes" rather than driving distances measured in "miles" provide a very important insight into how far your customers are willing to travel in order to patronize you.

For most suburban businesses, the critical drive times are typically five to seven to ten minutes. In urban areas your drive times are likely to shrink a little while in rural areas they are likely to increase. As for walking, most people will only walk about three to five minutes in order to get to their destination. If they happen to go bar hopping or decide to visit a pedestrian friendly shopping area, the time they spend walking will increase but not significantly.

Unlike ring demographics, drive time demographics tell us a lot about a very important factor - convenience. The importance of this element should not be lost on business owners unless they operate what can unequivocally be classified as a destination type business. Businesses such as cinemas, jewelry stores, pubs, and bookstores, as well as specialty and/ or higher end restaurants, qualify to wear such a mantle. However, they represent a significant minority of the businesses which populate our cities, towns, villages, and unincorporated areas.

Free Rent. This is a great way for landlords to maintain desired property valuations while providing a strong incentive for tenants to lease space. Oftentimes tenants are given free rent as a means of reducing their initial financial obligation. In other instances, landlords can provide free rent in exchange for a tenants' making a series of interior improvements ranging from upgraded HVAC and electric to extra plumbing and additional walls. In certain instances, free rent can extend to having tenants make one or more exterior improvements such as the provision of patio seating, awnings, building lighting, and facade enhancements.

The provision of free rent is an especially effective tool when a tenant's financial statement and/or credit is subpar and results in a landlord's unwillingness to invest some or any money in making one or more interior and/or exterior improvements. It is also an important incentive when a landlord is unwilling to drop his or her initial rents below a certain level but realizes that being able to lease space can't be achieved without some provision for free rent - perhaps two or three or four months of free rent.

Frontage. Whether you are looking at street frontage, building frontage, or window frontage, make sure you memorize these four words: "the more the better." Retail and restaurant space which contains minimum amounts of frontage, especially those with excessive depth, should be avoided at all costs! A good standard to keep in mind is the aforementioned three to one ratio - a maximum of three feet of building depth for every one foot of frontage.

Highest & Best Use. This is a favorite term of real estate appraisers, bankers, developers, and city planners. It refers to land uses and focuses on which uses are the most appropriate for a particular area. In many instances, most appropriate refers not so much to land use compatibility as to tax base enhancement. In most highway interchange areas and most commercial corridors, highest and best use means that retail, restaurants, gas, banks, motels, and offices are preferred land uses.

Ingress and Egress. In Chapter Two the importance of access is discussed. Access is all about being able to get into and out of a site both conveniently and safely. Typically, convenience and safety are influenced by the number and placement of curb cuts. If "easy in, easy out" isn't characteristic of the location you are considering then you are advised not to waste any more of your valuable time.

Market Analysis. Market analysis is an important first step for many multi-unit retail and restaurant companies - especially when they are considering expanding into new markets. Determining how large the market is, identifying key competitors, determining competitor strengths and weaknesses, determining competitor market share, analyzing customer demographics and psychographics, determining if and where voids exist, and projecting future sales are all components of a detailed market analysis.

Median Strips. Avoid not only evaluating, but selecting sites where these types of physical barriers exist. They are literally "the kiss of death" when it comes to not only attracting but maximizing customer traffic. Remember, one mistake in site selection can realistically make the difference between success and failure.

Nighttime Population. This important term refers to the resident population which lives in a particular area. It is one of the first and one of the most important factors which needs to be evaluated in the site selection process.

Typically, the more rooftops which surround a potential business site the better. Rooftops are especially important to restaurants which attract a significant amount of dinner business. A pizza restaurant is a prime example. Whether it offers customers dine in service or focuses on pick-up and delivery, rooftops are absolutely essential to generating high levels of customer traffic as well as repeat business.

Nighttime population is the focus of most demographic reports. These insightful reports provide existing as well as prospective businesspeople, consultants, and commercial realtors with detailed data and projections which are based upon the most recent Census of Population. Whether reported by political jurisdiction, drive times, radii, or zip codes, such data is essential to understanding the characteristics of the people who live in the surrounding trade area.

Parallel vs. Perpendicular Building Space. Always look for a location which sits parallel to the street. Parallel buildings are not only more visible to motorists and pedestrians than buildings which sit perpendicular to the street, but are also more inviting to them. While tenants in parallel buildings will enjoy good visibility, with the exception of end cap and corner locations, buildings which sit perpendicular to the street will provide substantially less visibility.

Never, ever let cheap rent for lease space in a building which sits perpendicular to the street become a factor when making your location decision. While space in a building which sits parallel to the street will almost always cost you more, the bottom line is that it will generate higher sales levels - something which could end up making the difference between your staying in business or going out of business.

When you think about these two types of buildings make a simple apples and oranges comparison. In this case, the apples are parallel sitting buildings and the oranges are perpendicular sitting buildings. Don't forget this comparison - that's how much different they are from one another!

Some shopping center developments with one or more large anchor tenants will periodically violate **the parallel is preferred rule** and build "B" shop space which sits perpendicular to the street in order to accommodate a cluster of small to mid-size tenants. While these types of shopping centers are frequently able to attract and keep a mix of tenants, their future success is largely attributable to being located in close proximity to one or more anchors. Therefore, they represent the exception rather the rule.

When you think about it, when is the last time you remember seeing an anchor store which sits perpendicular as opposed to parallel to the street? The answer is very, very seldom. As such, why wouldn't you want to make the same type of site selection decision?

Percentage Rent. While scorned by most small businesses, percentage rent is looked upon as a value enhancement by owners of malls and shopping centers throughout the United States. Consequently, it is a common lease requirement for retail and restaurant companies who wish to occupy "prime" real estate.

The "bonus" theory behind paying percentage or overage rent is that landlords should be rewarded financially for establishing a synergistic tenant mix - a feature which, if done correctly, should account for higher sales levels. In such situations, in addition to paying a base rent, tenants pay their landlords a percentage of their sales beyond a certain predetermined figure.

For example, a retailer may be required to pay a landlord anywhere from two to perhaps seven percent of annual sales revenues exceeding

$1,000,000. In instances where said retailer produces annual sales of $1,250,000 and is bound by a percentage rent requirement of five percent, the landlord will end up receiving an additional $12,500 in annual rents. Capitalized at ten percent, this translates into an increase in real estate value of $125,000. That's the power of percentage rent!

Most tenants who end up paying their landlords percentage rent don't do so grudgingly. That's because business is good. Nonetheless, they are advised to "cap" how much extra rent they pay their landlord.

Pickup Window. An increasing number of restaurant businesses are incorporating pickup windows in the end caps of their buildings and space in order to provide additional convenience for their customers - the great majority of whom call ahead or either order online or order via a mobile app.

Unlike drive thru windows, pickup windows do not require either a menu board or a speaker system. In addition, they are less likely to have a long line of cars, trucks, SUVs and mini vans waiting to pick up their food and/or drinks.

Given the popularity of customers increasing use of mobile apps and the internet to place food orders in advance, pickup windows are becoming much more commonplace. They are time savers, a real convenience. Examples of how popular pickup orders have become are illustrated by Chipotle and Chick-fil-A. Chipotle does not have a drive thru. Rather, it has a Chipotlane reserved exclusively for preorders. Chick-fil-A is building dedicated lanes exclusively for pickup orders placed thru mobile apps. Doing so gives it the capability of supporting a greater number of vehicles than is typically found at a standard Chick- fil-A.

In the future, expect to see more and more restaurant businesses adding pickup windows as a means of increasing customer sales.

Pull Aside Lanes. More and more, customers who place their orders at fast food drive thru windows are encountering longer wait times before they receive their food and drinks. As a result, they are being asked to pull aside in order to allow other customers to place their orders. It won't be too long before their order is delivered to them.

Safety. If the neighborhood you're looking at isn't safe, then don't waste your time looking for retail or restaurant space, even if the asking price is right. Safety can be a tremendous influence on sales, especially whenever women constitute a large percentage of your customer base.

One of the best crime deterrents is lighting - whether it is located on a building or in a parking lot. Another important deterrent is the amount of nighttime activity in both the immediate and surrounding areas, whether pedestrian or vehicular. In both cases, the more the better.

Site Distance. Too many people look at visibility from a head on perspective. In other words, they evaluate site visibility from directly in front of a particular location. Doing so should only be a starting point. What you also need to observe is visibility from approximately one, two and three hundred feet away. Your objective is to determine how many seconds the site you are considering is clearly visible to someone who is either stopped at a traffic signal or who is driving the speed limit. **The longer your site is visible the better.**

Too often what impairs clear and sustained visibility is slope, other buildings, and trees and shrubs. At a minimum, you want the locations you are considering to be clearly visible to the driving public for at least three to five seconds. This is usually a long enough time frame for someone to not only read your sign but to deposit your business name in their memory bank.

Site Grade. Flat or relatively flat sites are the only types of sites that you want to spend time evaluating. Be especially cautious when looking at sites which sit more than a few feet below street level. Otherwise, you will sacrifice visibility, especially signing visibility - something which you cannot afford to do!

Slightly elevated sites - those which sit no more than a few feet above street level - are also worthy of your consideration.

In the long run, you want to secure sites whose grades do *not* exceed five or six percent of slope as measured over a distance of one hundred feet. Sites which exceed this time - honored standard risk creating not only unwelcome uphill and downhill walks for their customers but the prospect of having to deal with potential drainage problems.

Site Selection Coach. Many operating small businesses and most start-up retail and restaurant owners would learn a lot if they invested what amounts to a relatively nominal amount of money to hire an experienced and knowledgeable site selection coach. Site selection coaches act as mentors and typically have backgrounds in commercial real estate, consulting, teaching at the college/university level, or running a successful business similar to the one you want to establish.

Speed Limit. The higher the speed limit on the street where you are considering opening your retail or restaurant business the less time someone will have to see and remember both your storefront and your signing. In this case, "less is more."

Generally speaking, streets with posted speed limits of twenty-five, thirty, and thirty-five miles per hour are more attractive and more viable locations than streets where the posted speed limit is higher. As stated previously, speed affects visibility. The more likely your business can be seen the more you are ahead of the curve. Don't ever sacrifice visibility. If you do you could find yourself being behind "the eight ball" right off the bat.

Synergy. Finding a location where businesses complement one another and have the potential to increase one another's customer base and sales can be "money in the bank." Locations where two or more synergistic opportunities exist is the ideal. Nonetheless, locations with only one such opportunity are better than locations with no synergy.

The best examples of synergy at work can be found at the many regional malls which are located across the United States. Observe how women's jewelry, clothing, and shoe stores like to be next to or near one another. Why is this? The answer is because they help generate customer traffic and sales for one another.

If you are in the ice cream business, selecting a location which is near one or more restaurants - especially family friendly pizza restaurants, a bookstore, and/or a cinema complex - can be a big boost to sales. If you are in the sandwich business, the best neighbors you can have are the other restaurants in the area, and nearby places of employment. While not every employee will eat out on a regular basis, chances are they will go out to lunch at least once a week. Hopefully you can capture some of the traffic they produce.

An often overlooked but outstanding example of synergy is food and gas. The two go together hand in glove. Similarly, jewelry stores, shoe stores, clothing stores, cosmetics stores, and beauty salons can boost sales for one another.

Tenant Mix. If you are considering opening your business in a shopping center one of the first things you should consider is the type of tenant mix that exists. Are there tenants whose business is compatible with your business? Are there tenants who are likely to attract the same types of customers as your business? Is the mix of tenants likely to increase the number of people walking through your front door? Is there an anchor tenant who will not only provide an immediate identity for the shopping center but generate a significant amount of customer traffic? Are there tenants whose customers will compete with your customers for convenient parking opportunities?

Traffic Quality. Factors such as traffic congestion, restricted turning movements, multiple traffic lanes, frequent traffic stops, the lack of turning lanes, the opportunity to travel at high speeds, and limited or poor site access can singularly or collectively discourage or harm customer patronage.

Traffic Signalization. Being at or near a traffic signal is usually, but not always, a potential advantage for your business. Traffic signals typically mean that lots of vehicles will be driving by your front door as a result of the critical mass (for example, large numbers of offices, retail, and restaurant businesses) which is located in both the immediate and nearby areas. It also means that cars, trucks, and SUV's will typically be either slowing down or stopping - something which should result not only in increased visibility, but increased customer traffic.

The one caution about locating your business at or near a traffic signal is the amount of vehicle stacking which is likely to occur. Being too close to a traffic signal may result in long lines of backed up vehicles, all of which can combine to prevent easy turning movements into as well as out of your site.

When looking at "near" corner locations (as opposed to "far" corner locations) always count the number of vehicles which are stacking during the hours when your business will be the busiest. If stacking appears to be a problem, then you are advised to start looking for another location - even if everything else appears to be fine. **There is no room for gambling when it comes to site selection.** "It is better to be safe than sorry."

Windows. Typically, the more windows your business has the better. If you are in the retail business you need windows for display purposes. If you are in the restaurant business you know for a fact that people tend to gravitate to window seats. At a minimum, approximately seventy - eighty percent or more of your building frontage should feature glass.

Some locations feature floor to ceiling windows, others feature windows above a low wall - typically what is referred to as a knee wall. And, of increasing significance are glass garage type roll up doors. Does one type of window have an advantage over another? The answer likely depends on your preferences.

While front windows are absolutely essential, windows which extend along a portion of the side of an end cap space or a freestanding building will benefit some businesses, especially restaurants. Glass wrap helps to bring in more natural light and can make your business more appealing, more inviting to customers. Also, the number and amount of window space you have can help to differentiate your business from other nearby businesses.

In certain instances, having a section of high glass located along the back wall of your space is recommended - especially if you are in the retail service business and are in need of some small office space, or, desire more natural light in your customer space. For safety and privacy purposes, high glass should never be installed lower than approximately seven feet off the floor.

Older business districts in particular often feature recessed storefront entryways flanked on either side by large windows. These provide retail and restaurant owners with something which is critically important - additional display and/or seating space. While newer strip centers almost always overlook incorporating this type of amenity, many mall stores as well as many lifestyle centers routinely incorporate them into their building designs.

One word of caution: be careful to provide either an overhang or awnings for windows which face south or west. Otherwise, you will experience not only the potential for display items to fade, but customers who may become uncomfortable due to the glare of the sun. In the restaurant business this is especially critical because every seat needs to be occupied as much as possible. If the noontime, afternoon, or early evening sun is especially bright, chances are good that your window seats will not be seen as "the best seats in the house."

Any architect, developer, or businessperson who is involved in new development needs to take the location of the sun into consideration when contemplating the design and construction of a new building or building space. Unfortunately, this is something which, from time-to-time, I've seen get overlooked.

Appendix B
Words and Terms You Need to Know About

Cannibalization. This term refers to the sales transfer impact one location has on another. Whether you operate a mom and pop retail store or restaurant, a small chain, or, are a franchisee owned business, you should be concerned about the potential for cannibalization. Because there is no room for guessing, the best way to prevent the unwanted transfer of customer sales from one location to another, ideally no more than 3-5%, is to have a very good understanding of the extent of your existing customer trade area and who your primary customers are.

Captive Customers. Airports are a great example of places where captive audiences exist. Here, customers are likely to find only a limited number of restaurants to eat at and even a smaller number of retail stores for shopping. Here, there's no mistaking that "convenience is king."

Cheap Rent. How many "home run" locations do you know of which are characterized by cheap rent? The answer should be very few if any! Yet, cheap rent is frequently the reason why many business locations are selected.

Rental space is typically cheap for reasons such as deferred property maintenance, lack of an anchor tenant, the need to make one or more repairs to the roof and/or the HVAC system, little or no landlord build out contribution, excessive depth, high vacancy rates, limited signing opportunities, minimal visibility, limited or inconveniently situated parking, impaired ingress and egress, poor tenant mix, functional obsolescence, etc.

One or a combination of these drawbacks can end up costing a retail or restaurant owner something very important - customer sales. Yet, such drawbacks can be overlooked by people who have not done their "homework", are overly anxious to open a new business, or, don't grasp the fact that their competitors have superior locations.

Unless you have a unique or destination business, it is important to remember that cheap/low-cost retail and restaurant locations usually are guaranteed to produce only marginal sales. In the long run, there is no getting around the fact that "you get what you pay for."

Collector Streets. These are the types of streets which feed large amounts of traffic onto major roads, streets, and highways. While they carry a lesser amount of traffic than arterial streets, they typically generate many more cars, trucks, and SUVs than do local streets. In comparison with local streets, collector streets typically permit not only higher speed limits, but feature more moving lanes of traffic.

Color. Both your business and the property where you are or will be located need to stand out. Typically, this can best be accomplished as a result of attractive building design, attractive and/or unique signing, attractive landscaping, the use of awnings, and, color schemes which attract lots of attention.

Two colors always command attention: red and yellow. Perhaps this explains why businesses with a worldwide presence such as McDonald's, Wendy's, and Shell feature red and yellow in all of their signs. Color, especially with respect to signs and awnings, oftentimes is responsible for creating a customer's first impression. As such, don't be shy about incorporating one or more bold colors into your storefront design as well as into the image that you want to project.

Concept Plans. Architects and Landscape Architects, rather than Engineers, typically provide drawings to clients and developers to help

187

better visualize a new development or redevelopment project. They should be regarded as a starting point for site planning.

Congestion. Traffic which is regularly backed up can have a negative impact on store and/or restaurant sales. People tend to avoid locations where gridlock is a common occurrence, especially if turning movements can result in periodic accidents.

Consultants. Companies such as *Location Decision Advisors,* the author's site selection company, can be an invaluable resource when it comes to making "smart" location decisions. Consultants who specialize in offering site selection services typically have years of experience in "weeding out" the *winners* from the *losers*. In addition, some of them are capable of providing clients with zoning assistance.

Costs. What a business can afford to pay for rent and common area charges is a direct function of sales - something which is lost on many prospective and first-time businesspeople. For most businesses, the combination of these two factors should represent approximately ten percent (10%) of total sales.

Curb Cuts. Here, we're talking about ingress and egress. Curb cuts which permit two-way traffic to come and go as well as left turn movements leaving a site are far more preferable than right turn in and right turn out only curb cuts.

Decay Curve. This little-known phrase refers to the fact that as driving and/or walking distances from a retail or restaurant business increase, customer traffic ends up diminishing. In this case, reference is made to miles as well as minutes. You need to take this important factor into consideration when conducting your site search. This is where a site selection consultant can be an important resource.

Developers. Many times, the best way to secure a "home run" location is to work with developers. The absolute best time to meet with them is before any ground is broken for a commercial or mixed-use development.

This way you can get a better understanding of not only their concept plans but one or more location options. If you start early enough you may even be able to influence how certain amenities such as outdoor seating and glass wrap can be incorporated into the project in order to better serve your specific needs and requirements.

The best link to the development community is commercial realtors. For many of them new development, as opposed to existing commercial space, is a critical focus area. In many instances, they will have preestablished relationships with developers - something many small businesspeople don't. This important resource group also understands the commercial marketplace and is well positioned to provide you with the kind of negotiating tools and assistance which can lead to the creation of a win win opportunity for both you and the developer.

Drop Lane. Having the opportunity to make a right-hand turn into a site from a separately dedicated traffic lane extending for one hundred or more feet is not only driver friendly but a welcome safety feature.

Education Levels. This is both a demographic and psychographic variable which can be a very important influence in the site selection process. For upscale retail shops and restaurants, the higher the education levels are within a trade area the better. Conversely, higher levels of customer patronage for some businesses will consist primarily of people with lower education levels.

Egress. Locations where it is difficult to exit, whether turning left or waiting behind a stack of cars, mini vans, SUVs, and trucks, present a potential problem. This is because if it is difficult to turn left personal safety becomes much more of a concern. In cases where traffic ends up stacking, a person's patience will be tested and, if bad enough, could result in business avoidance. The best way to mitigate these concerns is to have your site served by a traffic signal. Remember that convenience is not only the name of the game, but something which can have a profound influence on both customer traffic and customer sales.

Entryways. These are the "gateways" into your location. As a result, they need to stand out. Attractive, well-maintained entryways heighten anticipation and create the impression that something worthwhile awaits a retail or restaurant visitor. Yet, appealing entryways are not only often overlooked, but are simply forgotten about. The ultimate loser, of course, is your small business.

Façade Enhancements. Making your storefront standout is an important means of not only increasing your visibility, but attracting customers. This can be accomplished in a variety of ways. Some of the most common are colors, lighting, awnings, and unique designs.

Front Door Parking. If you are in the convenience business, front door customer parking is absolutely essential to attracting customers and propelling sales. How much parking is required depends upon the nature of your business and its size. In urban locations, on-street parking which is located either in front of or in close proximity to the front door of your business is highly desirable.

Unfortunately, too many business owners think that front door parking is reserved for them. This situation becomes intolerable if employees also park in front of or as close to the front door as possible. Owners are advised to require that all of their part-time and full-time employees park well away from the front door. In addition, business owners need to hold themselves to this same high standard. If owners and employees want to park near a door then they need to get used to parking at or near the rear door.

Grid Streets. This is a very desirable type of street system because it provides added convenience for your customers. Grid streets are synonymous with interconnecting streets - something which enables customers to get to and leave your place of business more quickly. Unfortunately, in most suburbs, especially in newer suburbs, this kind of street system is largely absent. On the other hand, grid streets are much more common in urban areas and in older suburban communities.

Growth Indicators. In order to gauge the dynamics of an area, you need to look beyond factors such as traffic counts, anchors, rents, and vacancies. You need to learn about important growth indicators such as new postal drops, new building permits, new housing starts, recently approved subdivision plats, projected increases in school enrollment, and, new residential, commercial, industrial, educational, and institutional construction activity. Without knowing about what's planned for the future of an area how can you justify making a significant financial investment?

Gut. This one word describes the popular decision-making process which is used by far too many people when it comes to site selection. Remember, picking "home run" locations is a lot more about science than art - a message which is oftentimes ignored.

Hole in the Fabric. This terminology refers to the importance of finding a site which is located within, as opposed to outside, a business cluster - one which enjoys a continuous flow of customer traffic as opposed to one which is characterized by either leapfrog development or incompatible neighboring uses.

While especially important to businesses which rely primarily upon pedestrian traffic, determining whether a hole in the fabric exists is absolutely essential when considering sites which are totally dependent upon vehicular traffic. In the case of the latter, simply being located five hundred or one thousand feet away from a neighboring business may make the difference between staying open or closing your doors.

Hours of Operation. This important factor can easily be overlooked when evaluating sites for your business. For all but a handful of businesses, you want to locate in an area where your planned hours of operation are similar to the majority of other nearby businesses. If you are looking to maximize customer traffic until 9:00 pm and find that most of your neighbors and most nearby businesses are not open past 6:00 pm, then you are most likely going to be disappointed unless you operate a destination type of business.

Image. Not only does your place of business need to project curb appeal, it needs to make a positive impression from the moment someone walks through the front door. This means that, in addition to attractive signing, inviting windows and convenient parking, your business needs to be bright, clean and well laid out. Furthermore, customer service needs to be courteous, friendly, and helpful. Remember that a customer's image of your business is what helps drive sales. If it isn't positive, you risk losing customers.

Income Levels. In order to avoid expensive mistakes, it is important to match the income levels in either a new or a potential trade area with those which have been previously identified in your customer profile. An upscale restaurant or retail store, for instance, should concentrate its site selection efforts primarily in areas with lots of moderate and upper-income households.

Infrastructure. Besides streets, the availability of sewer, water and gas are absolute prerequisites for retail and restaurant development. Two other vitally important improvements which can have a significant impact on boosting future sales are the number of curb cuts and proximity to nearby traffic signals.

Lighting. Having high levels of both storefront and parking lot lighting is an absolute must, especially if your retail store or restaurant hopes to attract significant numbers of women. Out of a concern for personal safety, women will not make site visits to businesses which are not well lit.

Lower-Level Space. This type of space has a real visibility problem. Like basement space, it should be avoided unless money is no object and failure is an acceptable risk. The only time such "stigmatized" space might be justified is if your business is highly specialized - like a consignment shop, a used bookstore, or an exercise or fitness studio.

Loyalty Rewards Members. These are people who are among your most loyal customers. They are your repeat customers - people who are likely to account for the majority of your business. Indeed, you might even recognize some or many of them. As a result of signing up and providing you with a little bit of personal information they earn rewards points. FYI, Panera and Starbucks have the highest customer loyalty programs in the restaurant and retail business.

Neighboring Land Uses. By all means, pay attention to which types of land use are located either next to or very close to your business. Certain types of land uses are not compatible and can have a negative impact on both your customer traffic and sales. Especially unappealing neighbors are vacant parcels of property and businesses which generate loud noises, odors, and what could be construed to be the wrong type of customer.

Number of Traffic Lanes. The best locations for retail and restaurant businesses are those with one or two lanes of slower moving traffic in either direction. Traffic arteries with three or four lanes of fast-moving traffic in either direction may potentially end up discouraging, as opposed to encouraging, business patronage.

Observations. There is no substitute for not only making but recording personal observations. Simply visiting a site and leaving impressed afterwards is not enough. Having information which you can periodically reference is, indeed, the "name of the game."

On Street Parking. Being able to provide customers with conveniently situated on-street parking, regardless of whether it is angled or parallel, is highly desirable. While free on-street parking is much more preferable than metered on-street parking, the latter is ok if it allows people to park for both short and long periods of time and is reasonably priced. Nothing chases away existing or potential customers faster than being issued a parking ticket.

One Way Streets. Communities of all sizes may contain one-way streets in certain sections of their business districts. They are not, however, highly desirable from either a customer convenience or customer intercept perspective. In addition, they appear less pedestrian friendly to people than two-way streets, in part because they can encourage motorists to drive at higher speeds.

Outdoor Seating. This amenity is increasingly becoming a visible feature in both shopping centers and lifestyle centers. Many fast casual restaurants, in particular, are beginning to require that outdoor seating be incorporated into the design of their spaces.

This is an especially important amenity during warm weather months- one which provides a definite boost to business. Outdoor seating, whether at a table or bench, enables people to relax outdoors while indulging in a favorite pastime: people watching. Similarly, it provides customers with the opportunity to be entertained by everything that is happening around them. In short, it revels in being a happy place.

Outdoor seating also provides another notable benefit, something which is absolutely priceless - free advertising. However, you need to be very careful about the placement of outdoor seating. Because sitting in the hot afternoon or evening sun can be uncomfortable, you need to make sure that only limited or no patio, deck, courtyard, plaza, or sidewalk seating faces either west or south. Indeed, unless shaded by canopies, umbrellas, trees, or a building, primarily east and north facing outdoor seating is recommended.

Parking Garages. Both parking lot and on-street parking are preferred alternatives to garage parking. However, parking garages, especially those located in downtown and regional mall areas, are a desirable option for providing conveniently situated customer parking. The primary drawbacks of structured parking are their cost, the perception that they may be unsafe, and the potential to forget where you parked.

194

Parking Lots. Large surface parking lots have become ubiquitous. To the dismay of many, they have become asphalt jungles - places which are uninviting because they typically lack humanizing amenities such as landscape islands, crosswalks, and trees.

Whether located in the front, back, and/or sides of buildings, large parking lots can turn out to be hot, poorly maintained, and even unsafe places to be. Yet, there is no denying that they provide customers with an abundance of convenient retail and restaurant parking and will continue to be an essential element of the local landscape.

Parking Ratio. In suburban settings it is especially important to understand how much parking your business requires. If you are already in business, you should have a pretty good idea of how many parking spaces are needed, not just for customers but also for employees. If you are starting up a business or are moving to a different type of location you might spend some time checking out how many parking spaces your competitors provide.

In no instance should you rely solely on zoning requirements, in part because they are often stated as minimum requirements. Retail uses, depending on size, will almost always require fewer parking spaces than restaurants. Generally speaking, retail and restaurant businesses will require anywhere from five to twenty parking spaces per one thousand square feet of floor area.

Remember that insufficient parking could have a negative impact on customer sales. Indeed, without adequate on-site or off-site parking you not only are guilty of gambling but risk staying in business.

Primary Streets. These streets comprise a network of well-known travel arteries in every community. They not only carry high volumes of vehicular traffic but are typically associated with congestion, numerous as well as frequent curb cuts, and lots of traffic signals. Still, they are where most businesses want to locate.

Sales Transfer. See Cannibalization.

Sidewalks. While every business, large or small, will benefit from having sidewalks, not every property features this kind of amenity. Sidewalks provide an important means of helping link businesses and customers, especially in pedestrian friendly areas such as downtowns and neighborhood business districts. Sidewalks can be covered or open to the sky - each has its advantages and disadvantages. Typically, the wider a sidewalk is in front of a business the more inviting it becomes not only for customer traffic, but for outdoor display and seating purposes.

Site Model. Anyone who is involved in site selection should have a model or a system in place in order to standardize as well as guide his or her site selection search, analysis, and conclusions. Spending "time and money" on developing such a resource tool is a far superior way for making decisions than the "fly by the seat of your pants" approach embraced by so many start-up and small businesspeople.

Slope. This refers to a site's grade. The less slope/grade the better.

Standards. In order to start your quest for a "home run" location you need to establish quantifiable standards. **How many** parking spaces will your business require? **How much** store frontage do you need? **How much** window space do you need? **How many** square feet do you need? **How large** does your outdoor patio need to be? **How many** signs can you display on the property? **How much** traffic passes by your front door every day?

The answers to these and other similar questions will enable you to not only determine whether the minimum site selection standards you have identified have been met, but permit you to begin comparing sites. Accordingly, you will be able to measure how Site A stacks up against other site options.

Without identifying standards prior to beginning your site search efforts, you are not only "rolling the dice" but you are charting a course to fail

- something which, with a little bit of "homework," is very preventable!

Surveys. See Customer Interviews in Chapter Five.

System for Success. Securing the right location will not, by itself, be enough to make your business a success story. This may surprise you. However, the right location is only one of several factors which will influence how successful your retail or restaurant business becomes.

What you need to understand as early in the business cycle as possible is that **you need a system for success.** This is one of the reasons why buying a franchise is attractive to so many start-up businesspeople. While by no means an automatic guarantee for success, by investing in a franchise which has a track record - meaning that it has been in business for several years and has multiple locations - you are investing in an entity which has established a **formula for success.**

A system for success, at a minimum, includes not only having a good location, but a strong drive to succeed and being either a good or a great operator. If you don't have these three "building blocks" you won't be able to create a strong foundation for future business success.

Target Customer. Quite simply, **if you don't know who your target customer is then you shouldn't be in business.** Yet, the sad truth is that way too many small businesspeople have absolutely "no clue" about who their customers are.

Your target customer group will consist of your best customers - the ones who patronize your business the most often. While eighty percent (80%) of your business will likely not come from only twenty percent (20%) of your customers, the lesson to be learned is that your *repeat customers* are the ones who you need to focus your efforts on. *Repeat customers* are also the one group who should be at the top of your marketing contact list. Hopefully, these are people who are members of your loyalty rewards program.

197

If you are already in business and you want to learn who your target customers are **you are strongly advised to periodically conduct customer surveys**. Doing so, along with both demographic and psychographic data collection, will provide you with lots of reliable information and permit you to create a profile of your target customers.

If you do not currently operate your own business, then you need to understand as much as possible about the customer profiles of your competitors. This is not an easy task, but is something which starts with your becoming a customer of your competition and making as many observations as possible. Also, don't be afraid to speak with the hired help. Without realizing it, they can often be a "gold mine" of useful information.

Traffic Count. Knowing how many vehicles pass by your site each and every day is important. While lots of traffic may lead to periodic traffic congestion, it is certainly preferable to having only a small amount of vehicular traffic pass by your front door on a daily basis.

This important information is usually available at city and county offices as well as at your state department of transportation office. In addition, planning organizations represent another good source for such information. Recorded traffic counts may or may not be up to date. However, they will usually be fairly current and will allow you to compare two or more locations.

Traffic Generators. Unless your business is either a convenience or destination business, one which will attract customers regardless of how many other retail stores and restaurants are located nearby, you should strive to be in the same general area as one or more major traffic generators. Examples include malls, lifestyle centers, big box stores, cinemas, restaurants, grocery and drugstores, office buildings, hospitals, schools, hotels, recreation complexes and industrial parks.

Traffic Stacking. While regulated by zoning and typically associated with congestion, traffic stacking needs to be considered if you are the owner or the operator of a restaurant which features an order/menu board and a drive thru window. Being able to safely stack multiple vehicles one after another is very important. Perhaps even more important, however, is the ability to quickly move each vehicle through the line. Ideally, the best way to prevent unnecessary traffic stacking is to create a bypass lane. These approximately 12-foot-wide lanes enable vehicles to either get out of line or continue driving around a building without becoming stuck in line.

View Corridors. All too often, developers and property owners permit buildings to be built on outlots in front of their shopping centers. While one or more outlots will maximize visibility for their end users, they typically end up blocking visibility for businesses which are located behind them. This is a preventable problem.

If zoning doesn't require that a good-sized uninterrupted view corridor be maintained between buildings, then developers and property owners are advised to adopt such a standard. The open areas which separate outlot buildings are ideally suited for parking, outdoor dining, and landscaping. If not excessively landscaped with trees, especially evergreen trees, these open areas can provide the types of view corridors which will help ensure that the identification signs of the individual shopping center tenants located behind them will remain visible from the street.

If visibility becomes a problem for one or more shopping center tenants their business will suffer, tenant turnover will occur, vacancies will increase, rents will decrease, and property values will decline. Furthermore, once customer traffic at a shopping center begins to decline, typically what happens next is that outlot users will also experience reduced customer traffic. Thus, by simply maximizing the extent of view corridors a vicious cycle of decline can be prevented.

View Time. When you are driving, your rate of speed will determine how long you see a building or a sign. The faster you are driving the less opportunity you will have to read names and make out details. Conversely, the lower your speed the greater the opportunity you will have to make out names and details. For most businesses, being visible for just three or four seconds is sufficient time for name recognition to occur.

Voids Analysis. This is an exercise which many businesspeople conduct. Where voids exist, they oftentimes explain why people elect to open their businesses where they do. While conducting a voids analysis is a good starting point it is just that – it should not prevent you from doing additional "homework."

As you should be aware from reading the contents of this guidebook, making "smart" location and "smart" site selection decisions is not an easy task. While the process may be time consuming, it is absolutely essential to being able to secure "home run" locations.

Windshield Survey. Also known as drive-bys, this is a good way to scout retail and restaurant properties. By using the **PASTA V** method which is described in detail in Chapter Two you can quickly determine whether a property merits further evaluation or should be eliminated from your site search.

Zip Codes. Many big box businesses regularly track customers by zip codes - something which is ok if your trade area extends beyond three miles and ten minutes. However, for those businesses whose customers either live or work within one to two miles and are coming from three to five to seven minutes away, relying primarily on zip code information to begin building a customer profile is not recommended.

From a comparability perspective, one reason for not being overly dependent upon zip code information is that zip codes encompass a variety of both geographic sizes and population totals - from large too small. Viewed individually, they are likely to identify only a fraction of the customers who frequent your business.

Zip code research can, however, serve as an invaluable introduction to the different types of population groups residing within a particular area. In addition, such research allows you to quickly gain an understanding of where your customers are coming from.

When I look at zip codes, I focus my efforts on learning about a select group of variables. For instance, if I'm working on behalf of a premium ice cream company, I want to quickly learn about median income levels, housing values, the percentage of people working in professional capacities, and the percentage of people with college degrees. Doing this kind of research enables me to almost effortlessly understand where I need to initiate both my location and my site selection efforts.

Zoning. Every urban and suburban community is likely to have adopted zoning regulations in order to control land uses, parking, signing, building setbacks, and much, much more. As such, one of the first things you need to do when conducting your site evaluation is to identify its zoning classification.

While many businesses are classified as Principal Permitted Uses, others may be classified as Conditional Uses. If your business falls into the latter category, chances are you'll need to secure permission from a local Planning and/or Zoning Commission rather than from administrative staff. In such instances, be prepared to live with one or more restrictive conditions.

Site plan requirements are another familiar provision of local zoning codes. While mostly associated with new development, they also apply to retail and restaurant businesses intending to expand their existing space. In such instances, you will need to employ the services of a local architect or engineer.

Signing is heavily regulated. From window to building facade signing to freestanding multi-tenant and/or monument signing either you or your sign company need to check with local zoning officials in order to make absolutely sure that your proposed signing complies with local zoning requirements.

In certain instances, zoning restrictions will govern business hours of operation, especially in areas where nearby rooftops exist. In other instances, zoning will require the provision of landscape buffers, trash enclosures, and parking lot lighting. Even outdoor seating is very likely to be governed by zoning.

Many retail, restaurant, and shopping center properties are designed to satisfy minimum zoning requirements - something which can be a huge mistake, especially with respect to businesses which require higher levels of parking.

Typically, five (5) parking spaces per one thousand (1,000) square feet of building space is a common zoning standard for retail stores. On the other hand, for restaurants, parking standards are typically based on the number of seats - for example, one for every two seats. In neither case do these parking standards consistently take employees into consideration. While this may be ok for most retail uses it can prove to be inadequate for restaurant businesses.

Quite frankly, parking is a "hot button" issue amongst local planning and zoning staffs and the elected and appointed bodies they advise.

Before you sign an agreement to either purchase or lease property, please make sure that you visit or call local planning and zoning staff. Doing so will not only prove to be informative, but will end up being time well spent.

Appendix C
Other Sales Influences and Related Factors

The following represent a list of influences and factors you should become familiar with as you do your site selection "homework." You'll find that they are process focused. As such, they should be considered influential rather than essential factors when you are busy conducting your research.

Aerial Photographs & Google Street View. Looking at these is a great way to become more familiar with the area surrounding the site you are considering. Pay special attention to proximity to anchor retailers and restaurants, site connectivity, and nearby competitors.

Ambiance. These are the things that make your business more memorable. Simple things like a fireplace, ceiling types and levels of lighting, flooring, wall coverings, decorative touches, booth and couch seating, and music can, individually or collectively, help create a positive and lasting impression. Examples of businesses who understand the intricacies of this important influence include Panera and Starbucks.

Analog Model. Initially developed by grocery store giant Kroger, this analytical system relies upon variables like square footage, population, income levels, trade area size, site accessibility, traffic counts, critical mass, competition, and parking to forecast retail and restaurant sales.

Areas of Dominant Influence. Just as each restaurant and retail store has its own customer trade area so does each metropolitan area. In the television, radio, and newspaper worlds they are known as Areas of

Dominant Influence (ADI).

Today, some franchisors will look to Areas of Dominant Influence in order to determine the number of people who not only live in a particular area which they would like to have a presence in, but how many store or restaurant locations such areas could potentially support. As an example, a standard of one restaurant for every two hundred thousand people might be identified. It is this type of information which is then used to help determine which types of media to use for television, radio, and/or newspaper advertising.

Awnings. A great way but often overlooked means of drawing attention to your store or restaurant is to use awnings. They come in many different colors and shapes, can be made out of a variety of materials, and can easily accommodate the use of lettering, symbols, and lighting. Especially effective are striped awnings.

Bay Windows. The presence of bay windows is especially important whenever there is a limitation on the amount of natural light coming into your business, or, the need to create additional window display opportunities exists.

A secondary but important benefit of having one or more bay windows is that they help draw attention to your business. In this regard, they function a lot like awnings and signs.

Benchmarks. This is a comparative tool, something which enables you to evaluate how different locations stack up against one another.

Primary factors such as total population, income levels, education levels, and housing values should be compared. In addition, other benchmarks like traffic counts, critical mass, number of parking spaces, and the number and size of nearby anchors should also be evaluated.

Big, as in Building. Is the space you rent or own or want to be in easily identified from the street or the parking lot, or does it somehow blend in and, as a result, get lost? For most retail and restaurant buildings design materials, colors, and amenities can be big positives.

Big, as in Space. Most businesses don't need a whole lot of space. Indeed, if spaces were to be classified as being small, intermediate, and big, by far the largest number of retail stores and restaurants would be grouped into the former category while the least number of businesses would be grouped into the big category. A good way to remember this classification system is to think of a pyramid.

Board of Advisors. Every big corporation in America has a Board of Directors. However, if you ask small business owners if they have a group of advisors who aren't involved in day-to-day operations and decisions the overwhelming answer, you'll get is no. A word of advice-don't be overly concerned about sharing or giving up decision-making responsibility. Instead, think of adding a Board of Advisors as a way of achieving greater success.

Don't think twice about asking your attorney, your accountant, your primary supplier, your lender, your marketing company, and even a well-respected site selection consultant to periodically meet as a group in order to help advise you on a variety of important matters. Their counsel will teach you a lot while costing you very little money.

Brand Equity. Name recognition is helpful and can be a powerful influence in building or improving customer patronage. While this may not be a problem locally, the lack of brand equity in a new market can initially inhibit store sales. While increasing your marketing budget may help build brand equity the best solution is to embark upon a program to open new "home run" locations - something which will result in expanding your local market share.

Brand Recognition. Defining your business and differentiating it in the marketplace is what brand recognition is all about. As you embark upon expanding your business footprint you will find that brand recognition helps build customer awareness as well as customer patronage. And, it can generate not only more site and location opportunities, but also create potential franchise opportunities.

Build To Suit. Periodically, retail and restaurant companies will look to one or more developers for build to suit opportunities. Instead of purchasing land, bidding the construction job, and building a new store or restaurant these businesses choose to contract with a developer in order to provide them with what amounts to a turn key building opportunity. Two of the major benefits of this type of development are that retail and restaurant businesses save both time and money. This, in turn, enables them to not only open for business quicker but to realize a variety of cost savings - especially if they utilize the services of a preferred developer.

Business Plan. A business plan is essential for anyone who is contemplating going into business - especially if they are either going into business for themselves or need to secure a bank loan. Business plans should not be done on a one-time basis. Rather, they should be updated at least annually.

Among other things, a good business plan will clearly state your business objectives, list and describe start-up costs, identify your target customer, indicate how you plan to market your business, identify one or more funding sources, spell out location specifics, and describe sales projections.

Business plans are one of the most overlooked tools for business success. If you want to learn more about business plans you should visit your local library or go to a good bookstore. Otherwise, browsing Amazon.com or conducting research via Google is recommended. An overlooked but tremendously helpful business plan educational contact is your local SCORE (Service Core of Retired Executives) chapter. You should definitely consider calling and scheduling an appointment with a counselor. It will be one of the best investments you ever make.

Camera. Whenever you visit a site or an area always have your camera or phone camera with you so you can take a series of pictures. The human mind can only remember a limited amount of detail. Having pictures to study will definitely help you do a better job of evaluating the pros and cons of a site and its surrounding area.

Census Tract. This is a geographical area which the U.S. Census Bureau uses to gather a variety of household data. Census tracts serve as the basis for assembling important demographic information - something which, while only current for a short period of time, helps companies formulate their site selection criteria.

Chambers of Commerce. These are organizations which are pro-business. They do a great job of promotion and have a membership roster which may become a valuable resource for not only data mining but business development. In many small communities Chambers of Commerce can be very helpful to the owners of start-up as well as existing retail and restaurant companies. However, in large cities and metropolitan areas where attracting large numbers of office and industrial jobs is the highest priority I've found these business organizations to be less of a resource.

City Hall. The planning, zoning, and economic development departments at City Hall should be one of your first stops when considering locations and site options. The public servants who work in these departments can provide you with answers to a wide variety of questions related to such things as permitted uses, curb cuts, parking requirements, permits, licenses, and signing. In addition, they can provide you with valuable statistical information.

Comparative Analysis. Never look at a site without comparing it to one or more additional sites. The same goes for comparing demographics, parking, signing, etc. This important exercise not only eliminates emotion and gut from the decision-making process, but helps businesspeople differentiate great sites from good sites and good sites from average sites.

Corridor Dynamics. Ask yourself if the commercial area you are looking at is growing, stable, or beginning to decline? This is one of the first questions that needs to be answered. Areas which are characterized by business turnover, more than a little vacant land, bargain rents, empty storefronts, and aging properties are areas which present a "red flag." They are areas which present a high level of risk and should be avoided. The same advice applies to one dimensional areas and areas with little or no nearby housing.

Covered Walkways. These can be both a blessing and a curse. While they permit shopping center customers to walk or sit outside without any direct exposure to rain, snow, or the hot sun they can also make buildings and display windows look less inviting to customers- especially if they are either north or east facing.

Creating A Memorable Experience. Creating a memorable experience for your customers is important, especially in the restaurant business where differentiating your business from your competitors is so important. Yet, creating a memorable experience is not only challenging but doesn't happen overnight - the proverbial "easier said than done." You'll know it when you feel it is the best way to describe what a memorable experience is. That means feeling something special, something unique, something to cherish.

A hospitality attitude combined with factors such as memorable building and interior design, quality products, a variety of selection options, and the opportunity to observe (watch) other people are some but not all of the components which help to create a memorable experience - something all of us want more of. A great example of a company that understands the importance of creating a memorable experience better than just about any other company is Starbucks.

Credit Scores and Financial Statements. These constitute the litmus test for most landlords who end up leasing space to small and start-up businesses. They are looking for high credit scores and financial statements which show that you have little debt and an attractive net worth. The combination of these important factors will automatically elevate not only landlord interest levels but your ability to negotiate better terms for yourself with respect to rent, buildout, and/or a tenant improvement allowance.

Customer Addresses and Data. This is relatively easy to accomplish if your business accepts checks, issues "loyalty" cards, does catering, and/or makes deliveries. With a little bit of effort, it can also be used in conjunction with credit cards. Other ways to capture this important information is to create a customer loyalty program which will enable you to obtain addresses, and by conducting customer surveys.

Once this important information is available you will have established the basis for a market data base which can be used to stay in touch with customers via periodic mailings. In addition, it can provide you with a wonderful opportunity to create a spotting map which identifies where your customers live. This, in turn, will give you an excellent idea of the geographic reach (trade area) of your business.

Customer Frequency. Repeat customer business is much more important to your success than the business which is provided by the occasional or infrequent customer. This, unfortunately, is a little understood success dynamic.

Someone who spends money in your store or restaurant once a month as opposed to 2-3 times a year should be your target customer - the customer who you want to continue doing business with on a regular basis.

Customer Interviews. Periodically talking with your customers is absolutely essential. Nonetheless, my experience reveals that very few businesses ever spend time doing this type of research. Whether face-to-face interviews or interviews over the telephone are conducted they are easy to do and can be relatively inexpensive.

Businesses which fail to conduct customer interviews forfeit a tremendous opportunity to learn as much as possible about their customers. Besides observing whether they are male or female and what their general age group is, you should ask questions which reveal where they live or work, whether they rent or own a home, their education and income levels, where else they shop or eat, how long it took them to get to your store or restaurant, and how many times a month they patronize your business.

The number of questions you ask is up to you and is dependent upon how much customer information you wish to obtain. Interviews can last from less than a minute to several minutes. They can be conducted either in person or over the telephone. They can be conducted not only by you, but by one or more employees, by local college students, or by a market research company.

Afterwards, it will be important to not only tabulate, but thoroughly analyze the interview results. Once these important tasks are completed you will have a much better understanding of who your customers are. In addition, you will be able to use this kind of data in order to seek out other store or restaurant locations where similar types of customers are most likely to reside.

Customer Lists. Every small business should have an understanding of their customer base. In addition to individuals, you should know if certain groups, organizations, and/or other businesses help generate sales for your business. If so, they should be added to your customer address file and may even become a component of your customer interview effort.

Customer Profile. See Target Customer.

Customer Relationships. If you don't do a good job of establishing and maintaining customer relationships you won't be in business very long. Remember something very important: these are the people who pay for your car, your mortgage, your vacations, and your kids college educations. Ignore them and you are inviting trouble.

Customer Service. Most businesses only get one opportunity to make a positive first impression. Therefore, it is absolutely imperative that you *train* all of your employees on becoming customer focused, starting with a friendly greeting and a smile. Something so simple is, regrettably, one of the most overlooked opportunities for generating sales as well as repeat business.

High levels of customer service are absolutely essential for business success. If you are looking for a true competitive advantage your top priority should be customer service. In the long run, it could well turn out to be your holy grail!

Customer Spotting Maps. These are a critical but vastly underutilized resource tool for businesses of all kinds. Knowing where your customers originate their store or restaurant visits, whether from home, school, place of work, etc., is very important information.

Customer spotting maps are easy to do. They can be completed by either asking customers questions or by having them locate, on a map, where their trip originated. This can be a fun exercise if you remember not to ask customers, especially females, for their home address - something many of them will be reluctant to reveal. Instead, ask them for the name of the street where they live, followed by the name of the closest intersecting street.

By using dots to indicate locations, you can easily develop a map which shows where your customers are coming from. This will enable you to define the geographic reach of your store or restaurant - otherwise known as your trade area.

Customer Surveys. Such surveys are distinguished from customer interviews primarily by the fact that they are not conducted in person.

Rather, they are conducted through table top surveys, point of sale information, delivery records, a mailed survey instrument, or, an on-line internet survey.

While these other types of surveys can ask more questions than is typically the case in customer interviews whether a person chooses to respond or not is completely discretionary. Therein lies a potential problem because the universe of responses is likely to shrink - sometimes considerably - in comparison with face-to-face interview opportunities. Thus, the reliability of such surveys is diminished.

One of the best means of achieving survey "buy in" is to offer something to the respondent. For instance, an incentive might be the chance to be entered into a drawing for a prize. Another might be a gift certificate. Yet another might be to reward them with a small amount of money. If you aren't in a position to offer very much, then think about making a two for one offer, or, provide some type of discount, like fifty percent off their next purchase.

Daytime Businesses. If your business is primarily a daytime business you want to pay special attention to who else in the immediate and nearby commercial area operates a daytime as opposed to an evening business. Why? Because the owners, managers, and employees of local businesses should be encouraged to become customers of your business. Similarly, you should become one of their customers. Such patronage will lead to something very positive - an increase in customer traffic for everyone.

Daytime Visits. When you are conducting your site search the best time to do so is intermittingly throughout a several days period of time for perhaps one or more weeks. A good rule of thumb to follow is to make an early morning, noontime, and late afternoon visit at least twice during the weekday and once or twice over the weekend.

Every time you make a field trip be sure to spend the majority of your time on-site. However, don't neglect spending time making observations in both the immediate and nearby commercial areas as well as in the surrounding residential areas. Otherwise, you won't be able to obtain a good understanding of the dynamics which are likely to impact potential store or restaurant revenues.

When you conduct each of your daytime visits you should plan on spending an hour or more making recorded observations, talking with people, and taking pictures. There is absolutely no substitute for doing this type of comprehensive research. Indeed, the more time you devote to making such trips the better prepared you will be to make a "smart" site selection decision.

Desirability. There is an old expression that "birds of a feather flock together." When conducting fieldwork, you should place an early emphasis on the desirability of not only the site you are considering but its general location. By way of example, if you are looking to cater to upscale customers you should only consider sites and areas which are attractive and appealing. To go into a less desirable setting is risky- very much a "role of the dice."

Destination Uses. This is a type of use which is the opposite of a convenience business. As an example, quick service (fast food) restaurants, unless highly specialized, draw people who either work or live in, or visit the nearby area. By contrast, casual dining and fine dining restaurants attract customers from a much larger area - one which instead of catering to people who are located within a five - minute drive time caters to people who may be coming from as far away as ten, fifteen, or twenty minutes and more.

Differentiated Storefronts. One of the best ways retail stores and restaurants can boost their identity is to differentiate their storefront facades from neighboring businesses. In older shopping centers, most facades look the same. On first glance, the only thing that separates them from their neighbors is their storefront signing. In older downtowns, malls, and newer shopping centers - especially lifestyle centers - just the opposite is true. Here, unique retail and restaurant storefront facades are the rule not the exception. Your storefront facade should be designed to create a memorable first impression - one which immediately differentiates it from your neighbors. Think of your storefront façade as an extension of your brand image. The best way to accomplish this is through the use of a combination of tasteful but attention getting materials, shapes, and colors.

Drawing Power. Every business needs to know about its drawing power - in this case, the geographic extent of its trade area. Knowing whether your store or restaurant is attracting customers from beyond the nearby surrounding area - the equivalent of three minutes or approximately one mile for neighborhood types of businesses - is important. The further your reach the larger your customer base and potential sales should be.

Early Termination/Escape/Kick Out Clause. If you decide to rent space having your attorney incorporate an early termination provision into your lease agreement is the best way to protect the substantial investment you are making. Simply stated, such a clause allows you to terminate your lease obligations prior to the conclusion of either your base term or option term if there is some compelling reason to do so. An example might be a loss of business due to the closing of one or more shopping center anchors. Another might be a substantial increase in the amount of vacant space in a shopping center.

Other reasons for invoking this type of protective clause might be attributable to the continued postponement of needed capital improvements such as roof replacement and parking lot repairs and resurfacing, or common area maintenance problems such as continuous delays in snow removal and the replacement of burned- out parking lot lighting. Such problems can result in diminished customer counts.

Having a Kick Out clause in your lease can also provide you with a platform for requesting temporary rent relief - something that most good landlords will consider if you have a history of being current with your rent.

Similarly, you need to make sure that you can invoke such a lease clause if your landlord wishes to relocate you to lease space which may not contain the same types of amenities which your present space has - things like substantially similar visibility, store frontage, signing, windows, convenient as well as sufficient parking, building improvements, and interior finishes. In such instances be careful to also not overlook the potential for loss of business due to the lack of synergy or compatibility with one or more adjoining or nearby tenants.

Ego. Never, ever let ego get in the way of making an informed site selection decision. That being said, it happens from time-to-time.

Emotion. Perhaps the biggest mistake people make in site selection is falling in love with their choice of a particular place or location. There is no room whatsoever in site selection for emotion. Literally, emotion can be likened to a "red flag," the "forbidden fruit," and the "kiss of death." Trust me: "smart" location decisions are always made without emotion.

Employee Parking. This is less of a problem in suburbia than it is in downtown and neighborhood and older business district settings. In the former instance, parking is usually plentiful and free. However, away from suburbia just the opposite is true.

In instances where customer parking is at a premium, employees are encouraged to park off-site. Sometimes on-street parking is available. In other instances, employee parking is available in either no cost or low-cost public parking lots. In most instances, however, shared parking with a nearby bank, office, or church can help solve the problem of where employees can park.

In certain instances, locating your business on or near a bus line or mass transit route is another way of addressing the dilemma of employee parking. While not a primary consideration, such access can be especially important in not only attracting but in retaining good employees.

Employment Occupations. It is helpful but by no means essential to know what types of jobs your customers have. While some may not be employed at all, good examples are stay-at-home moms and dads and retirees, others will be employed in white as well as blue collar jobs. Also, knowing whether your customers are employed in a professional, sales, technical, or clerical capacity can influence the design of your store or restaurant, the types of merchandise or food which is sold, price points, marketing, etc.

Entrepreneur. You may think of yourself as being an entrepreneur - something which has its good points as well its bad points. For the most part entrepreneurs are ambitious, hardworking people with a huge drive to succeed. They have "can do" attitudes, enjoy challenges, like being their own boss, and frequently question conventional thinking. However, they can also be notoriously stubborn.

Two of the biggest drawbacks facing entrepreneurs are their unwillingness to embrace the concept of "team" and their inability to master the art of delegating responsibility. As a result, they sometimes end up being their own worst enemies.

Exceptions and Excuses. If you are one of those people who think you can find a "home run" location on your own, then all I can say is please be sure that you not only read this guidebook but master the entirety of its contents. Otherwise, I would urge you to seek some kind of professional guidance. Doing so has the advantage of demonstrating that "two heads are better than one." If you don't read and don't absorb the significant amount of information detailed in this guidebook and subsequently decide to go it alone then you must accept full responsibility for any site selection decision(s) you make. As my old Spanish teacher used to remind us about not having completed our "homework" assignments, "no hay excusos" - there are no excuses.

216

Float. This is a term which is used to measure unmet opportunity within a neighborhood or community. It is defined as the difference between buying power (demand) and retail or restaurant sales (supply).

Floor to Ceiling Glass. Many suburban retail stores and restaurants are located in shopping centers where floor to ceiling glass is the norm. While this type of glass has advantages for retailers, it is somewhat less desirable for restaurants. In the case of restaurants, it is better to have glass which starts two to three feet off the floor. Doing so affords not only a greater degree of dining privacy, but creates fewer cleaning problems. In addition, having elevated windows can help a business minimize safety problems.

Focus Groups. These are an important means of learning about customers as well as for obtaining their feedback. Many companies use focus groups as a means of gauging potential customer satisfaction with new products. In other instances, focus groups can be an effective way to learn about customer tastes with respect to such things as desired ambiance, price points, and store and restaurant layouts. The key to relying on focus group input is having a trained and knowledgeable facilitator.

Free Rent Incentives. Do not, under any circumstances, take the posture that the site selection decision which you are about to make is dependent on whoever gives you the best deal - for instance two or more months of free rent. Simply put, this is a surefire method for winning the negotiation battle while losing the sales war. Given the sizable investment in time and money that you will be making the only responsible action is to focus on locations which will produce the most sales revenues not the most savings. On the other hand, if you have done your "homework" carefully and the site you have chosen is at the top of your list then, by all means, go for it.

Ghost Kitchens. These are places which are known as virtual restaurants. They offer pick-up and delivery based upon phone and online orders.

There are no dine-in options. They operate out of an existing restaurant's kitchen or from a separate kitchen located somewhere else. FYI, Door Dash Kitchens are customized spaces where restaurants can operate delivery and pick-up services thru Door Dash.

Gimmicks and Freebies That Pay Dividends. Chips and salsa are standard freebies at Mexican restaurants. Similarly, some restaurants where alcohol is served like to offer customers free popcorn. Whether intentional or not, both of these gimmick types of freebies are likely to lead to an increase in alcohol sales which end up helping "fatten" profit margins.

At Five Guys Burgers and Fries, free peanuts are available to customers to snack on. Some restaurants offer free pie on select days. If you want free soft serve ice cream, Jason's Deli is the place to go. At Chicken Salad Chick, every sandwich order comes with a free cookie. Endless salad and breadsticks are free at Olive Garden restaurants.

To underscore the value of freebies, Kent Taylor, the CEO and founder of Texas Roadhouse Grill says: "Our free hot bread and peanuts are our best advertisements."

Meanwhile, many restaurants and hotels offer senior citizen discounts in hopes of winning their business.

From an "icing on the cake" perspective, gimmicks such as the aforementioned can help build not only repeat business, but enhance long-term customer loyalty.

Goodwill. In many businesses the personality of the owner is responsible for building the types of customer relationships which result in more frequent and higher sales. This is one of those site selection factors which is difficult, if not impossible, to accurately quantify. However, it is essential that you not only recognize its importance, but that you evaluate its impact carefully if you decide to either start, buy, or invest in an existing retail or restaurant business.

Grand Opening. The importance of having a grand opening event is lost on many businesses. Why this is the case is somewhat puzzling, especially since it can help to generate not only a lot of positive publicity for your business, but can create name recognition as well as introduce you and what you are selling to lots of potential customers.

At such events, many businesses choose to donate either all or a portion of their sales or profits to a charitable organization. In addition, they present an outstanding opportunity to donate food or prizes and items to local schools, athletic teams, and organizations - some or all of whom might represent a target audience. Almost everybody enjoys going to such gala events, in part because of the socializing and networking opportunities they present.

Gravity Model. This sales forecasting system has been around for a very long period of time. It looks at the size and composition of nearby critical mass in order to determine the trade area of a store or restaurant as well as how critical mass influences customer traffic. Hypothetically, the larger an area's critical mass the further its trade area extends.

Ground Lease. In instances where the cost of purchasing real estate is high, or where an owner is unwilling to sell, a ground lease can be an attractive opportunity for retail and restaurant companies to either enter the local market or expand their existing presence. Typically, the annual cost of leasing a developed lot is the equivalent of ten percent of its potential purchase price. The catch, however, is that the base term for a ground lease is typically twenty or more years. This helps to explain why ground leases are not for the "faint of heart."

Higher Level Glass. See Knee Walls.

Holdover Clause. This is an important lease clause that your attorney can help you with. It enables you to temporarily remain in your space for a short period of time (anywhere from a week to two or more months) once your lease has expired. However, in order to invoke this important privilege, you will be obligated to pay your landlord a rent premium. Accordingly, count on your holdover rent to increase by as little as ten percent or as much as twenty five percent or more.

Judgment. The odds of securing "home run" locations improve with experience - a lesson which, unfortunately, is lost on too many small businesspeople. "Two heads are better than one" is an old adage which also contains a lot of truth with respect to making "smart" location and "smart" site selection decisions.

In the long run, whether a site selection decision is made by an individual or a real estate committee, the need to do a significant amount of "homework" is absolutely the best foundation for exercising good judgment as well as for achieving future success.

Kick Off Event(s). Every retail company and every restaurant should incorporate a kickoff event when they open for business. When planning for such an event you should think about inviting more than friends and family to visit your new store or restaurant.

Chamber of Commerce officials love attending a ribbon cutting ceremony. Radio personalities enjoy making remote broadcasts. The local press is a l s o interested in informing their readers about a new business opening. And, of course, mayors and city officials cherish the opportunity to welcome new businesses and be the center of attention.

Knee Walls. Many shopping centers which are built today feature building space with floor to ceiling glass. This is in sharp contrast to the facades of retail and restaurant buildings which are located in older neighborhoods and urban areas. They oftentimes feature glass which starts at a height of a person's knee. Knee walls add more character to a building - something which has not been lost on the developers of the lifestyle centers which are currently in vogue and are being built all across America.

Landscaping. A simple way for retail and restaurant businesses to add curb appeal is to provide attractive landscaping. The provision of a variety of colors which are attributable to the planting of flowers, shrubs, and/or trees, is important. However, be careful to avoid renting a storefront or buying a lot where trees, especially street trees, will end up blocking visibility. While city planners and the commissions they advise are correct in wanting to create attractive corridors they sometimes forget that planted too close together street trees can block a store's visibility and therefore negatively impact not only sales, but business longevity.

Lease Agreement. This is a comprehensive document which spells out the terms under which a tenant agrees to rent space from a landlord. It is a complex, very detailed, and somewhat intimidating document - something which should definitely be reviewed by a real estate attorney before being executed.

Leakage. This refers to money which is being spent in neighborhoods and areas which are different from where people live. Oftentimes this means that people will travel from an underserved area, one with some retail and restaurant establishments, to areas where a cluster of such businesses exist. From a municipality or local government perspective leakage results in lost sales taxes - something which means that less money is available for public services and/or improvements.

Marketing. Businesses which budget money for marketing are much more likely to remain in business than those who don't. Indeed, such businesses are much more likely to increase customer counts and sales revenues. Nowhere is the need for marketing better understood than at the franchise level. Typically, franchisors require franchisees to spend anywhere from three to five percent of their sales on marketing. Thus, a franchisee with annual revenues of $500,000 will be required to spend $15,000 - $25,000 per year on marketing. Choosing to spend three to five percent of annual revenues on marketing your business is a good rule of thumb even if you are not a franchisee.

Many different forms of marketing exist. However, effective marketing starts with your understanding something very important - who your target customers are. Afterwards, your objective is to build awareness, create desire, and to get customers in the front door. Once customers visit your business your immediate goal is to keep them coming back. In order to accomplish this, you need to commit yourself to constantly promoting your business.

At a minimum, you need to invest some of your marketing budget for print and website advertising. In addition, becoming involved in sponsoring one or more athletic teams or school events is a good way to keep your name in front of people. Doing so is also an effective means for creating both repeat business and loyal customers. Other proven ways for you to market your business include being featured in news articles, creating introductory offers, offering loyalty cards, holding contests, sponsoring family nights, using coupons, periodically offering discounts, and advertising periodic sales.

In some instances, you will find that landlords will require that a tenant not only spend money on a marketing program but evidence to them, on a monthly, quarterly or annual basis, just what kinds of marketing initiatives have been undertaken. From a landlord's perspective, requiring that money be spent on marketing is not only in the tenant's best interest, but a proven method for increasing customer traffic at the property which the landlord owns.

Market Penetration. Most small businesses, especially mom and pop businesses, aren't too concerned about market penetration. Indeed, their focus is on remaining in business. When business owners expand the number of locations they operate they increase market penetration. Doing so enables them to build more name recognition - something which is absolutely essential in order to not only survive but thrive in today's extremely competitive business environment.

Market Share. Simply stated, market share refers to the percentage of sales within a market which a restaurant or a retailer captures or owns. By way of illustration, in the hamburger marketplace McDonald's has by far the highest percentage of market share for fast food restaurants.

Median. Median refers to the midpoint of a variable like household income or home prices. It is often confused with but is different from the word average (or mean). When looking at demographic data, median is a better reference point than average is.

Merchandising. This important term is often associated with how products are displayed. While display is a primary component, merchandising consists of much more. It incorporates a comprehensive set of influences which are critical to establishing an image and creating a tenant mix which can prompt sales. Developing an effective merchandising strategy starts with market research and includes such things as customer profiles, gap analysis, advertising and promotion, store design, demographics and psychographics, packaging, and product introduction.

Mobile App Data. Data collected via your smart phone is the source of a huge amount of important data. Mobile apps track consumer behavior and location history, including places you've visited, such as shopping centers, bookstores, grocery stores, drug stores, restaurants and retail stores - not just locally but wherever you travel to or from.

It may be hard to believe, but according to PMQ Magazine, nearly 25% of all food orders are placed on mobile devices. Because of the convenience they provide, mobile apps lead to more sales. As a result, restaurants with drive thrus are increasingly adding exclusive pick-up lanes for mobile orders only.

Mystery Shoppers. Every retail and restaurant business owner who is interested in building repeat business and building either a good or great customer experience might consider investing a small amount of money to employ the services of mystery shoppers.

These are people who are charged with a very important responsibility: visiting a retail store or restaurant unannounced on one or more occasions for the purpose of recording their thoughts and impressions. Such feedback will subsequently be packaged into one or more report cards and be presented to a business owner.

After receiving mystery shopper feedback business owners will be better positioned to not only understand customer impressions, but be better prepared to make the types of decisions which are critical to not only improving the customer experience, but to building an absolutely essential element of success - repeat business.

Name Recognition. Chances are the more name recognition your business has the better positioned it will be for success. Building name recognition should be an immediate focus area both before and after you open your doors for business.

New. Today, the word new is a part of our national fabric, something which has become imbedded in our national psyche. As consumers we have become accustomed to buying new cars, new homes, new clothes, etc. This is an important standard to remember and respect if you are either a businessperson or are considering going into business for yourself. Keeping your retail store or your restaurant current is no longer a choice, it is absolutely essential.

McDonald's is a prime example of a company that knows the value of making their restaurants look new or current. In many instances they are reinventing themselves by upgrading what were once standard looking (cookie cutter) restaurants into not only richer looking but more welcoming places - places where you can still bring the kids but can also hold business meetings. For McDonald's, periodically spending money on modernization translates into not only increased business but increased profits. If you want to increase sales McDonald's is the model that you should definitely consider emulating.

Another example of a company that understands the meaning of keeping their interiors looking fresh and current is Starbucks. Many mall stores are also super conscientious about having their interiors look new. Mall owners have long understood that **new is oftentimes equated with success**. As such, many of them require tenants to update their stores at least once every five years.

New is the "in" look! It is the equivalent of "money in the bank."

Niche. Looking for niches and voids is one way to go about looking for locations and making site selection decisions. While this translates into being the "pioneer" in the market it also means that you might initially have the market to yourself.

A word of caution is necessary. Just because a niche or a void exists, doesn't necessarily mean that you should make a business investment. Besides making sure that you have a "home run" location, what you need to do is spend time determining the size of the market, estimating potential sales levels, and deciding whether the price you will be paying to rent or purchase a retail or restaurant property will create a reasonable return on your investment.

Nighttime Businesses. If your business is evening oriented then it is to your advantage to be near other nighttime businesses. For instance, if you are in the ice cream business, being near a pizza restaurant, a bookstore, or a movie theatre is a good bet to generate additional business revenue.

Nighttime Visit. Anyone who is checking out potential locations needs to make one or more nighttime visits to not only the potential site but the surrounding business area. In the process of visiting, they should pay particular attention to two important items: nighttime lighting and signing. These are factors which can either negatively or positively influence customer perceptions and patronage.

Numbers vs. Percentages. When evaluating demographics never, I repeat never, base your impression of a trade area on percentages rather than numbers. For instance, while most everyone would be impressed to learn that seventy percent of the one thousand people living within a trade area earned $100,000 or more in annual income, they should be even more impressed to learn that demographics for a competing site indicated one thousand of the two thousand people living within the competing trade area annually earned $100,000 or more. If you do the math, one thousand trumps seven hundred. On the other hand, some people might be misguided into thinking that seventy percent was the more impressive figure.

Operations. There are no shortcuts to becoming a good operator. The first step in this important process is on the job training. It is the equivalent of paying your dues. It is something that doesn't happen overnight. Oftentimes this means that you will be starting at the bottom of the ladder and working your way up. This kind of "hands on" training will provide you with invaluable experience. Indeed, it could turn out to be the best teacher you will ever have.

Good operations are absolutely essential to achieving business success. While not very often thought of as an influential site selection factor the simple truth is that **good sites coupled with good operations can go a long way towards guaranteeing business success**. However, a good site without good operations could, potentially, be destined for failure. The influence of good operations is so strong that it can, in fact, pave the way for average locations to become better locations.

Overage Rent. See Percentage Rent.

Pass Through Costs: See Triple Net Rents.

Patience. If you have ever heard the phrase "patience is a virtue," I hope you took it to heart. All too often new businesspeople are impatient to get going. They want to do something now as opposed to later. This is a dangerous attitude - one which can not only result in a poor site selection decision, but, end up contributing to a lack of business longevity; in other words, business failure. Doing your homework and being not only patient but selective can go a long way towards determining future business longevity; in this case business success.

Peak Periods. All businesses experience certain periods of the day or evening when customer visits are at their maximum. For restaurants selling sub sandwiches this is often over the lunch hour. For retailers selling women's clothing the peak period could be either during the day or evening on a weekend. In order to cope with such peak customer traffic and maximize sales opportunities every business needs to make sure that, in addition to appropriate staffing levels, sufficient as well as conveniently situated customer parking exists.

Pedestrian Friendly. Most urban areas have neighborhoods and downtowns where people feel welcome to walk to retail, restaurant, and entertainment locations. These are places where the automobile has lost its power of intimidation. However, with the exception of older suburbs and lifestyle centers, very few pedestrian friendly locations can be found anywhere in suburbia.

All great shopping districts, like the Miracle Mile along Michigan Avenue in Chicago, Madison Avenue in New York City, and Rodeo Drive in Beverly Hills feature busy pedestrian friendly streets.

Whether you are in the retail or restaurant business don't dismiss pedestrian friendly locations. They are capable of generating lots of customer traffic morning, noon, and night as long as they are close to conveniently situated parking.

Pedestrian Traffic. Pedestrian friendly older business districts and downtowns have long differentiated themselves from suburban business corridors where strip shopping centers and big box stores and huge surface parking lots are the dominant landscape features. During the past decade, pedestrian friendly lifestyle centers have become an increasingly popular destination, in part because they have been able to recreate the building, street, and sidewalk vernacular which is characteristic of so many older, inviting business areas.

Designed effectively, these welcoming features can collectively encourage pedestrian traffic and help generate high levels of sales - one of the major reasons why many chain retailers and restaurants have increasingly been willing to leave mall and strip shopping center locations.

Perpendicular Building. Buildings which sit perpendicular to the road often have only one "prime" location - the end cap space which is closest to the street. Such space maximizes visibility, signing, and parking for its retail or restaurant user. With few exceptions, all of the other spaces in perpendicular buildings are at a disadvantage because they don't have the same levels of visibility, signing, or parking as their end cap neighbor enjoys.

Whenever possible, businesses should seek locations in buildings which sit parallel to the street. Doing so will enable them to not only have a much better opportunity for maximizing visibility, signing, and parking, but will most likely lead to higher sales levels. Furthermore, chances are pretty good that they will also experience less turnover from neighboring stores and restaurants - something which can not only result in reduced customer traffic to a shopping center but result in reduced customer sales.

Per Capita Income. This measure of per person income can be a good indicator when comparing the attractiveness or appeal of two or more business trade areas. However, no informed decision should be made based solely on this important statistical factor.

Pictures. See Camera.

Previously Occupied Space. Not everyone can afford or wants to occupy new space. As a result, a lot of start-ups as well as expanding businesses are good candidates to go into used space. You need to be careful, however, when considering these types of locations. This is one instance where you really need to do your "homework!" There is a reason why some of these sites continue to underperform and ultimately result in a cycle of business failure. With that in mind, the first thing you should do is reread Chapter Two in this guidebook - The Six Keys to Making "Smart" Site Selection Decisions.

Please keep in mind that while low entry costs and cheap rents and sometimes the presence of furniture, fixtures and equipment (FF&E) can be very tempting reasons to consider occupying recycled or older space, they are not sufficient justifications for making an investment, whether big or small. Yet, many start up as well as existing businesspeople think that they will be able to change this repetitive problem and that they will, despite the long odds, succeed. My experience is that, for the most part, these are overly optimistic and somewhat misguided people who are only fooling themselves. Indeed, given a five-year time horizon, many of them will either no longer be in business or will have moved to a different location. So, decide whether you are a risk taker or a gambler. And, remember to "look before you leap!"

In those instances where cheap space and/or low entry costs and/or the presence of FF&E represent too big a temptation to pass up, the best thing you can do is sign a short-term lease - nothing longer than three years. And, make sure that your lease contains an escape clause which allows you an early exit if, among other reasons, adequate retail or restaurant sales don't materialize.

Primary Trade Area. See Defining Trade Areas in Chapter Three.

Property Maintenance. An oftentimes overlooked influence on retail and restaurant sales is the level of service which is delivered by a property manager. A person who regularly makes on-site visits as opposed to someone who is seldom on-site is more likely to deliver a higher level of service. Furthermore, a property manager who looks at his or her tenants as "partners" and communicates with them regularly is much more likely to build meaningful long-term relationships than someone who is simply an investor or someone who doesn't employ the services of a trained professional. Good working relationships can lead to not only less tenant turnover, but the need to spend fewer dollars on tenant space refurbishment as well as on new leasing commissions. As a result, landlords end up saving money.

Most tenants judge property managers and their employees by two things: responsiveness and the quality of the work they do. With the exception of occasional plumbing, heating, and air conditioning problems, very little property management is actually performed inside a tenant's space. Most maintenance responsibilities occur outside, primarily within a property's common areas.

In colder climates snow removal is typically the top winter priority for property managers. Not removing snow in parking areas on a timely basis or not doing a good job of keeping pedestrian access points open and free of ice can not only cost tenants business, but is a surefire way to create adversarial relationships between tenants and landlords.

During warmer months, landscaping and landscape maintenance, followed by parking lot striping and parking lot repair require the most attention. Throughout the year, trash removal and maintaining high levels of parking lot lighting will be a property manager's focus areas.

Regardless of what needs to be done, an effective property manager will take good care of his or her tenants because he or she realizes that not only establishing but maintaining long-term tenant relationships as well as maximizing tenant business opportunities is good business, especially in today's very competitive commercial marketplace.

Proposal. See Exhibit A - Sample Letter of Intent.

Public Transportation. These days, fewer and fewer businesses are dependent upon public transportation for generating any significant amount of customer traffic. Nonetheless, some of them may be dependent on such transportation in order to attract and retain employees. As a result, some businesses may wish to add securing a location which is either on or close to a bus, rail, subway, or rapid transit line to their list of site selection factors.

Quantitative Analyses. Gathering factual information is absolutely essential. The more you can put your hands on the better. Yet, beyond obtaining traffic count information and demographic information very little quantifiable data is ever collected by most small businesses. Why not make it a point to avoid this mistake? Do your "homework!"

Questionnaires. See Chapter Five - Customer Surveys and Customer Profiles.

Radius. Typically, data is evaluated on the basis of the 1-2-3 mile radii which surround a particular site. This is informative information and is a convenient way to compare apples and apples.

I would like to offer a word of caution, however. Don't you or don't let anyone else make the mistake of defining your primary customer trade area simply by assigning it a mile marker. While this is frequently done it is an oversimplification that can lead to false assumptions about future sales. Personally, I much prefer evaluating drive times of 5-7-10-15 minutes.

Real Estate Agent. This is a licensed person who can provide you with information about lease space, property that is for sale, and such things as comparable rents, traffic counts, competition, lease terms, incentives, etc. Real estate agents can also assist in preparing proposals as well as negotiations. Nonetheless, remember that only a minority of real estate agents are qualified to provide you with the kinds of comprehensive site selection skills and guidance which are promoted in this guidebook.

Recessed Entryways. Many older neighborhood business districts feature these types of storefronts. Unfortunately, with the exception of some mall stores and some lifestyle centers, recessed entryways have been left out of the design of almost every suburban strip center which has been built during the last fifty years. This is unfortunate because these types of storefronts are not only more interesting but more inviting. Recessed entryways create additional window display areas as well as more opportunities for people to window shop.

While a traditional 20-foot-wide storefront in a shopping center may be all glass, a recessed storefront may contain as much as an additional eight - ten feet of glass. What a great way to increase your business exposure without having to pay any additional rent. This is one of the reasons why I like to classify having extra window area as a "bonus" opportunity.

Ask yourself which building type would you prefer to occupy? Which building type do you think your customers would prefer to patronize?

Rent. Always think of rent as a function of sales. Depending upon the type of business you have and the quality of the location you are considering, you should count on paying anywhere from seven to ten percent of your annual gross sales in rent. If your sales are forecast to be robust then you can afford to be at the high end of this range. Whenever your projections reveal more modest sales then you need to be in either the middle or lower end of this range. If you forecast a low level of sales, especially during Year 1, then you need to negotiate a beginning rent which is as low as possible. If you succeed, chances are you will need to help pay for some tenant build out improvements.

Return On Investment (ROI). Calculating a return on investment is an exercise that very few start-up businesspeople devote any time to. Consequently, they may not have a good handle on whether the money they invest and the profits they achieve will result in a generous, modest, or skimpy return on the money they've invested.

A good accountant or a SCORE counselor are two good resources you can turn to for help in calculating ROI. While a low cost of investment might be attractive to many small business owners the only way they can earn an attractive return on their investment dollars is to generate above average sales and profits. With that in mind you might want to keep in mind the old saying "it takes money to make money."

Royalty Fees. If you operate a franchise then you will be obligated to pay a portion of your weekly, monthly, or quarterly sales to your franchisor. While these fees are typically locked in there is no harm in trying to negotiate a payment schedule which enables you to start off paying lower royalty fees while agreeing to gradually increase them over time to the standard percentage fee. Doing so will enable you to reinvest more of your sales revenues during the start-up and most difficult phase of your business, which is usually the first three years after you open your doors.

Sale Leasebacks. This popular vehicle permits the eventual sale of a retail or restaurant property in exchange for a long-term lease. Such transactions permit the seller to receive cash and the buyer to lock in a fixed return on investment. Sale leasebacks are a great way to create win win opportunities for both parties.

Sales Per Capita. This is a very simple way to measure sales on a person-to-person basis. For example, if 5,000 people live within the trade area of a business and annual sales reach $1,000,000, then per capita sales of $200 per person will have been realized.

Sales Per Parking Space. This is another important means for measuring sales performance. By way of illustration, if a retail store or restaurant has fifty parking spaces and records annual sales of $1,000,000, then each parking space represents $20,000 in customer sales.

Sales Per Seat. If you are in the restaurant business this is a great way for learning the value of each customer seat. If your business seats 100 people and you achieve annual sales of $1,000,000 then each seat represents $10,000 in customer sales.

Sales Per Square Foot. Simply stated, this is the number of annual sales divided by the size of the retail or restaurant space you are renting or own. My own rule of thumb for projecting retail store and restaurant success is to look at what I call the $100, $200, $300, $400, and $500 per square foot sales levels.

If your business does or is forecast to do sales of approximately $100 per square foot, chances are it isn't providing you with any meaningful return on investment. You are most likely barely able to pay your bills. As a result, you're not likely to have any "jingle" in your pockets.

Where sales or forecasted sales are in the $200 per square foot range a business may be turning a small profit. When sales are elevated to the $300-$400 per square foot level businesspeople should be making a decent profit - one which may encourage them to begin thinking about the possibility of opening another location "down the road."

If your sales are reasonably good, say approximately $500 or more per square foot, you should not only be thinking about expansion but begin considering the opportunity to franchise your restaurant or retail business in the not too-distant future. Nonetheless, don't rush.

Should your sales either reach or exceed $600 per square foot you've got a "winner" on your hands. Stated differently, you have created the formula for business success. Given your talent and success, you have the potential for building not only a local chain but one which could, with the right team in place, potentially grow into either a regional or national chain. Congratulations!

SCORE. The Service Corps of Retired Executives is a tremendous resource for both start-up and existing small businesses. If you need help with your business plan or your marketing plan or some other business advice this is a group you should definitely contact. SCORE is made up of retired people who have either run their own businesses, been in charge of major departments and divisions for big businesses, or have been successful entrepreneurs.

An added bonus of working with SCORE is their affiliation with the Small Business Administration: the SBA. As a result of both one-on-one and group counseling services, SCORE can be a big help to you in not only applying for but obtaining SBA financing through local lenders.

Seating. The question is not how much or how little customer seating you have but what kind of sales each seat generates. Is it $5,000, $7,500, or $10,000 or more per seat? If you don't know the answer to this question then you don't have all of the information you need to better assess the performance of your existing restaurant as well as the potential performance of future restaurant opportunities.

Which kind of customer seating should you prioritize? Which is better tables or booths? If you only have one choice the answer is booth seating. Quite frankly, people perceive booths as being not only more comfortable, but offering more privacy. Adding more booth seating is guaranteed to not only improve the initial impressions that customers have of your restaurant, but increase the amount of repeat business you do.

Whenever you can add outdoor seating please do so - even if it is only a table or two and just a few seats. During warm weather people absolutely love to eat and drink outdoors, especially when they can indulge in a favorite pastime - people watching.

One piece of advice for restaurant owners: take advantage of each and every opportunity to maximize window seating for your customers.

Secondary Streets. These are streets which are located off of the "main drag"- the primary street. Unless you are considering opening a destination business within approximately three hundred feet of the "main drag," you are advised to proceed with lots of caution - especially if visibility from the primary street is less than optimal.

Second Floor Space. For retail and restaurants, this is the type of space you should avoid - even if it is cheap! Unless located in a mall, only destination/service type businesses are likely to survive a location on the second floor.

Secondary Trade Area. See Defining Trade Area in Chapter Three.

Sensory Appeal. Some café style businesses have demonstrated that they are capable of creating special places. These are inviting places, places where people not only enjoy coming but want to linger. These are places where everyone feels welcome and comfortable. They are places where individuals are not only happy to meet family and friends but to conduct business.

The opportunity to relax, to purchase food and drinks, and the potential for people watching is a great combination - one which has the ability to create something very powerful, something which is very memorable - an experience. It is this ability to create an experience that not only produces loyal customers but leads to significant sales and enhanced profits.

When you are looking for a business location you also need to understand that what you do inside your four walls is capable of playing a very important role in whether your business thrives or simply survives. Accordingly, you are encouraged to pay significant attention to creating an appealing interior design, one which is capable of creating an atmosphere which customers want to experience over and over again. The better you do this the greater the opportunity you will have for building long-term business success.

Service. See Customer Service.

Service Drives. These are easy to spot. They parallel major thoroughfares and usually sit back fifty or so feet from the edge of the street right of way. They have become very popular with traffic engineers because they minimize the number of curb cuts which are permitted along heavily traveled streets. Consequently, they are seen as a safer alternative for accommodating large scale commercial developments and the retail, restaurants, gas, and banks which typically follow.

One of the drawbacks to service drives is that traffic frequently stacks in front of a signalized intersection. This results in drivers sometimes having to wait longer than they would like in order to turn off of the service drive and get in line to be able to turn onto the major thoroughfare. Thus, convenience-oriented businesses are not always well-suited to locations on service drives.

Another drawback associated with service drives is that the green space area which sits in front of them can become a popular candidate for beautification. This can result in regulators becoming overzealous about planting street trees. While street trees may look attractive, they oftentimes end up blocking building and signing visibility - something which can negatively impact business sales.

Service Type Retailers. Dry cleaners, chiropractic businesses, travel agencies, tutors, insurance offices, financial/brokerage offices, optical stores, real estate offices, and barber shops are all examples of service retailers. While not glamorous or sexy, they are all good examples of businesses which tend to stay put for long periods of time and routinely pay their rent on or before their due date. Thus, they definitely shouldn't be overlooked when planning your tenant mix.

Two of the qualities of most service retailers are that they do not require significant amounts of off-street parking, and are very compatible neighbors.

Shadow Businesses. Oftentimes businesses will commence their site selection efforts based upon the success of a "model" business they want to be close to. For instance, many businesspeople like to follow anchors such as grocery stores, drugstores, and big box stores like Target, Walmart, and Home Depot. In the fast food and convenience businesses many companies want to focus their efforts in areas where Panera, McDonald's and Starbucks have a presence.

The thinking on the part of people who want to shadow a business is that they can not only tap into the customer traffic which is generated by one or more of these businesses but, that they can reduce their risk of failure. While such shadowing is understandable and has, in fact, worked for many decision-makers, what cannot be overlooked are the possible differences that potentially exist in not only the quality of individual sites but the quality of individual operators. Indeed, **the most successful businesses are always characterized by a combination of quality sites and quality operations.**

Shared Parking. In exchange for a small monthly fee some property owners will permit one or more nearby businesses to utilize their parking lots during non-peak periods in order to accommodate employee and/ or customer overflow parking. Churches, office buildings, and banks are prime candidates for authorizing shared parking. If you decide to pursue such an arrangement, please be advised that it is in everyone's best interest to sign an agreement which identifies the terms under which shared parking is permitted.

Site Plan. This is something which is relatively easy to obtain. Any property owner or real estate agent should be able to provide you with a site plan. It will show not only how the building you are considering leasing or purchasing is situated on the property but where parking is located, how many parking spaces are available, points of ingress and egress, tenant locations, etc., etc.

Site Selection Snob. This is a term which can be used to describe a relatively small group of people. Site selection snobs are people with high standards. As a result, some would classify them as perfectionists. They have a track record of making "smart" location and "smart" site selection decisions. **They know how to consistently pick winners and avoid losers.** With few exceptions, they work in corporate real estate, commercial real estate, real estate consulting, and for businesses with multiple locations.

Given his significant experience and track record in real estate, the author considers himself to be a bit of a retail and restaurant site selection snob. Nevertheless, his interest in **helping people to succeed** remains his greatest satisfaction - his primary joy.

Site vs. Location. While often used interchangeably, these words really describe two different types of places. Think of macro and micro. In this case, location is the macro and site is the micro. Stated differently, location typically describes an area such as a street, a neighborhood, or a community. Site, on the other hand, refers not only to a specific property but to a specific place (space).

The distinction between location and site is important because **while it is relatively easy to decide on a desired location for your business it is much more difficult and much more time-consuming to reach a decision on what constitutes the right site.**

Choosing a location is something that many people are capable of doing. Choosing a site, on the other hand, is something that only a relatively small group of people ever end up mastering. It is important to realize that most small businesspeople fall into the former group and that a minority of them end up being a part of the latter group.

Small Business Administration (SBA). The SBA is a division of the U.S. Department of Commerce. Its primary function is to work with small and start-up businesses in order to help them secure conventional financing from a variety of sources, from large regional and national banks to small community banks. What the SBA does is act as a loan guarantor, thus making conventional lending more attractive to the lenders involved. The SBA's involvement also means that the borrower is eligible to borrow a higher percentage of loan monies. Of particular importance to the small business community are SBA's 504 and 7A loan programs.

If you are contemplating becoming a franchisee, you should know that the SBA maintains a Franchise Registry. The beauty of having a franchise organization listed in the Registry is that applications can be processed more efficiently and quickly by the SBA and the lenders that it works with.

As previously mentioned in this chapter, SCORE is affiliated with the SBA and offers counseling services to the small business community *prior* to their approaching lenders. You may be interested to know that lenders often refer applicants to SCORE for additional counseling prior to completing the loan application process.

South & West Facing Space. If you are looking to be on the "sunny" side of the street - usually the preferable side of the street - then you want your entry door(s) and windows to face either south or west. If the entirety of your business is conducted indoors the only two things you need to be concerned about are whether the sun will cause any of your window displays to fade or cause any discomfort for customers who are seated in immediately adjoining window areas. Covered walkways and window awnings are the two most common options for mitigating these concerns. On the other hand, if your business features outdoor seating, umbrella tables are highly recommended.

Space. For retail and restaurant business owners who plan on going into multi-tenant space it is not enough that you have already picked the "right location" and the "right site." Now you need to determine whether the inline or end cap space which you are considering is the "right space" - the one most capable of maximizing customer sales.

If you have previously read and applied the advice which is contained in this guidebook you shouldn't have any difficulty making a good decision. However, for those individuals who haven't done their "homework," it is important that you realize that the odds of making a bad decision will be significantly increased if you have either a lack of information or only limited information. While a good decision can put money in your pocket a bad decision can not only take money out of your pocket but can seriously jeopardize your ability to remain in business.

Space Plan. Drawing up a floor plan for your business is relatively easy. It should show sales areas, the location of the front counter and cash register, restrooms, the kitchen, dining areas, storage rooms, utility and office areas, changing rooms, etc.

Space Size. Be careful not to bite off more than you can chew. In other words, don't commit to more space than you need. If you are a company with multiple locations or a multi-unit franchisee this won't be a problem. However, knowing how much is enough or too much is often a dilemma for many start-up businesses.

If you are in the bakery, dry cleaning, or jewelry business, you typically need space which doesn't exceed one thousand square feet. In the case of chiropractic offices, specialty retail stores, ice cream, frozen custard and yogurt, gelato shops, nail salons, florists, insurance offices, sandwich shops, travel agencies, pizza pick-up and delivery establishments, small gift shops, and bagel and coffee shops, spaces which range from approximately twelve hundred to eighteen hundred square feet are generally all the space you need.

The space needs for convenience stores, beauty salons, liquor and wine stores, tanning salons, fast casual and fast food restaurants seldom exceed four thousand square feet. Dine in restaurants and sports bars need to be bigger - typically ranging in size from four thousand to six thousand square feet. It isn't until you get into categories such as carpet, tile, and golf stores, discount clothing stores, dollar stores, and mattress stores that square footage begins to push or exceed ten thousand square feet.

Subdivision Plats, Building Permits and School Enrollment Projections. The best way to explain the importance of each of these factors is to mention the fast food restaurant behemoth McDonald's. No one does more "homework" than McDonald's. Their real estate department literally leaves "no stone unturned" when it comes to being informed and knowledgeable. This is one reason why so many fast food businesses want to be in the same area as McDonald's.

When McDonald's begins its site search it looks at many, many factors. One of these is growth. Therefore, knowing how many new residential subdivisions have been approved, how many lots have been platted and recorded, and how many building permits have been issued is important when projecting future sales levels. The same is true with respect to school enrollment. Finding out whether one or more area elementary, middle, and/or high schools are growing is an important site selection consideration.

Everyone can learn from the McDonald's approach to data collection and sales forecasting. Sadly, most businesspeople as well as very few prospective businesspeople will ever consider, let alone utilize, such a time-consuming approach. This lack of interest in or inability to conduct comprehensive area and site evaluations helps partially explain why business failures will continue to be "a fact of life."

Subjectivity. There is little room for subjective thinking in the site selection process. Instead, you are advised to focus your efforts and your energies primarily on collecting and interpreting factual data-information which is measurable and can be easily compared.

For the most part, subjective thinking is only likely to confuse you or to cloud your thinking. Therefore, you are advised to (a) seek the advice of one or more successful businesspeople, (b) hire a site selection consultant, and (c) talk with a SCORE counselor.

Surplus Space. Unless your business can grow into unneeded space within a relatively short period of time you should avoid buying or leasing extra or surplus space. In many instances, landlords have space which is deeper than you require but don't understand that it is not only space you don't have an immediate need for but that you don't want to pay for. Therefore, unless you are offered a shorter base term (for instance, one year as opposed to three years) or either a blended or discounted rate, you should avoid signing on the dotted line for surplus space.

Oftentimes small retailers such as bakeries, dry cleaners, and jewelers are unable to find space in a highly desirable location which is no larger than eight hundred or nine hundred or one thousand square feet. Because of this unfortunate circumstance they are often left with a difficult decision. If you are in "the same boat," you need to consider whether renting or purchasing excess space can be justified from a sales and profit perspective. If it can, then go ahead and lock it up. If it can't be justified then you should consider either extending your site search or try negotiating either a lower rent or securing one or more financial incentives.

TEAM. Many times, businesses are started because people want to be their own boss. While there is certainly nothing wrong with wanting to be "the master of your own destiny," there is one potential limitation: not relying on others for advice and/or help. My advice is to consider adopting what I like to call a TEAM mentality. Briefly, this important acronym stands for **Together Everybody Achieves More**.

When you are out scouting locations and sites for your business, please don't overlook potential resources like commercial realtors who specialize in retail and restaurant site selection and/or site selection consultants. Think about adding these types of resource people to your team, much like you would your banker, your accountant, and your attorney. In the long run you'll be thankful because these are people who can help prevent mistakes - the kind that can not only significantly shorten the duration of your business career, but leave you with major debt.

Tenant Build Out. Most landlords typically provide tenants with two kinds of rental space. For new space the standard is a "vanilla" box finish. This typically includes the basics: unpainted drywall, concrete floor, one restroom, ceiling, lighting, electrical outlets, HVAC, and a hot water heater. For restaurants, upgrades in kitchen and restroom plumbing, electrical, and HVAC will all be required - how much depends upon the type of restaurant use.

In certain instances, a landlord may agree to deliver unfinished space or "cold, dark shell" space while providing a build out allowance to the tenant who will then assume responsibility for completing the build out. This removes the landlord from the space planning and building permit processes as well as from bidding the job and hiring one or more contractors.

Older or second-generation space is usually delivered to tenants in either "as is" condition or with some minor improvements. Such improvements might include low-cost items such as freshly painted walls, new flooring, new ceiling tiles, etc. Alternatively, some landlords will be happy to simply provide a new tenant with some form of free rent in exchange for the tenant coming "out of pocket" to refurbish the subject space.

Tenant Improvement Allowance. Landlords will consider providing a desirable tenant, one who has good credit and good financials, with some form of build out allowance. Physical build out covering standard items is the key. Landlords don't want to spend money for things like furniture, fixtures, and equipment. Nor will they consider providing money for decorative items.

Upgrading the HVAC, electrical, and plumbing systems may be candidates for improvement dollars. Adding glass wrap or an outdoor patio represent other possibilities. These improvements will ultimately add value to a property. Remember that landlords want tenants to have "skin in the game." In other words, they typically want to see tenants come "out of pocket" for a long list of costly upgrades to flooring, lighting, HVAC, electrical and plumbing.

Third Place Environments. No company understands how to create a Third-Place mentality better than Starbucks and Panera. These are businesses which encourage customers to not only visit, but to stay as long as they like, whether that means eating, drinking, reading, people watching, conducting business meetings, spending time online, or any combination of the above.

Third Places are special. They are places where you want to linger, where you want to hang out. They are places where you feel comfortable and welcome and don't want to leave right away. These are places which are designed to make you feel at home, places you want to take family and friends to. They are places which breed something which is very important - intense customer loyalty. It is this loyalty which leads to lots of repeat business - something every business wants but doesn't always achieve.

Trees. Trees have their place in certain settings. For instance, they are quite commonly used to not only dress up older business districts but revitalize "main streets." In addition, trees help establish character and help provide curb appeal, especially in pedestrian friendly business areas.

Nonetheless, if not properly evaluated, trees can end up creating visibility problems by blocking storefront signs and windows. This, in turn, can end up costing merchants not only sales, but negatively impact their ability to remain in business. Therefore, you need to make sure that something as welcome as a tree doesn't, in fact, turn out to be "hazardous" to your pocketbook.

Trip Origin. Understanding where your customers are coming from is very important, especially if you intend to create one or more trade area maps. While most customer visits begin from home, some originate from work, some from visiting family and/or friends, some from school, some from recreational facilities, some from church, some from entertainment venues, some from restaurants, some from shopping, etc.

Triple Net Rents: Most shopping center owners charge their tenants what is known as a triple net rent. Sometimes referred to as pass through costs, triple net rents require a tenant to pay his or her pro rata share of real estate taxes, insurance and common area maintenance.

Turning Radius. Determining what is a proper vehicle turning radius into/out of a shopping center or place of business is typically the responsibility of an engineer. Make them too tight and curbs and landscaping are likely to get run over and damaged by delivery trucks and large vehicles. This not only looks unsightly but ends up costing money to fix.

Two Hundred to Three Hundred Feet Away. Unless your business is strictly destination oriented and will be located on either an intersecting or parallel street which is already home to a cluster of other nearby retail and/or restaurant businesses, the maximum distance you should consider locating your business off of "the main drag" is two hundred to three hundred feet. Otherwise, opening "just around the corner" means that you are likely to experience a significant drop off in customer traffic in comparison with the amount of customer traffic which either walks or drives by the multiple businesses which account for "where the real action is."

Urgency. While the pros are very thorough in conducting the research which is required to make "smart" location and "smart" site selection decisions, oftentimes small and start-up businesspeople are in a hurry to get the ball rolling. Maybe they've been out for a drive and saw something they liked. Or, perhaps a developer or a commercial realtor has contacted them about an opportunity. They may even be motivated by the fact that a competitor is expanding and they don't want to concede a loss of market share.

Please don't be guilty of reacting or making quick decisions with respect to site selection. In site selection, urgency typically leads to mistakes. While there is nothing wrong with finding a location for son "Joey" or for cousin "Vinny" what is important is that you take your time and **follow the advice which is spelled out in this book.**

Valet Parking. Casual and fine dining restaurants that are located in areas with limited amounts of on street parking are the businesses which are most likely to offer this type of convenience service. Nearby parking lots, such as those which serve churches, offices, and banks are typical recipients of such "overflow" parking. If offered, valet parking can end up being a big boost to restaurant sales.

In many communities, shared parking arrangements are permitted only if two or more property owners sign an agreement and evidence said agreement to local zoning officials. In other instances, zoning will require the issuance of what is known as a Conditional Use Permit - a written authorization which permits shared parking based upon a set of conditions governing such things as days and hours of operation.

Vanilla Box Space. Developers and landlords typically deliver space to tenants complete with walls, ceilings, lighting, HVAC, and one or two restrooms. The tenant is then expected to decorate the walls and provide floor coverings. Extras such as additional HVAC, electrical, and plumbing are, along with improvements such as outdoor patios, awnings, signs, and additional glass, typically paid for by the tenant.

Website. Please don't overlook this important sales tool. Today websites are the single most important investment every small business can make in order to increase not only name recognition but sales revenues.

Women. In case you don't already know, women are the key decision-makers when it comes to shopping as well as deciding where to go to eat. They tend to not only be more loyal to a particular business than men, but attach greater importance to curb appeal, cleanliness, ambiance, and nighttime lighting. If you can, please do not overlook what is important to women. If you do, you definitely risk "taking money out of your pocket."

Written Impressions & Observations. Whenever you visit a commercial property or talk with a commercial realtor or property manager be sure to either jot down or record notes, thoughts, and/or buzzwords. The human mind can be much frailer than we think, especially when it comes to processing numerous observations, conversations, and multiple properties.

You. Are you ready to go to work? Do you have a business plan? Do you have a marketing plan? Are your finances in order? Is your credit score high? Are you prepared to make a big investment of time and money?

These are some of the questions you need to ask yourself before deciding to either lease or purchase property. Being thorough and "looking before you leap" are key attributes of people who know what they are getting into and are prepared to meet the challenges of the future.

In the long run, I hope you'll remember that **"business success is about doing not only the right things, but doing things right."**

EXHIBIT A

Letter of Intent (LOI). Proposals and Letters of Intent are synonymous. They identify the terms under which a landlord (Lessor) and a tenant (Lessee) agree to enter into a business relationship. The location and size of space, term, rents, pass through costs, buildout and/or remodeling obligations, hours of operation, tenant improvements, the amount of security deposit and signing form the core contents of a Letter of Intent.

Letters of Intent can be prepared by either a prospective tenant or his/ her representative (more common) or a landlord (less common) Typically, they identify a response deadline of five to seven to ten days. In many instances, the original LOI is where the negotiation process begins. Accordingly, it is highly likely that a Letter of Intent will be modified in some manner prior to being executed.

Once an LOI is signed, either the landlord (more common) or the tenant (less common) will provide the other party with a standardized lease agreement. At this point the landlord is likely to insist on obtaining financial statements. Depending upon whether the prospective tenant is a start-up, a small multi-unit company, or a regional or national chain, the landlord may ask for authorization to run a credit check.

Because of their detail and complexity, one or both parties are likely to employ legal counsel as a means of advising them prior to executing what typically ends up becoming a revised lease agreement.

Sample

LETTER OF INTENT

Contents

DATE: _____

LEASE SPACE: Address
                               Amount of Space

BUSINESS USE.   Description

GUARANTEE: (if applicable)

SECURITY DEPOSIT: $ Amount

BASE TERM RENTS: Years
                               Cost per square foot
                               Cost per month

OPTION TERMS: Number of

OPTION TERM RENTS: Years
                               Cost per square foot
                               Cost per month

PERCENTAGE RENT: Preferably none
                               (or % over a specified
                               $ amount)

PERCENTAGE RENT CAP: Not to exceed $/sf/year

PASS THROUGH COSTS: Cost per square foot + annual
                               bumps not to exceed

250

RE TAXES: Cost per year + yearly pro rata adjustments

POSSESSION: Date

CONDITION: List Landlord improvements or Tenant allowance or "As is"

HVAC SYSTEM: Landlord warrants that HVAC system is in good working order

START OF RENT: x # of days after delivery

BUSINESS HOURS: # days/week for not less than x # of hours except holidays

EXCLUSIVE: Excludes or limits competition

PATIO: Seating #

AWNINGS: Tenant right to display

SIGNING: Subject to Landlord + local jurisdiction approval

UTILITIES: Tenant cost responsibilities

TRASH PICK UP: To be included in CAM charges

KICK OUT: After # of years if sales do not exceed specified $ amount with advance written notice

RIGHT TO RELOCATE: None

RADIUS RESTRICTION: None

BROKERAGE FEE: None. Otherwise, to be paid by Landlord or Tenant

251

EXPIRATION: Date.

Signature

_____

        Name

EXHIBIT B
Sample
Real Estate Representation Agreement
Agreement

WHEREAS,_____ a restaurant
                      name of business

company headquartered in_____ is rapidly expanding
throughtout _____, and is looking to build a relationship
with a real estate brokerage company which has significant experience
as well as a track record of success in the specialized area of site
selection, and

WHEREAS,_____ agrees
                      name of business

to share, on a confidential basis, its Site Selection Guidelines and
Site Selection Checklist with a commercial real estate brokerage firm
which understands that we are committed to leasing only "home run"
locations, and

WHEREAS,_____ agrees
              name of real estate company

it can assign a dedicated, trustworthy, responsive resource person who
is committed to helping _____
                              name of business

achieve its market penetration goals.

253

NOW, therefore, be it resolved that _____,

name of person

fully understands and agrees to perform all of the following duties and responsibilities at no cost, and with the understanding that all compensation will come from the Landlord of the property where

_____decides

name of business

to sign a multi-year lease agreement:

1. Conduct periodic **drive tours** with our franchisee in order to identify potential "home fun" locations

2. **Contact** landlords, property managers, listing agents, and developers on behalf of _____

   name of business

3. **Complete** required Site Selection Guidelines and Checklist information for subsequent submission to Franchisee and Franchisor

4. Identify **drivers** of weekday lunchtime business, evening business, and weekend business, all within a 5 and 10 minute drive time.

5. Conduct **market research** as directed by Franchisee and/or Franchisor

6. Provide demographic data and maps based upon 5 and 10 minute drive times

7. Obtain current **traffic counts** at or in close proximity to candidate locations

8. Identify **competitor restaurants,** and, if possible, their respective annual sales

9. Prepare **Site Selection Information** Packages for candidate sites

254

10. **Communicate** with franchisee not less than once a week via email, phone calls, and/or text messaging

11. Provide a 1-2 page **written progress report** to franchisee two times a month

12. Identify **strengths and weaknesses** for each location option

13. Rank potential location options based upon **Area, Site & Space**

14. Identify Landlord **incentives** such as free rent, extra build out allowance, site amenities, etc.

15. Obtain Landlord **Build Out** Exhibit

16. Develop **Letters of Intent** after obtaining franchisee input

17. With direction from Franchisee and Franchisor, **negotiate** with Landlord and/or Landlord Representative, all terms and conditions required to finalize a lease agreement

In exchange for abiding by the aforementioned obligations, you are hereby appointed our sole real estate broker and granted the exclusive right to represent us in the following market:_____
Said exclusive right shall be in effect for a _____month period, and shall be extended for another _____month period if Franchisee and Franchisor are mutually satisfied with the progress which has been made and the results which have been produced.

We hereby agree that, subsequent to the expiration or termination of this Agreement, to continue recognizing you as our exclusive real estate broker, in accordance with the provisions herein, with respect to any and all of the locations for which you have submitted a detailed package of information in writing during the term of this Agreement.

It is hereby acknowledged that Franchisor and Franchisee will each be responsible for conducting due diligence as well as determining if a particular property is safe and not subject to any environmental hazards or concerns.

Franchisee and Franchisor consent to publicizing your role in any real estate transaction which is agreed to.

Both parties agree to act in good faith and to work with one another in both a timely and responsible manner.

Based upon the aforementioned, should either party become dissatisfied with the other party, it shall have the right to terminate this Agreement upon providing thirty (30) days advance written notice to the other party.

In the event franchisee or broker commences litigation against the other party to enforce the rights identified in this Agreement, the party prevailing shall be entitled to recover from the other party all costs and expenses, including reasonable attorneys' fees which have been incurred.

AGREED by Franchisee   AGREED by Real Estate Broker

_____   _____

Date: _____   Date: _____

EXHIBIT C
Meaningful Quotes & Educational Pictures

The purpose of adding a brief section on Meaningful Quotes is to offer both advice and inspiration to would be as well as existing businesspeople. Furthermore, the purpose of the series of Educational Pictures which follows is meant to familiarize readers with a host of options related to Differentiated Storefronts, Memorable Signing, Memorable Design, and Amenities. Collectively, what follows should prove insightful, especially when readers understand that, according to the Small Business Administration (SBA), *only half of small businesses survive past the five-year mark!*

"You need to focus your efforts, your energy, and your money on finding only one type of location - the Home Run." *Frank Raeon*

"If you really look closely, most overnight successes took a long time." *Steve Jobs*

"Ambition is the path to success. Persistence is the vehicle you arrive in." *Bill Bradley*

"Patience, persistence and perspiration make an unbeatable combination for success." *Napoleon Hill*

"Coming together is a beginning; keeping together is progress; working together is success." *Henry Ford*

An old proverb says "If you want to go quickly, go alone. If you want to go far, go together."

"Incredible things in the business world are never made by a single person, but by a team." *Steve Jobs*

"None of us is as smart as all of us." *Ken Blanchard*

"TEAM - Together Everybody Achieves More." *Unknown Author*

"You don't build a business, you build people, then people build the business." *Zig Ziglar*

"Succes is where preparation and opportunity meet." *Bobby Unser*

"It takes a lot of unspectacular preparation to have spectacular results." *Roger Staubach*

"Failure to prepare is preparing to fail." *John Wooden*

EXHIBIT C
DIFFERENTIATED STOREFRONTS

EXHIBIT C
MEMORABLE SIGNING

EXHIBIT C
MEMORABLE DESIGN

EXHIBIT C

MEMORABLE DESIGN

EXHIBIT C
AMENITIES

INDEX

Canopies, 124

Captain America, 67

Captive audience, 122, 132

Capture rate, 139

Casual dining, 123, 136

Case studies, 143

CCIM, 143

Census, 33, 38

Central Business District, 126

Certificate in Retail & Restaurant Site Selection, xiv, 143

Certified Leasing Specialist, 142

Certified Shopping Center Manager, 142

Certified Site Selection Specialist, 11, 142

Chain Store Age, 130

Chamber of Commerce, 1, 117, 166

Chauffer mentality, 100

Cheap rent, vi, x, 8, 18, 111

Chicago, 11, 106, 128, 140, 141

Chicago Tribune, 11

Chick-Fil-A, 93, 99, 157

Chipotle, 99, 102, 147, 156

Christine Day, 12

Cincinnati, Ohio, 137, 147, 150,

151, 156, 161, 162

Citizen participation, 107

City Councils, 104

City Managers, 104, 117

City Planning Commissions/ commissioners, 104, 107, 117

City Planning Director, xiv, 105, 116, 117, 162

Cleanliness, 93

Clocks, 124

Cluster/clustering 31, 57, 116, 121, 122, 123, 125, 131, 138, 140, 149

Cold calling, 62, 66, 151

Colors/materials, 18, 19, 22, 115, 124

Coffee shops, 118, 123, 129, 136, 140

College/university faculty, 166

College/university locations, 122, 130

Columbus, Ohio, 130

Commercial developers/ development, 104, 110, 111, 159, 161, 166

Commercial realtor(s), xiv, x, xi, 10, 33, 34, 37, 59, 60, 65, 69, 79, 94, 97, 100, 101, 103, 108, 110,

---

NOTE: The Index does <u>not</u> include specific reference to important information which is identified in Appendices A, B, and C. To learn more:

See **Appendix A** (pages 167 – 185) for a detailed <u>list</u> of **Site Selection Influences**

See **Appendix B** (pages 186 – 202) for a detailed <u>list</u> of **Words and Terms You Need to Know About**

See **Appendix C** (pages 203 – 248) for a detailed list of **Other Sales Influences and Related Factors**

www.ingramcontent.com/pod-product-compliance
Lightning Source LLC
Chambersburg PA
CBHW071332210326
41597CB00015B/1420